To my mother and the children
of exiles and refugees everywhere –
may you find your way to the source.
The dead open the eyes of the living.

And to the lakes,
their boundless generosity.

TO THE LAKE

TO THE LAKE

A Balkan Journey of War and Peace

July 31, 2022

KAPKA KASSABOVA

Graywolf Press

First published in 2020 by Granta Books, London.

The author gratefully acknowledges permissions to quote from *Stone Voices: The Search for Scotland* by Neal Ascherson, *Children of the Greek Civil War: Refugees and the Politics of Memory* by Loring Danforth and Riki Van Boeschoten, *An Anthology of Modern Albanian Poetry: An Elusive Eagle Soars* ed. and trans. Robert Elsie, *Edward Lear in Albania: Journals of a Landscape Painter in the Balkans* ed. Bejtullah Destani and Robert Elsie, *The Heroic Age* by Stratis Haviaras, *Broken April* by Ismail Kadare, *Remnants of Another Age* by Nikola Madzirov, and *Black Lamb and Grey Falcon* by Rebecca West.

This publication is made possible, in part, by the voters of Minnesota through a Minnesota State Arts Board Operating Support grant, thanks to a legislative appropriation from the arts and cultural heritage fund. Significant support has also been provided by the National Endowment for the Arts, Target, the McKnight Foundation, the Lannan Foundation, the Amazon Literary Partnership, and other generous contributions from foundations, corporations, and individuals. To these organizations and individuals we offer our heartfelt thanks.

Published by Graywolf Press
250 Third Avenue North, Suite 600
Minneapolis, Minnesota 55401

www.graywolfpress.org

Published in the United States of America

ISBN 978-1-64445-026-0

2 4 6 8 9 7 5 3 1
First Graywolf Printing, 2020

Library of Congress Control Number: 2019949938

Cover design and art: Kimberly Glyder

A lake is the landscape's most beautiful and expressive feature. It is earth's eye, looking into which the beholder measures the depth of his own nature.

Henry David Thoreau

CONTENTS

PART ONE: SPRING

PART TWO: AUTUMN

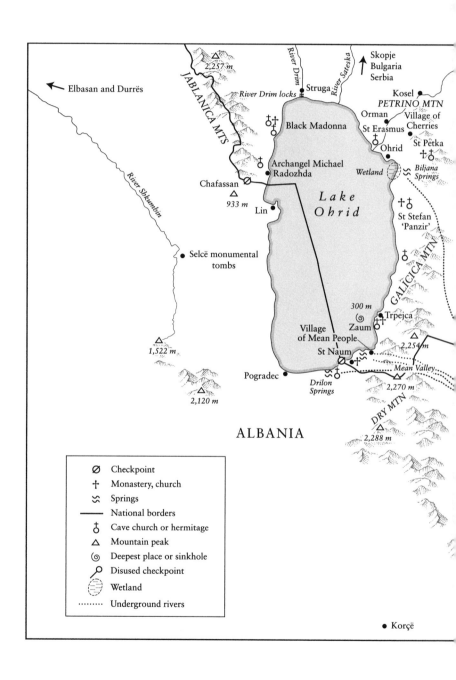

Elbasan and Durrës

JABLANICA MTS

2,257 m

River Drim

River Drim locks

Struga

River Sateska

River Shkumbin

Black Madonna

Archangel Michael
Radozhda

Chafassan

933 m

Lin

Selcë monumental
tombs

*Lake
Ohrid*

Wetland

Skopje
Bulgaria
Serbia

Kosel
PETRINO MTN
Orman   Village of
St Erasmus Cherries
St Petka
Ohrid

Biljana
Springs

St Stefan
'Panzir'

GALIČICA MTN

300 m

Trpejca

Village
of Mean People
St Naum

Zaum

2,254 m

Mean Valley

Pogradec

Drilon
Springs

2,270 m

1,522 m

2,120 m

DRY MTN

ALBANIA

2,288 m

Ø   Checkpoint
✝   Monastery, church
𝔖𝔖   Springs
─── National borders
⚲   Cave church or hermitage
△   Mountain peak
ⓢ   Deepest place or sinkhole
ℴ   Disused checkpoint
⬭   Wetland
······ Underground rivers

● Korçë

The Lakes

River Daljan

REPUBLIC OF
NORTH MACEDONIA

• Resen

≈ Gjavato Pass
△
2,010 m

• Bitola
(Heraclea Lyncestis)

Ezerani
Wetland

• Asamati ☦✝
• Pretor

P e l a g o n i a

• Oteshevo

Marsh
• Stenje

*Lake
Prespa*

BABA-PELISTER MTS
△
2,600 m
△
2,350 m

Nakolec •

Village of
Immigrants ✝ St Petka

Zaver ✝
☦ Golem Grad island

Thessaloniki →

• Agios Germanos

Dry
Village
•
☦✝ Psarades

✝ Virgin
Eleusa

Zachariadis
Cave

Vigla Pass
≈
△
Vitsi Peak

Florina •

☦ St Achillius

Mali Grad
island

△
1,332 m

Vidronissi

Antartiko • 1,931 m

GREECE

△
1,457 m

*Little
Prespa*

△
1,470 m

Lake Kastoria ↘

Via Egnatia

BALKAN MTS

BULGARIA

Black Sea

RHODOPE
MTS

TURKEY

Istanbul

Sea of Marmara

Aegean
Sea

INTRODUCTION

This book tells of two ancient lakes. Some places are inscribed in our DNA yet take a long time to reveal their contours, just as some journeys are etched into the landscape of our lives yet take a lifetime to complete. So it is for me with these lakes.

Lake Ohrid has exerted a pull on me since early childhood because my maternal grandmother was from there, and she was an influential figure in my early life. As an adult, I often thought of returning to the Lake properly, but sensed that I wasn't ready. To journey to the place of your ancestors, you must be prepared to see what it is easier to deny.

What finally propelled me was a concern that as time passed, something might happen insidiously. That unless I understood my maternal family's existential landscape, I might repeat old patterns. That as we continue to witness in this century conflicts of a civil and fratricidal nature, divisive politics between and within nations, patriarchal autocracy and revisionism, mass emigration and displacement – as we witness this, unless we become aware of how we carry our own legacies, we too may become unwitting agents of destruction.

Generations of my predecessors had lived by the Lake. I hoped they could serve as a gateway to the Lake and to this surprisingly little-known corner of Europe. The lake region is home to epic landscapes and rich histories. It is a realm of high altitudes and mesmeric depths, eagles and vineyards, orchards and old civilisations, a land tattooed with untold histories. A couple of years earlier, I had explored Europe's far south-east to seek out the human stories of a triple border zone between Bulgaria, Turkey and Greece. The lakes occupy the south-west of the Balkan peninsula and are likewise shared by three countries.

The twin lakes of Ohrid (hard 'h') and Prespa are embedded diamond-like in the mountain folds of western Macedonia and eastern Albania. They are relatively close to the Adriatic and the Aegean, but whichever way you approach them, they don't feel close to anything, not even to each other. Forbidding ranges must be traversed, and lonely roads travelled. Here passed the strategic Roman Via Egnatia (or Egnatian Way) on its way from Dyrrachium on the Adriatic to Constantinople on the Bosphorus. Later, Orthodox hermitages and churches were hewn into the limestone, later still Islamic caravanserais and dervish monasteries appeared. Thanks to the Via Egnatia, built in the mid-second century BC to connect the Roman world and used for nearly twenty centuries, the lake region became for a while, in the words of the historian Alain Ducellier, 'the nerve centre of the Balkans'.

The Via that shaped history was itself shaped by geography. It followed the valley of the River Shkumbin between the great mountains of Illyria, bypassed the twin lakes, snaked between mountain ranges that now straddle the (North) Macedonian–Greek border, before descending into the Pelagonian plains; reached the Aegean and continued, parallel to the coast, all the way to the Bosphorus.

The lakes are engendered by springs, surrounded by springs, and connected to each other by underground streams. They are at the juncture of two and in places three national borders – Greece nibbles at the southern end of Lake Prespa and almost swallows up the teardrop lakelet at the bottom of it, Mikri (Little) Prespa. Here, at the confluence of powerful civilisational forces from antiquity to the present day, mingle the currents of two warm seas and the icy winds of mountains nearly 3,000 metres (9,000 feet) high.

Ohrid and Prespa are Europe's oldest lakes. Ohrid may even be the world's second-oldest. Ordinary lakes last only a hundred thousand years at most before they fill up with sediments, but a handful – Tanganyika, Baikal, Ohrid-Prespa – have endured for over a million years. Despite recent probes, scientists cannot be precise about the age of Ohrid-Prespa; they may well be up to three million years old.

Lake Ohrid is fed by tributaries, sublacustic springs, and most remarkably – by underground streams from Lake Prespa, which travel through the limestone Galicica Mountain (pronounced Ga-li-chi-tsa, 2,254 metres high). These sister springs account for a quarter of the lake's incoming water. The porous karst ensures that the icy waters arrive at Lake Ohrid naturally filtered. This extraordinary transfusion, along with the bubbling lacustrine springs, can be seen at the St Naum Springs in Macedonia and the Drilon Springs in Albania as it happens, second by second.

Prespa sits 180 metres above Ohrid, and seen from the air, the pair look like eyes in an ancient face. The area of the lakes and the Galicica Mountain between them form a reserve with an extremely rich biosphere. Brown bears, wolves and golden eagles inhabit the higher parts. Some say that the lakes' geomagnetic location creates a very high vibrational quality. Some even believe that Ohrid Lake is inside an 'energy vortex', and a popular, if scientifically null, local hyperbole fancies yet another lake under the mountain – a 'buried' lake. There is also talk of a subaquatic mountain, caused by ongoing tectonic shifts in the region – which is not unlikely. But what is certain is that the subterranean communication system of the two lakes is the only one of its kind in Eurasia.

Ten years ago on a visit to the Lake, I encountered a young monk who asked me where my grandmother was buried. I said Sofia. He said that it didn't matter, that her spirit had returned here, because Lake Ohrid is a 'gathering point'.

On that same visit, I witnessed a freak accident. It was a warm

September day. I stood on the cliffs of Kaneo above Ohrid town. From there, you could see the entire shore. I photographed a tourist boat gliding over the mirror of the lake. Thirty minutes later, the boat capsized and sank without trace, as if the lake had swallowed it. The people on it were visitors from Bulgaria. Fifteen drowned, the rest were rescued by locals. With eerie symbolism, that boat was called *Ilinden*, after the tragic Ilinden (St Elijah's Day) Uprising in 1903 which had aimed to free Macedonia from Ottoman rule. Ilinden is commemorated every year in Bulgaria and the Republic of (North) Macedonia, though in an instance of retrospective nationalism the two countries' governments periodically argue over who took part in it – Macedonians or Bulgarians, or both, and whether and to what degree there was a difference between the two.

Tourists come to Lake Ohrid each summer, but the region's deeper currents remain hidden. The Balkans are a complex civilisational weave into which diverse and sometimes conflicting versions of reality are read by the natives, and projected by outsiders. This Rorschach-test phenomenon has produced and endured more than one apocalyptic war. In the Balkans, as in many places across the world where a new–old nativism is rising again, melting pots are endangered. The lacustrine realm that is shared today by the three countries is one of the oldest surviving civilisational melting pots in Europe and the Middle East.

A *salade macédoine* in French means the ultimate 'mixed salad'. 'With luck a traveller in Macedonia may hear six distinct languages and four allied dialects spoken in the same market place,' wrote the British journalist Henry Noel Brailsford in 1905, when the region of Macedonia was part of a decayed empire and my great-grandparents were Ottoman subjects. A century later, as an indirect result of this tower-of-Babel effect, the former Yugoslav Republic of Macedonia was embroiled with Greece in a generation-long dispute over patrimony. It finally reached a formal resolution during my journey, with the Prespa Agreement, which saw the country's name change – rather quickly, and for some, painfully – to Republic of North Macedonia. Although the region continues its tradition of confusion, complication and conspiracy, (North) Macedonia and Albania cling by the skin of their teeth to an old habit of tolerance.

Since the end of the Yugoslav Wars (1991–2001) 'the Balkans' have been erroneously conflated with the former Yugoslavia, which occupies the western Balkans only, and the name has been widely replaced in international bureaucracy by 'South-East Europe', but in this book I call them the Balkans. This is in a spirit of reclaiming the natural, once neutral, name of the peninsula, after the epic Balkan Mountains in Bulgaria. Although the toponym was initially imposed from the outside, it has become over the centuries a self-designated cultural identifier conferring a transnational kind of citizenship on its diverse people, even when they disagree on other matters.

'The Balkans, that's us,' my grandmother used to say – meaning her family. But in as far as 'the Balkans' came to be equated with the fragility of peace and tolerance, hers was a broader insight into the human condition. Our world is unstoppably connected, yet increasingly self-fragmenting. Some might say 'Balkanised'. In a term now a century old – it was first used in 1918 in the *New York Times* – to Balkanize is 'to divide a region or body into smaller, mutually hostile states or groups'. The French *se balcaniser* is self-reflexive, implying full agency, which hardly makes it happier. But before 'the Balkans' as a political designator acquired a negative hue, and contrary to the lazy and inaccurate stereotype of 'ancient hatreds', the peninsula had long housed a polyphonic, sometimes cacophonous, diversity. It still does.

In a wider context the two great opposing global forces at present, and I think at all critical times in human history, are these: fractiousness and harmony, war and peace, ignorance and understanding. Because of their transcontinental, transcultural geography, the southern Balkans have been a strategic theatre where these dichotomies have been played out with especial force, even ferocity. The geographic region of Macedonia sits in a highly seismic part of an already seismic peninsula. In 1963, the capital Skopje was destroyed by a massive earthquake. Thousands were killed and injured. My grandparents drove from Sofia to Skopje with supplies and camp beds – my grandmother's brothers and their families were left without homes, and my grandparents camped with them in the parks of the ruined city. They lay awake at night in their tents, listening to the earth roaring underneath them. To this day, the clock at Skopje's central railway station is frozen at the hour of the earthquake.

Sometimes, I feel like that clock. It's an irrational feeling, out of joint with the present: ruins all around, stuck in a long-ago moment of disaster. I knew that this stopped-clock legacy had come down from my mother but I wanted to find out where *that* came from, and how others carried it. I wanted to know what creates cultural and psychological inheritance, and how we can go forward with it, instead of sleepwalking back into the geopolitical abyss. The abyss is home to the bones of our predecessors who could not escape dark forces. Some of those forces are still with us – they never went away – the better to let us know that the abyss is always open for business.

Geography shapes history – we generally accept this as a fact. But we don't often explore how families digest big historio-geographies, how these sculpt our inner landscape, and how we as individuals continue to influence the course of history in invis-ible but significant ways – because the local is inseparable from the global. I went to the Lakes to seek an understanding of such forces. I knew from my *Border* journey that sometimes history's thoroughfares are disguised as geography's outposts, the better to fool us that the past is another country.

From roughly the time of Herodotus, the 'father of history' (fifth century BC), and for the next twenty centuries or so, the Greek word *historia* meant the multifaceted, multidisciplinary, often narrative exploration of a subject in the spirit of total enquiry. The subject of Herodotus' *Histories* was ostensibly the Persian–Greek wars, but his deeper subject is how human destiny plays out across vast stretches of time, memory and geography, and against the ever-moving canvas of the known world. Only in the late Middle Ages did 'history' come to be associated specifically with the past, and gradually as a discipline lodged entirely in the past, cut and dried, and separate from the rest of earthly experience – which is in essence boundless and not always linear. It was the original view of *historia* that I sought through this journey.

It was impossible to travel these ancient roads without seeking out earlier writers on the Lakes and the region. They have been delightful companions. Elsewhere in this book, some private individuals' names have been changed. When it comes to place names and terms describing national and regional identities, I have taken the utmost care to work with unbiased sources and first-hand accounts when writing about the past, and with current self-identifiers when writing about the present. The former Yugoslav Republic of Macedonia was renamed the Republic of North Macedonia in February 2019, which is why I use this new name in its current context only. Before this, the country was known locally and internationally as Macedonia or the Republic of Macedonia, and the varying usages in this book reflect this situation. I take the same approach with other place names that have changed over time.

Given the complexity and sensitivity of some of the material here, if anyone feels that their particular viewpoint is underrepresented despite my striving for inclusivity and fairness, I ask for forgiveness.

Kapka Kassabova
The Highlands of Scotland

Give me wings and I shall soar
Back to our lands, our shores
Set eyes on our places
See the faces of Ohrid and Struga
Where the lake is white and true
And when the wind blows – dark and blue.

Konstantin Miladinov, 1861

LONGING FOR THE SOUTH

It so happens that I am the fourth generation in a female line to emigrate. A hundred years ago, my great-grandmother emigrated from the Kingdom of Yugoslavia to the Kingdom of Bulgaria. Her only daughter, my grandmother, emigrated from the Federative People's Republic of Yugoslavia to the People's Republic of Bulgaria. My mother, an only child, emigrated with her family from Bulgaria to New Zealand, and I emigrated from New Zealand to Scotland. My sister moved back to Europe too. For each of us, emigration has meant separation from our parents.

As the changing names of the countries suggest, the uprootings in this family, as in numberless others, were triggered by cataclysmic historical forces: the fall of the Ottoman and Austro-Hungarian Empires, decolonisation, and the rise of Balkan nation-states; the Balkan Wars (1912–13) and the two world wars; the Cold War, its end, and globalisation.

In a more personal sense, this pattern of serial flight reminds me that the desire to travel, explore and indeed escape, has been with me since early childhood. Or even before – in the womb, I revolved ceaselessly, and emerged from my mother nearly suffocated by the umbilical cord which I had tied into a knot. Drawn early on to stories of adventure and the high seas, I longed for some place that would set me free – from the pressure cooker that was our small flat, from school with its compulsory patriotic parades, from the low-level oppressiveness that was indistinguishable from home and homeland. I longed for freedom before I knew what freedom meant, or who I was.

My maternal grandmother Anastassia longed for it too, or she longed for something at any rate. She was in my life for thirteen years, the last five of which she was ill with breast cancer. I loved her fiercely. She was in her fifties when she sickened. Although she wore a wig and put on lipstick, terrible things were happening under her clothes. She was also losing her sight. I sometimes read to her, as she had read to me. It was in my grandparents' flat in Sofia that I read my first book, aged five, with the blue outline of a mountain framed in the window.

My grandmother had an iconic book containing the lyrics of hundreds of folk songs. It was the work of two folklorists and linguists known as the Miladinov Brothers who had travelled across the Macedonian and Bulgarian lands – that is, the southern Balkans – in the mid-nineteenth century and gathered an epic collection of folk songs. The brothers were from Struga, a lake town not far from my grandmother's town of Ohrid, eponymous with the Lake. She told me their story, and I noticed that like all 'our' stories, it ended with brutal injustice but was retrospectively redeemed by the power of its ideal – freedom through learning and education. But the main point here was that the younger brother, a lyrical poet, wrote a poem called 'Longing for the South', *T'ga za yug*. It was inspired by his native lake while he was studying in cold, faraway Moscow.

> Does the sun rise darkly there
> As it rises darkly here?

To subsequent generations, this poem became symbolic of the Lake, of exile and loss, of some indefinable sorrow that was to do with Macedonia, with 'our places', with the Balkans and the South. It sat deep in our bones, like weather. Significantly, the word *t'ga* means simultaneously 'longing' and 'sorrow'.

Its last lines are:

There [by the lake] I'd sit, I'd play my flute a while.
The sun would set, I'd sweetly die.

To *sweetly die*. This was one of my first contacts with poetry. Already I felt the presence of something heavy and tangled in the atmosphere around me, something emanating from my mother who was an extension of my grandmother who had come from the Lake. How did she come to be here (urban and incomplete), yet often talked of there (watery and complete), where her family remained and where they spoke slightly differently from us, as if speaking an old dialect, but looked the same as us. There was a hard border between us. I'd often become absorbed in a heavy Soviet atlas of the world, where our Soviet world appeared in pink, and where you could see the geodesic features of faraway lands. On the main centrefold page, Europe appeared as a messy tangle of interbleeding colours, cramped and weighed down with multiple meanings.

Official history said that our southern neighbours were not the same as us, they were other – historically, they were agents of perfidy (the Greeks) and tyranny (the Turks). We, on the other hand, were long-suffering martyrs, passionate, poetic, unjustly wronged. But my grandparents' neighbours across the landing, the Vassilopoulovs, were not at all other. The mother, who was Bulgarian, beat her daughters and locked them out on the landing, and the father, who was Greek, tried to intercede. He was connected with what was mysteriously called 'the events in Greece'. My father, a university professor, had a Greek student I fancied. As to the Turks – my grandmother's years with a Turkish landlady in Ohrid were fondly remembered, and my father had grown up with much-loved Turkish neighbours. Besides, the poem mentioned Istanbul as one of 'our places'. Moscow, on the other hand, and contrary to what we were told officially, was not one of our places. True, the poem was over a century old and things had changed, but its heavy mood of separation and yearning resonated strongly, as if untouched by time.

On my grandparents' round living-room table covered by a fringed velvet cloth was a jar with pebbles from the Lake. They were smooth pebbles like any others, pink and white, but they were also talismanic objects that brought with them the breeze of a lighter, more spacious world.

Anastassia is a Greek name meaning Resurrection. With a girl's instinct, I could tell that my grandmother had been a great spirit as well as a beauty, a combination that had visited this family only twice in living memory: in Anastassia and in her beloved niece Tatjana who had just died of a brain tumour in Ohrid, aged thirty-six.

In the last years of her life, it was difficult to be around my grandmother. In Communist Bulgaria there were no hospices, and you relied on the mercy of family. Demanding by nature, my grandmother became downright tyrannical towards her husband and her daughter, who couldn't do enough even as she was doing too much: sewing clothes that had to be just so, organising birthday gatherings, because Anastassia had always been a proud hostess. In her suffering, my grandmother seemed to want life to be spoiled for her *loved ones* too, a favourite expression for the women in the family.

Meanwhile, the little pleasures still available to my mother, she denied herself. My mother couldn't eat in the terrible last few months of my grandmother's life, and became hollowed out by infections, a shadow ready to join her mother in the underworld. And if my mother died, I'd have to die too, because we were the same person. We had the same feelings and the same views. I mirrored her every move, sensed her every mood, mopped up every overspill of emotion, anxious to see her smile. By age ten, I spoke in my mother's grave voice and had her drawn face. I blamed *our* unhappiness on my father, twisting my natural love for him out of shape. Like my grandfather, he was outnumbered, held to account daily, and trying to atone for some unspecified failure. The emotional accounts were perpetually out of balance.

There is an abiding memory from those years. My mother and I sat on the bus home, after a visit to my grandparents at the foot of the blue mountain. From the bus window, we waved to them up on their seventh-floor balcony, tiny figures. But my grandmother was turned in the wrong direction because she couldn't see – and my grandfather gently redirected her wave. I waved and smiled. My mother was crying and I started crying with her.

She had done her best to protect me, I had done my best to protect her, but there it was – the loss couldn't be stopped. We were holding on to each other, keeping our heads above water, like those frescoes in Orthodox churches where the damned are drowning in a fiery soup, only their heads showing. And though we lived in a strictly atheist culture and I had never learned the word Damnation, I felt it bodily. By the age of ten, I was writing poems full of wrenching departures at train stations, doomed longings and nevermores. As if someone else was writing them through me.

It was not so much my grandmother dying – I could accept extinction, children do – it was the intolerable pain of parting I sensed in my mother. My mother said that she'd always lived in fear of something happening to her parents. I lived with the same fear. In the late Sofia summer in the year of the Chernobyl explosion, we bid goodbye to Anastassia. Among the red-gold leaves blown by the wind is my mother, a shadow dressed in diaphanous purple-black. A strong gust could sweep her away, like a leaf. She always felt to me precariously attached to life, as if born rootless, as if needing an external force to earth her.

The following summer I came down with an autoimmune disease, and spent weeks in a run-down hospital with blocked toilets where I wrote poetry, translated Baudelaire's *Les Fleurs du Mal*, and Longed for the South. My father was away on a fellowship, and my mother came every day, through dusty public traffic, after work as a data analyst, to bring me food she'd cooked at home and take me for slow walks in the hospital grounds. Although there was a Roma boy in the hospital I fancied, when I looked at the poems recently I was startled to see that they were addressed to my mother. Startling too was my discovery of love letters written by Grandmother Anastassia – beautifully worded, full of yearning to merge with the beloved, of seeing the beloved's green eyes and silken hair in the sea, in the sky. The sun would set, I'd sweetly die. They are addressed to her teenaged daughter.

Though I wanted to read the whole box of mother–daughter letters, I couldn't bear to go on. These romantic sentiments, the lover-like intensity that consumed her, were very familiar to me: they had travelled down to me undiluted, as had the need to express them through language. My grandmother wrote poems for the birthdays of family and friends and I still have a poem she wrote for my tenth birthday, five lines for the five letters of my name, even though by then she could not type and could barely see; she had dictated it to my grandfather. A journalist and script-writer for the Programme for Bulgarians Abroad – something like the BBC World Service but in a Communist context – her voice carried on the waves like a spell.

'Dear compatriots,' her seductive alto would begin. 'This song is for you.'

And some wrenching tune would reach for the heart-strings of the Bulgarian diaspora around the world. Of course, many of them could not return because they were blacklisted polit-ical émigrés. On occasion, I visited her in Radio Sofia's Bauhaus building. I'd wait at the security guard's kiosk in the main hall and look at the wall mosaic. It was in the shape of a proletarian sunburst, or perhaps a map of Bulgaria, but it also looked like Marx and Engels in profile, and Lenin, because they often appeared as a threesome. Then she would burst out of the elevator like the first day of summer. She occupied all the available space and had an uninhibited laugh that spread out in waves. Surrounded by the mediocrity, conformity and mendacity that a totalitarian system thrives on, Anastassia lived with zest, speaking her mind in a society where half the population didn't have a mind and the other half were careful to keep it to themselves.

Before she became her illness, she was like Demeter the goddess of harvests, the source of all things bountiful and delicious: shelves filled with books, a wardrobe of leather and fur coats which my grandfather procured for her from the state industry where he worked as head accountant. But then she got too sick to wear them. I brought one with me to Scotland though I've never worn it. It looks like the skin of a selkie, the mythical Northern creature who sheds her seal skin to assume human form on land and marry, but is destined to return to her watery home.

I have tried to reproduce my grandmother's recipes. The stuffed spinach filo with hand-pulled pastry, the baked lamb with yogurt called Elbasan *tava*; the *imam bayaldi*, aubergine roasts. You know what it means in Turkish? It means 'the imam has overeaten'. And like the imam, we overate together. Sometimes we slept together too, my grandfather abandoned next door. She ate to excess, smoked heavily, felt deeply, and what she found pleasurable was driven to a point of exquisite pain. Neutrality was not an option. Her health, like her emotions, was unstable long before the cancer, and my mother's has been labile too. I followed suit: as I became a woman, an all-pervasive malaise took hold of me. I didn't know how to feel good. In late adolescence, as we started a new life in New Zealand, I spiralled into anxiety, bringing every experience to a low point. If my parents went away, I imagined them in a fatal crash and drove myself into pre-emptive distress. I harshly judged myself and everyone else for perceived imperfections. Literature saved me from total self-destruction. Then my mother was dragged down by a raging depression that she projected onto her *loved ones*. After all, it was up to us to make her happy. When I look back, I see that my grandmother, my mother and I were taking turns in a pre-scripted drama. Though we tried to protect ourselves and each other from some unnamed menace, the protection didn't work. If anything, it seemed to attract the very thing it professed to ward off. Something pulled us down and compelled us to be unwell. The patients alternated, but the illness remained.

In childhood photographs with my grandmother, we have our hands on each other, proprietorially. The same in photos of her with my mother, a generation earlier, and with her nieces in Ohrid, the Lake behind them: you are an extension of me. But also: don't ever let me go.

Who do you love more, Mum or Dad? went the treacherous question adults asked you. Grandma or Grandad? Grandma or Mum? Secretly, I loved boys. Before I was ten, sensing my interest, Grandmother Anastassia warned me: never go with a boy who has the feet of a peasant or – I forget the rest, but there was a list which signalled that she didn't want me to enjoy boys at all. Not without her, for I was the apple of her eye. To be the apple of her eye felt like being irradiated. It made you glow, and it also made you tired. You wanted to close the door. But she had the key to the door.

Somewhere inside her was an abyss that could not be filled. It seemed to have its origins in Macedonia and the Lake. It's as if she was more than one person, a whole nation of souls, a clamorous hinterland of back-story. She carried some original matrix where the land masses were still moving, the fault lines stirred under the surface, the water level rose and fell, something was out of sync and could not be reconciled.

In my childhood, the family in Yugoslavia sent us a 3-D card of a blue lake and a town on a hill. Different aspects of the scene were revealed as you moved the card. It was compelling. I could do this for ages, enchanted by the blue of the lake – big as a sea – and the possibilities it represented. It was not clear why my grandmother had abandoned such a magical place. Why she had left behind her *loved ones.* But now you are my loved ones, she said. It was up to us *loved ones* to make her happy.

'I live between two worlds,' she said. 'When I'm in Ohrid I long for Sofia. When I'm in Sofia, I long for Ohrid.'

She always longed for something, so did my mother, and so did I. To be a woman was to lament an absence, a fault, an imminent loss. In short, to be in pain. Early on, I was certain that I didn't want to be anybody's mother or wife. I wanted to travel to distant lands, not to the school gates again; to live and die in peace, not surrounded by family. But some things follow us wherever we go.

The water dream began visiting me in late adolescence, shortly after our family arrived in the Pacific and just as Yugoslavia began to break up. In the dream, I watch a vast body of water rise on the horizon. I need to run but something is holding me back. I must bear witness. Now the water engulfs the shore, then buildings, electricity pylons, and people. Extinct species float in it. The mountains are ancient like pyramids, but they too are sinking. These are the waters of the Earth, immemorially old – and disturbed. They engulf the known world. My heart pounding, I swim through the wreckage, looking for those still alive, trying to help.

In Jungian psychology, water is the collective unconscious, and the calamity presaged in this dream does feel impersonal. I don't like this dream and want it to cease, but it has become only more frequent in the last years.

Three years after Grandmother Anastassia's death, in the oppressive summer of 1989, we travelled to Lake Ohrid: my parents, my younger sister, me, and my grandfather dapper in his suit. There was a sense that something was unravelling. In retrospect, that thing was our two countries, though at the time, it felt as if it was our family. With Anastassia and her niece Tatjana gone, it would never be the same. There was an awkward visit to a man with two sons: Tatjana's widower and boys, my second cousins.

There were silences and Yugoslav chocolates wrapped in gold foil, melting in the heat. My fascination with Tatjana's tragic trio felt like love. Fifteen and a virgin, I already understood the whole thing about sex and death. The Lake welled up with ripening figs and unbearable yearning. All my life, I'd be drawn to people and places that are damaged.

My grandmother's family had owned orchards for as far back as was remembered. Her father's family name was Bahchevandjiev, the Gardeners (from the Persian for garden, *bahcha*). Now my sister and I too were taken to see some peach orchards still owned by our uncles. That was the Lake – southern, bountiful, decadent, full of light, and also of a malaise that could not be named. A few years later, Yugoslavia lay in ruins. For the first time, Macedonia became the name of a fully independent nation-state. Of all the ex-Yugoslav republics, she escaped without a single shot being fired on her territory, though the war began with the mob murder of a Macedonian teenager whose ill fate had been to man a tank of the Yugoslav People's Army (JNA) in Split. When recruiters for the JNA came calling at Ohrid homes to seek volunteers, a surprise lay in store: 'Not here' was the answer at every door. Seeing which way the wind was blowing, the families of Ohrid's young men had dispatched their sons abroad, to relatives in other towns, or to the cellar. Fresh trouble came knocking on doors later, a year after the Kosovo War, when the violence spilled into Macedonia. And once again: 'Not here', came the answer.

Macedonia of the Lake had no taste for war. She had a way of surviving by the skin of her teeth.

Soon after that visit to the Lake, we emigrated to New Zealand. My parents put down firm roots there. My sister and I tried to do the same, but eventually I left New Zealand at the age of thirty to settle in Scotland and she did the same in Switzerland. But as life finally became easier for our family and the struggle of multiple emigration abated, of starting from zero over and over again in new places where they can't spell your name, peace became perversely elusive. Whenever we got together, something was twisted out of shape, brought to a painful point, and all our energy went into fixing it. Reunions became a crisis to be survived.

Repetitive overwhelming states don't always need a current object, it transpires: in transgenerational psychology, this is seen as a result of unprocessed trauma and is known as 'time collapse', which is how it feels. Time collapses. My mother stands in ruins – again – and I run to her. I'd listen to her bitter lament and weep with her as if we were freshly bereaved. Sigmund Freud called the masochistic compulsion to re-enact painful experiences 'diabolical', because it takes us away from life, and that's how it is: in such moments, you are just surviving. This draining cycle was repeated long enough so that eventually I stopped playing my part and began to draw boundaries for self-preservation. My mother and I grew apart. The no-woman's-land between us lay barren. Time after time, as in a nightmare, I looked into her eyes and saw not my mother but a mask out of an ancient tragedy.

Thirty years after my grandmother's death, and shortly before I embarked on this journey, I was grappling with a health crisis featuring mysterious widespread pain and fatigue. Like the dream of rising water, it felt oddly impersonal. As if I had tapped into a pool of negative energy and it was transmitting its waves to me for reasons I couldn't fathom. I felt the presence of universal death. But I slowly healed myself. Looking back, I am certain that had I not experienced this waterlogged night of the soul, I might not have had the courage of desperation which took me to the Lake.

Around the same time, my mother was struck down with an incurable disease. One of the symptoms was a severe neuralgia, which she called the pain, and soon it was The Pain. Overnight, my parents' lives were subsumed by it. It became the only thing there was. Yes, something was rising like a dark wave, time after time, trying to make itself known beyond any doubt, a shape-shifting presence that felt ancient. It had never been properly challenged, and with my mother's diagnosis it was promoted to legitimate member of the family. But by now, I was so sick of it all – the expression suddenly made sense – I could take no more. I just wanted it all to *cease*.

On my last visit to my parents in Auckland, I found it more suffocating than usual to be in the house with my mother. No doctors or healers could relieve The Pain, it was resilient and narcissistic, and had taken over her whole being. I had the same oppressive sensation I'd had around my grandmother: of subversive subterranean forces disfiguring a landscape. It brought to mind James Hutton's geological insight, in the mid-1700s, into how erosion, sedimentation and deposition had occurred over vast aeons beyond human comprehension: with 'no vestige of a beginning, no prospect of an end'. A chilling thought.

Not for the first time, I had the urge to just walk away. But I knew I couldn't do that, and anyway walking away wouldn't be enough. Under the Antipodean sun which my mother avoided, as ever, behind closed shutters, I saw it starkly: unless I understood why the two women I had loved and who'd had so much going for them (including caring husbands) had become tragic Furies, why we were martyrs to an unknown cause – I was next in line. The mask lurked behind my own face.

When I wave goodbye to my parents at the departure gates in Auckland and they stand there, still together after fifty years – my spectral mother folded in on The Pain, my stocky father propping her up – I wave and smile. My mother's face is collapsed, my father's eyes bright with tears but he is smiling for courage: two people who mean more to me than can be put into words because it precedes language. Soon we'll be oceans apart. Wave and smile. It is only once I pass through the gates that I cry.

I have travelled to distant lands. I have made my bid for freedom. Yet here I am, by the Lake, looking for answers.

PART ONE

SPRING

Ochrida [sic] hangs on a hillside, and trails along the shores of a lake that half Europe would flock to see were it not in this distressful country – a lake of surpassing beauty, second to none for wild splendour. The purple-and-silver glory of its snow-capped mountains fades into a mauve haze beyond the dazzle of its crystal waters. Its awful magnificence grips the imagination, and in mad moments awakes a thrill of sympathy for the unknown men who painfully hewed out tiny chapels in its flanking cliffs, and lived and died alone above its magic waters. There were times when I should not have been surprised to hear the white Vila of the ballads shriek from the mountains.

Edith Durham, 1903

MACEDONIAN GIRL

Over the Alps we flew, over Adriatic islands of all sizes and shapes, and over the highlands of Albania which rose quickly from the river-flats of the coast – mountain upon mountain, the hide of the land like hard-worn velvet. Rivers thickened and thinned into canyons and the roads ribboned between ridges lost in snow and cloud. The sun set over the blackening folds, a mythical landscape. Then suddenly, the blue light of the Lake.

Lake Ohrid is one of those places of the earth that make you feel as if something fateful awaits you. As if you were always meant to come and you can't believe it's taken you so long. When the lake appeared below, the whole plane went quiet.

It was not the tourist season yet, and aside from the wife of the British ambassador to Skopje and a few visitors, most passengers were chatty Macedonian and Albanian expats on a visit home. At the time, the former Yugoslav Republic of Macedonia was on the brink of civil meltdown. The newly elected prime minister and his cabinet had been attacked and injured in Parliament by rioters, some of whom were members of the outgoing government. The country had been in a political deadlock for two years, and everything had ground to a halt. The Pope was 'praying for Macedonia', and when the Pope starts praying for someone or something, you know it's bad.

I looked at the faces on the flight – the women's warm complexions, the men's homely round features. Is this how civil meltdown begins? One moment you're chatting and snacking, the next moment you're attacking the person beside you with a plastic knife. The person beside me was an Albanian hydro-engineer who had lived in London for twenty years. He was travelling with his elderly parents; they would take a taxi from Ohrid to the border crossing, where their car was waiting, and then on to Tirana. He too was worried, not about conflict but about the 'bottomless' corruption in Albanian and Macedonian politics that sabotaged progress.

'Politics is supposed to make life better,' he said. 'In the Balkans, it makes life worse. It's a tradition. Otherwise, we're rich,' he said. 'Look at this water!'

At the small airport, men with tanned faces pressed at the exit hustling for business, not a woman in sight. You could be arriving in the Middle East. I was dunked in a genotype soup: all the men looked like my cousins.

I picked a driver with a nice smile and we pulled away from the terminal. This former military airport was named after the apostle Paul, the first reminder that we had landed right on the Via Egnatia – Paul had been one of the travellers on the antique road. And along the potholed road into town, which closely shadowed the Egnatia, we passed the St Erasmus cave church – a memento of another traveller from the Jordanian desert with a message.

Then mile after mile of orchards that were wild, effulgent. And it was only May.

'*Bavcha*s,' the taxi driver said, gardens. Yes, I remembered them.

The lakeside flatlands on the outskirts of Ohrid looked the same as they had in the 1980s to me, and in the 1860s to a German writer: 'a giant abandoned garden'.

We entered the new town at the foot of the hill – though nothing was 'new' here. The first interesting thing I noticed was the thin white minaret of a small neighbourhood mosque from the Middle Ages. There was the scent of wood smoke. The evening call to prayer began: 'Allahu Akbaaar', a dusty, nasal Oriental chant of piercing melancholy. Half an hour later, the musical ringing of church bells carried down from the gated town on the hill. It was an Ohridian tradition, the taxi driver said. The mosque and the church took turns, they never clashed.

'Because we live in peace. If only politicians stopped hounding us.'

We climbed the winding road to the Upper Gate of the old town dominated by the rebuilt fortress of Tsar Samuil, also known as the *kalé*, Turkish for fort. For centuries following Samuil's dramatic end in the early eleventh century, rulers speaking diverse languages and wearing different headdresses had their residences up here.

We entered the inner town and its steep cobbled lanes ill suited to cars. Half-Levant with its blue lake views and shuttered windows, half-Balkan with its jutting wood-clad upper storeys and lush gardens, the gated town's spirit had endured. It was a spirit of stoicism and stubborn self-regard. The inner town was known as *varosh*, as opposed to the outer town, *mesokastro*, and the varosh looked down its nose at the mesokastro – to this day.

For a time, Greek was the official language here because the Greek Episcopalian Church dominated Ottoman Macedonia from 1767 until the mid-nineteenth century, pushing out the Ohrid archbishopric; but the millennial Slavonic influence kept asserting itself until it prevailed again, in a culture war a thousand years old. Confusingly, *mesokastro* didn't actually mean 'outer', but 'inner' – which suggests that whoever coined it was either dyslexic or not fluent in Greek. But then again, one man's inner town is another's outer.

A medieval-looking gate was still attached to the Upper Gate, and the taxi drove through it: a massive wooden slab panelled in wrought iron and studded with links like chain mail. In the olden days, the Upper Gate was open only on Mondays, market day still. In times of plague, the gate would be closed and movement discontinued till further notice. The wealthier Muslim families in the lower town would pack up their households and go to sit out the plague at the houses of Christian friends inside the gates.

Meanwhile, at the Lower Gate by the lake, travellers and returnees from long journeys were stopped and quarantined in two small interlinked churches: Virgin Mary Bolnichka and St Nicholas Bolnichki had been medical stations in the shape of churches. Hence their names – Virgin Mary and St Nicholas of the Ailing. When later I looked at the lifelike medieval faces in the sepulchral frescoes, they gazed back with expressions that can only be described as healing. Dozens of secret-holding churches dotted the lanes of the old town, tucked away in gardens, camou-flaged as small houses. The Church of the Holy Virgin Perivlepta, 'Most Glorious', with a magnificent panorama over the lake, has been the single continuously functioning church of the Ohrid diocese for a thousand years. It used to have residential quarters for those suffering from 'melancholy'.

The plague was anthropomorphised as the female *Panukla* (Greek for plague), who knocked on doors with deathly knuckles. The Panukla entered the house of such and such, people would say, and shudder. When things got really bad and the Panukla wouldn't leave, the old-town residents would conduct a proces-sion down to the lake.

'St Clement, our golden one!' went the plea, 'Deliver us from the Panukla.'

The priests carried large, long-handled icons of Clement, Naum (pronounced Nah-oom) and the Virgin Mary, typically double-sided so that a saint always faced the plague. The earliest-surviving processional icon, kept in the gallery of the Holy Virgin Perivlepta, dates from 1045 and depicts an Asiatic-eyed Basil the Great of Cappadocia on one side and St Nicholas the protector of fishermen on the other, the latter much needed by the people of the lake. The Muslims took part in these processions too, over the centuries, for the medieval monks Clement and Naum had less to do with monotheism than with talismanic protection.

Ailing and healing was clearly a motif of the lake.

The owners of Villa Ohrid where I'd booked a ground-floor flat with a garden looked familiar – but then everybody looked familiar here. After a brief exchange with my hosts, it turned out that we were in fact related. This was the nature of the town.

A man in the garden below was hacking off the branches of a plum tree with a vindictiveness out of place on such a peaceful evening, until almost nothing was left except the trunk, because – he said – it cast a shadow.

It cast a shadow.

My hosts' daughter was working in Dubai, her mother sighed. Because the young go wherever they can get a visa, she said, and the rest of us stay here and rent out our houses to visitors. Tourism had become the main livelihood.

The outskirts of Ohrid once buzzed with some of Yugoslavia's biggest industries – the iconic Zastava Automobiles among them – and overall, manufacturing employed tens of thousands. All of that collapsed in the 1990s when the era of shady privatisation and mafia barons arrived, furthered by war profiteering for some and war embargoes for the rest, as Yugoslavia combusted. A brain-drain that had begun in the 1980s intensified at the turn of the century as the Kosovo conflict spilled across the border, and has been accelerated in the last decade by a cynical, corrosive culture of extreme party politics. In one generation, Ohrid has lost fifty per cent of its population. One of my cousins, a doctor, recently moved to Germany after being dismissed from his hospital job here for failing to turn up for the obligatory ruling-party parades. Party loyalty was what made or unmade you.

Time after time, I heard people say 'it's worse than Tito'. The general state of morale and culture was worn thin by years of ruthless nepotism, kleptocracy, and grandiose ethno-nationalistic propaganda. The outgoing government had bankrupted the small country. Instead of renovating the waterworks of Ohrid, which were badly in need of investment, they had built gilded statues of Alexander the Great and turned the centre of Skopje into an internationally derided monument to gangster baroque. Some locals were so ashamed of what had been done, they stopped visiting the capital.

The Gladiator Restaurant in my street, above the antique theatre, had just opened for the season. When night fell, out came the dog walkers and the drunken philosophers, and after their dogs had pissed on the giant stone steps, they sat under the lime trees dripping with blossom and the still-green fig trees, and opened beers.

I ordered imam bayaldi and a Macedonian salad, although with the emotion of actually being here I could barely swallow. Seeing my notebook, the waiter asked if I was a writer.

'It's unusual to meet writers nowadays,' he said gravely. He looked about twenty. 'Regretfully, young people in this country don't read.'

He wrote poetry, and we agreed that whoever had literature in their lives would be fine (though clearly it wasn't true). I was the only customer, apart from a Dutch trio. There was something going on with the Dutch – great numbers of them visited the Lake, year after year. It turned out that they were drawn here by a cult Dutch novella set in 1930s Ohrid, *The Wedding of the Seven Gypsies* by A. den Doolaard, a writer and journalist who fell deeply in love with Macedonia and spent long periods here.

'I hope you'll find inspiration in our town,' said the waiter, with a respectfulness normally reserved for officials and the elderly.

And I did suddenly feel greatly aged at my white-napkined table, with my glass of Macedonian red and my memories, like a time traveller. When I looked at the wine label, I saw that it was called 'Longing for the South', after the poem. A quiet welcoming.

Ohrid made you feel the weight of time, even on a peaceful evening like this, with only the screech of cicadas and the shuffle of old women in slippers. Below me was a reminder that gladiators had fought here only two thousand years ago. The amphitheatre had been built by Philip II for dramatic use by the Macedons, converted to a gladiatorial arena by the Romans, and was now used for summer concerts. The theatre was only discovered in the last few decades. As a child, I used to scramble over the partially excavated hill with its houses on top yet to be demolished.

But what a civilised place, where waiters like literature, taxi drivers want peace, and wines are named after poems! The stillness was complete, as if the lake absorbed not only noise, but time itself. It was like the stillness of a deep forest, of something untouched by humans – an odd impression, considering humans had lived here for eight thousand years. The oldest-known inhabitants of the lake shores were the people of two tribes: the Dessaretae and the Illyrian Enchelei. In deep antiquity there had been five towns on the lake, and of those only one made it into the present day, albeit buried under subsequent layers: Lychnidos. Memorialised by a lapidary inscription from the third century BC that reads LYCHNEIDION HE POLIS, 'the place of light' in Greek, it was influential enough to be its own polis.

The creation myth resonates with a symbolism that has not gone away. The Phoenician Cadmus, king of Thebes and brother of kidnapped Europa, founded Lychnidos after he fled from Thebes and his misfortunes there, for the lands of the Illyrians and the Macedons. He established a town here that went on to prosper, though there were interruptions from around the sixth century onwards – long epidemics like Justinian's Plague, which killed half the population of the Roman Empire; invasions by Goths, Huns, Avars and Slavs who stayed and renamed the lake Oh-rid, 'on the hill'; and massive earthquakes caused by the same sulphurous fault lines in nearby Kosel that would cause thousands of tremors weeks after my arrival.

But misfortune continued to pursue Cadmus and his Samo-thracian wife Harmonia. They lost all their children and grand-children, and eventually grew scales and were turned into serpents by the gods, the better to escape their human suffering. As it happens, the two lakes are full of water snakes which I often saw in the shallows, in writhing knots, and shuddered.

The white houses and flesh-coloured medieval churches spilled down the steep lanes towards the lake, a thousand windows glinting in the sunset. There was something archetypal about the hilly old town above the lake, something you had seen a hundred times before, yet it was unrepeatably Ohrid. What I had come to seek was as simple as it was elusive – continuity of being through continuity of place. My grandmother had known every single lane, every hidden chapel. I wanted to rekindle some of that intimacy.

That's why, on this first evening, everything felt too rich and full of hidden meanings to process with the conscious mind. Darkness fell. The lake had gone hard as obsidian and looked like the surface of a vast catacomb. Not at all like that blue lake of the 3-D card that had winked at me in my grandparents' flat. Not at all inviting. For a moment, I was daunted by the enormity of the journey ahead.

Just across the water twinkled the lights of mountain villages. A giant neon-lit cross sat so high up in the hills, it floated in the darkness like an apparition. Smaller lit-up crosses sat atop the old churches in town. This fluorescence was new, a territorial response to the building of new mosques in the area. It made little sense in practical terms, because neither Christianity nor Islam was on the rise here, but I guessed it made sense in terms of culture wars and money-laundering. Here, as everywhere in the Balkans now, and across the world, the new church and the new mosque were part of the newly resuscitated ethno-nationalism, that brisk progenitor of new ruins, new medieval kings, new antiquities, and new age-old hatreds.

From under the cherry tree in my garden, I could make out

the jetty and the lit-up lake promenade. It looked small, yet in my childhood it had been majestic.

At the jetty, a high totemic pole dominated the harbour with its outsized flag of the Macedon sunburst, yellow on red. The sixteen-ray sunburst, initially used by the breakaway republic, had been trimmed down to eight, but too late. In its short life as a national flag since 1995, the sunburst had ignited conflict with Greece. Flagpoles like this had been planted in every town (except those with an Albanian majority) by the outgoing nationalist government. Like the neon crosses, the flag was a territorial marker in a small, vulnerable country whose identity was still a work in progress – as far as its neighbours were concerned. But the neighbours had serious blind spots.

The Bulgarians still didn't recognise Macedonian as a language separate from theirs, and nationalists still called it, patronisingly, a western Bulgarian dialect. Standard Macedonian was in fact only formalised in 1945, and in some ways official Macedonian literature begins on that date, making it the youngest European literary canon – though of course authors had been writing for generations in various regional dialects. Either way, a literary language it is, now, and a national one too. The Bulgarian denial is due to a historical trauma involving repeated border (and population) surgeries without anaesthetic, and whose resonance is akin to phantom-limb pain. Though the body has changed forever on the map, a sensation remains. At the same time, Bulgaria had been the first country to recognise the newly independent republic, back when Yugoslavia was breaking up and giving birth to small nation-states the world was yet to get used to.

The Greeks, by contrast, objected to the very existence of the country under its current name. This is how the trouble concerning the flag was most forcefully manifested in the 'name quarrel' that Greece had developed with the little republic. In the modern Greek-nationalist view, the heraldic sunburst of the House of Macedon belonged exclusively to Greece, because the royal seat of Philip of Macedon had been in what is now the village of Vergina, Greece, and the 'original' Macedonia was forever and exclusively Hellenic. Meaning Greek.

In this, as in many carefully constructed national narratives, one dug a long way down to excavate the precious evidence of historic precedence, but had to be careful to stop before deeper layers yet complicated the argument. Not so long before Philip and Alexander and their imperialism, the Greeks proper looked down on their northern neighbours, the Makednoi, as drunken barbarians. In the early fifth century BC the royal house of Macedon was recognised as Greek at the Olympic Games, but it remained on the remote northern fringes. The Macedons spoke a now lost language incomprehensible to the Greeks, and their political system was more similar to that of their immediate neighbours, the Illyrians in the west and the Thracians in the east, than to the Greek city-states to the south.

Looking at the giant sunburst flapping peacefully in the breeze, I wondered: what *is* Macedonia? A question that really asks: what is nation, what is geography? Meaning: what is history? Herodotus spent his life trying to answer this, but his long-view approach signalled that he had a deep understanding of why 'man is entirely a creature of chance'. He vowed to tell 'the story as I go along of small cities of men no less than of great. For most of those which were great once are small today; and those which used to be small were great in my own time. Knowing, therefore, that human prosperity never abides long in the same place, I shall pay attention to both alike.'

I could count no less than five historic Macedonias. Seen on the map, they move like live mercury around the lakes and between the Aegean, Adriatic and Pontic coasts.

The ancient kingdom of Macedon (ninth to second century BC) started off small – from the gulf of Thessaloniki to Lake Prespa – and ended up as a vast and influential civilisation. Its original contours overlap with today's north-western Greece and the southern part of the Republic of Macedonia. Alexander 'took' the Macedonian Empire all the way to India, changing the face of Eurasian culture forever. His father Philip built great towns all over the Balkan peninsula, often called after himself. The original name of Bulgaria's second city Plovdiv was Philipopolis. Bitola in the east had an impressive town complete with an arena, built by Philip and called Heraclea Lyncestis, after Hercules.

The Roman province of Macedonia (second century BC to seventh century AD) was extensive: from the three-pronged Halkidiki peninsula to the Adriatic in the west, and covering much of modern Albania, mainland Greece and the Republic. It came to an end with the decline of the Western Roman Empire.

The Byzantine *theme*, or province, of Macedonia (seventh to fourteenth century) took over, but it turns up in a bewilderingly different place: much further east, not even overlapping with the preceding Macedonias. It looks like an administrative error made by some clerk who never left Constantinople.

The Ottoman region of Macedonia (fourteenth to twentieth century) shaped what became known as geographic Macedonia today: a large and extraordinarily varied territory with an Aegean outlet, whose main watercourse is the Vardar River. This territory is now divided among four countries (a sliver of it is inside Albania). But only one of these, Greece, has made exclusive claims to the name.

Yugoslav Macedonia (1944–91) was the briefest and smallest, and the one I knew as a child. Its boundaries have remained the same since it declared independence but its evolution was stunted by the quarrel with Greece. On the face of it, at least, the quarrel seemed to stem from an over-identification with an antique empire, and a symbol of this over-identification was the flag at the jetty.

Which results in a sixth Macedonia – an imaginary one, one that does not exist anywhere except in the desperate collective desire for a great past that is required to infuse the diminished present with meaning and value.

★

I'd brought with me a handful of photographs of my grandmother by the lake. In a 1943 photo on the jetty, she wears a rather thin coat and smiles. In her papers in Sofia, I'd found a couple of cards from admirers, written during parties in Ohrid where men wrote messages to the ladies they hoped to dance with. One was from an Albanian aristocrat from the family of King Zog who sent her Christmas cards even after she married another. Another card was inscribed: 'To the most beautiful Gypsy'. There was also a small photo of my grandfather, who was not present at those dance parties. I found many sensually posed photographs of her, with poetic inscriptions and always the lake in the background – often so full of light that the water was invisible. But this was the only photograph of him sent to her: a fair young man with a look of constitutional sadness.

The jetty featured in my own past too. I'd had an encounter here in the late 1990s. The war in Kosovo had just ended. I had travelled from New Zealand back to Europe for the first time since our emigration to the new world in the early part of the decade. It was my first solo visit to Ohrid. An aged man in a Panama hat was throwing bread to the swans. He wiped his hands needlessly with a handkerchief.

'Forgive me for asking, but whose are you, young lady?' he said.

Whose are you? The Ohridian question. I said my grandmother's name and maiden surname. For a moment, I thought he hadn't heard. Then he said:

'I knew her. I heard that she passed away, too young.'

He asked if I would meet him later in the evening, at the same spot. His words became rushed. He was taken by surprise. As was I – I didn't know anyone here, outside the family, who had known my grandmother. In Sofia, she was remembered among the intelligentsia of her generation from her radio days. But a long time had passed since she'd left Ohrid. Fifty years.

We met at the appointed time. He wore a cravat and for a

moment it felt like a date. We walked by the water. He was a retired doctor and had that cared-for look of affluent middle-class Yugoslavia, a country that no longer existed.

'I was in love with her and I wasn't the only one,' he said without preamble. 'More than that, I admired her.'

'She missed Ohrid,' I said.

'She wasn't made for small-town life,' he went on. 'She had met someone in Sofia, an officer in the cavalry. A wartime romance. I heard she had a daughter. But I never saw her again. And one marries, life goes on. Small-town life.'

Nothing moved except the light. I was twenty-five, he was seventy-five, and we each embodied the past for the other.

My grandparents were an odd match, temperamentally. She wrote poems and radio plays, he wrote accounts. She was full of appetite; he was a poor eater. He was resigned, she was turbulent. He suffered quietly, she was a drama queen. If there were a motto that sums up one's chief request from life, hers might have been 'Love me!' whereas his might have been 'Leave me alone.' Then again, perhaps they were no more of an odd match than most. She didn't seem fulfilled with him, that much I knew, and she felt entitled to fulfilment – all the women in this family do. We become enraged like elephants if we don't feel fulfilled by our *loved ones*.

But I couldn't say this to the suitor. On family visits to Ohrid, Anastassia had instructed her young daughter to answer the question *Whose are you?* with 'A child of love'. I picture my mother cringing as she said it to please her mother. You couldn't displease your mother.

'After the war, when she left, things changed,' he went on. 'The narrative changed, and with it, national identity. But these things remain inside you. We are the last generation to speak the old language and remember old Ohrid.'

The mountains at the Albanian end of the lake had turned indigo.

'We take these things to the grave with us,' he said, and gave me his number, to look him up next time.

Ten years later, when I returned to the lake, I called the number. A woman answered and told me that he had died. I hung up and a wave of loss washed over me. I had selfishly expected the suitor to live forever — because he held the memory of the young Anastassia before something had been twisted out of shape.

My grandparents came to Ohrid every summer, to spend long days on the beach with her family. As I knew him, my grandfather was a slender man, easily upset, a poor sleeper who would cry out in the night. His stomach ulcer bled and he was deaf in one ear: mementos from the war. He was a low-key presence, in the shadow of my grandmother. I was very attached to him. One of our routines was to watch him peel and slice an apple, and pass it to me from the tip of the knife. I relished the peacefulness of it: he gave me the apple slices and asked for nothing in return.

He had been a reluctant officer in the cavalry, and fought in Kosovo in 1944. For the previous three years, the Bulgarian army had been an occupying force, not a fighting one. Occupying and annexing a large part of geographic Macedonia, and helping the Nazi project by deporting thousands of Macedonian Jews who were never to return. The main reason Bulgaria had joined the Axis was its claim to Macedonia. Almost all of geographic Macedonia had been included in the territory of newly autonomous Bulgaria by the Treaty of San Stefano (1878), to be breezily revoked only three months later by the Treaty of Berlin — at the behest of Britain and France, alarmed by the size of this new Slavic (meaning pro-Russian) state in the Balkans — and resulting in dramatic shrinkage for Bulgaria and the re-plunging of Macedonia into late-Ottoman abuse, which in turn resulted in the epic Struggle for Macedonia. The consequences of this volte-face by the European powers have reverberated down the generations with some force. This heralded the onset of what would become a chronic Balkan border disorder.

This is why, for the Balkan nations, the Second World War was about either reclaiming territorial losses or hanging onto territorial gains that harked back to war treaties. But when the Bulgarian monarchy saw the Red Army massing on the horizon, it declared war on Germany. Once Nazi allies, the Bulgarians now fought alongside the Yugoslav resistance. My grandfather's 2nd Cavalry Squadron, until then stationed at home in the Balkan Mountains, won a historic battle at Kosovo against the Germans, even though Bulgaria lost Macedonia. Again. For the fourth time in sixty years.

On their way out of Kosovo, knowing the battle was won but Macedonia was lost, my grandfather's squadron looted abandoned houses. In one house, there was a piano. Some of his men, peasants from remote villages, had never seen a piano. They ripped the lid off and made something useful from it: a bench. I wouldn't be amused if someone ripped off the lid of *my* piano, I said, and he said: It was war. War is stupid and ugly. It chilled me that someone as gentle as my grandfather could be a soldier in some stupid, ugly war.

Although he never complained when his wife sickened, it broke his heart. Even before, I felt as if something in him was not strong. I was ever tuned into the undercurrents between him and my grandmother, as between my parents. Driving the hot dusty road to the Black Sea one summer, me sitting in the back, the song 'Et Si Tu N'Existais Pas' came on the radio; my grandmother sang along with Joe Dassin and translated for us:

'If you didn't exist, tell me, for whom would I exist?
If you didn't exist, I'd invent love itself.'

My grandfather, who was driving, wiped a tear but said nothing. Even now, that song brings a lump to my throat.

He accompanied her loyally to the gates of the underworld and returned bereft but also, perhaps, relieved that it was all over – the illness, the marriage, the struggle. She had wanted too much, what he'd offered hadn't been enough, even though it was all he had. Many years later, living in self-imposed solitude in their apartment on the outskirts of Sofia with a view to the blue mountain, as if immured in a tower – with hundreds of books annotated with comments and dates in his neat accountant's hand, and surrounded by photographs of his daughter and her two daughters far away in the Pacific – he must have felt that he could no longer resist the melancholy that had shadowed him all his life. He put his affairs in order, placed his old watch on the round table with the small jar of pebbles to which he'd added the two coins he'd placed on his wife's eyelids when she died – and took his own life.

Out of nowhere a breeze arose, and a shiver ran through the trees of the old town. The cherry tree stroked my head. The lake quivered, chord after chord played by the wind.

When I lay in bed, I could hear the splash of waves on the shore as if they were outside the door. I dreamt of the lake rising in the night and engulfing the town, like an old prophecy.

In the morning, the sound of music woke me. It came from the lake radiant with sunshine. The happy-sad song 'Macedonian Girl' blasted through the loudspeakers of an early tourist boat. It celebrated the women of cosmopolitan Macedonia:

'Macedonian girl, you are a many-coloured blossom.'

Then the refrain, with its undertones of loss foretold:

'Will there ever, never ever be,
a lovelier blossom
than you, Macedonian girl.'

Like the tune, the lyrics were more sad than happy, because the precious blossom is plucked from the mother-tree and given away to some inferior garden–family that would never cherish it enough.

The amphitheatrical town with its glinting windows picked up the melody and echoed it back, as if the houses themselves were humming.

Biljana washed her linens
in the Ohrid springs.
A caravan of vintners passed,
vintners from White Town.

'Vintners from White Town,
gently with your caravan
or you'll crush my linens,
my linens for my dowry.'

'Biljana, blossom-girl,
we promise if we crush them
we'll pay for them in wine,
wine and fiery spirits.'

'I don't want your wine,
I want the young lad over there,
who wears a tilted fez
and looks at me just so.'

'Biljana, blossom-girl,
Our lad is finished,
we'll marry him on Sunday.
That's why we carry wine,
wine and fiery spirits.'

Ohridian folk song

WHOSE ARE YOU?

If you spend time in Ohrid, you'll end up hearing 'Biljana Platno Beleshe' in a more-happy-than-sad D major, because it is the unofficial anthem of the town.

Its first known performance was by the legendary troubadours of Ohrid. With their lutes and guitars, they were a blend of Venetian influence and possibly the medieval Bogomils – the much-persecuted Eastern Christian sect who rebelled against the tyranny of ecclesiastical and feudal landlords, lived in communes, and were famed for their minstrels. Many migrated to Bosnia to save themselves, where some later converted to Islam, and others moved to Western Europe, blending into the Cathars. My mother saw the last troubadours in 1956 when she first visited with her parents. The occasion called for a clan gathering, and the Sadilov Brothers were hired. They played all day and night as seventy members of Anastassia's family sang and drank till dawn.

What intrigues me about Biljana's song is the role reversal: she stands and speaks for herself, while the vintners are the chorus. The groom-to-be remains speechless – 'finished' means betrothed – and though Biljana is left disappointed, she is fully in charge of her linens. The locals have made up a coda, told as a legend: once the vintners went on their way, Biljana's engagement ring – ah, she was already engaged! – was thrown in Lake Prespa, as a gesture of protest. But it popped up in Lake Ohrid, to prove that everything is connected. And that, no matter how assertive you are, you can't escape your fate. Biljana has some springs dedicated to her, near the last protected wetland of the lake, by the marina, where you can sit under the vast plane trees and listen to the frogs' chorus in the reeds for many happy hours.

My first week in Ohrid was spent humming 'Biljana Washed Her Linens', panting up lanes, looking up relatives, and browsing books on the lake promenade where a gently spoken *bouquiniste* with patched clothes, called Elijah, set up his stall in the afternoons. Thunderstorms interrupted the days and made you run down the slippery cobbles in search of shelter, while Elijah deployed his emergency plastic sheets over the books.

On warm days, I'd swim at the tiny Sarayishte beach by the Lower Gate. It was named after the now vanished Ottoman *saray*, or mansion, that had been built here by the ruler Djeladin Bey. Earlier, a medieval money-printing press had occupied the spot. For generations, in their basements by the water, locals had been digging up valuable old coins – or were suspected to have been digging by their neighbours.

With apt symbolism, the old Sarayishte boat jetty had faced eastwards, while today's jetty on the promenade faces west. Planted with weeping willows, Sarayishte sat on land reclaimed from the lake. Well into Anastassia's time, the water lapped against house walls and flooded gardens, sometimes entering windows, bringing in the detritus of the lake: carpets and shoes, barrels and pots and coins from different eras. It was here that the girls of the old town would swim, but only at night and fully clothed. The first Ohrid woman to swim here in a bathing suit, in plain daylight, caused a scandal. I met her great-granddaughter. Her name was Trena, after her great-grandmother.

Trena was my age and a gifted social entrepreneur. Though she'd had opportunities for an academic career abroad, she had returned to the Lake. No matter how hard it was to make a living here.

'Each time I went abroad, I'd start dreaming of the Lake. Like it was calling me. It's in my blood. If I had a thousand lives, I'd still choose the Lake.'

Trena was from a family of strong women, as she put it. Her great-grandmother Trena, the swimmer, had been the first female owner of a taverna, where the town's bohemians gathered. Widowed early, she ran her business alone, and – one presumes – her love life too, because there was a song dedicated to her. Trena had forgotten the melody, but not the lyrics:

'Three years I lay sick for you, Trena,
    and you didn't come to visit once.'

Trena took me back to where she lived with her mother and her young son in a leafy neighbourhood. Her father had died of alcoholism. As had her grandfather, and possibly the great-grandfather.

'Alcoholism is the family trauma. I want no man in my life,' Trena said. 'I'm strong enough to cope.'

She supported her mother too, who couldn't survive on her pension.

'I suppose I'm still carrying the family trauma,' Trena said. 'While telling myself that I've managed to avoid it, by avoiding men.'

Her mother seemed pleased with this arrangement. She showed me her garden full of fruit, vegetables and flowers, filled bags with cherries for me, and was in awe of her daughter – like a housewife proud of her successful husband.

'Come and see your son,' she said to Trena, implying that Trena was not spending enough time with him. But that was because Trena was worked off her feet.

'When Trena was invited to teach abroad,' the mother said, and lit a cigarette, 'I told her: if you go, I'm coming with you. I'm not staying behind like a cuckoo. *Yok.* You'll take me with you.'

I was surprised to hear her use the old Turkish *yok* for 'no', an emphatic negative. But I was not surprised that Trena had stayed in Ohrid.

We sat in the garden and ate last season's hazelnuts with honey, and the mother told me a family story which struck me as symbolic.

It was the late 1800s, the time of the *komita*s, or guerrillas, who fought for the liberation of Macedonia from the Ottomans. In the mother's native village north of the Lake – now a ghost village – there were four clans of which three had komitas up in the hills. Being a komita instantly made you a local hero and absolved you of seasonal work, so it was a popular if deadly occupation. It also meant that you and your mates could descend on a village and raid it – the peasants were obliged to serve the insurgency. The son of the fourth clan, one Velyan, was a pastoralist, too busy with his flock to join the komitas; he travelled seasonally between Elbasan in Albania and the Aegean. One day, Velyan got word of an imminent attack on the komitas by Turkish soldiers at a crossroads above the Lake. He sent word to the komitas, to warn them. But they were drunk and felt invulnerable, and dismissed the messenger. The soldiers attacked them, as planned.

When the dust had settled, the dead were buried, and the surviving komitas had to report to the regional leader. The finger of blame was pointed at Velyan. A vendetta began against him, and since he was always the first to get word, he escaped with his family to Romania. So the komitas murdered his brothers instead – at the same crossroads. After many years, Velyan returned to his village, but nothing was forgiven or forgotten. Not long after, the komitas' sons ambushed him at the same fateful crossroads and killed him.

'At the same time,' the mother went on, 'misfortune pursued the dishonest komitas' families. Children and young people died, as if cut down by a plague.' Until there were just two young people left in the village: Velyan's nephew and the daughter of one of the komitas. Velyan's clan had lost its fortune as well as its men in the vendetta, while the komita clan had grown rich from plunder; rich, but wretched. It was decided that the two young people should be married, as a reconciliation.

'That was my grandparents,' said Trena's mother. 'But what galls me is that the truth was never spoken. Velyan's name is still associated with betrayal. When they betrayed *him*. Why do we shoot the messenger?'

Because it is easier that the shadow lies with the other, not with the self. What struck me about this tale is that the village didn't need 'the Turks' to wreak destruction. They were quite capable of destroying themselves.

Every time I went into the water, I felt instantly happy. Emotion and memory dissolved, only the present moment remained. And it was enough.

Then I'd drag myself out of the water, put on my clothes, walk to the jetty and then to the square by the harbour, and once again feel weighed down by the town's complicated past. A large mosque once stood here. During the interwar Serbian government (1918–39), a statue of King Alexander of Yugoslavia was erected in front of the mosque, facing the lake. When the Bulgarians returned during 1941–4, they dumped the statue in the lake. When Yugoslavia returned under a red flag in 1945, the mosque was blown up to make room for a square, now full of cafes. A statue of St Clement holds the town in his hands.

While buildings and statues rose and fell, the Chinar remained a constant witness. Standing at the junction of the *charshia* (market) lanes, the Chinar was a huge plane tree, allegedly planted by Clement himself in 893. It was of 'immense magnitude', the English painter and polymath Edward Lear observed when he spent time here in 1848 – though at some point it had been split by lightning, and I found its branches clipped and its trunk held together by a metal corset. Over the centuries it accommodated cafes and barbers. This is where Christians and Muslims, men like my great-grandfathers and their Turkish and Albanian friends, came to get a shave, click their worry beads, drink coffee brought on a copper tray by a boy, crunch salted chickpeas, and shake their heads at the folly of politicians.

Across from the Chinar used to be the Radich Hotel, a barometer of Ohrid's mercurial twentieth century. Under the Serbs, it was renamed the 'King of Serbia'. When the Germans arrived in 1941, the owner Radich displayed a swastika, and later that year when the Bulgarians took over, the hotel became 'Hotel Great Bulgaria', that country's tricolour was hoisted, and Radich sent Tsar Boris III forty kilos of lake trout. All the while, Radich went on greeting visitors with the Japanese 'Banzai!' – May you live a thousand years! Radich's own son, in the resistance, didn't live to see thirty; he was killed by the Germans. Then the Communist state 'nationalised' the hotel and turned it into an officers' club for the Yugoslav People's Army, and the only reason Radich wasn't shot as an 'enemy of the people' was because of his dead partisan son. The building was demolished in the 1960s and the land restored to the Radich descendants in the 1990s, who are apparently still arguing over it.

Next to the Chinar is a public drinking fountain with multiple spouts. Surprisingly for a town set on the water, there was no drinking water until 1821 when the Albanian Djeladin Bey commissioned this fountain; previously people in the gated town bought it from pedlars. There was no sewerage, either – on rainy days, each household would pour their collected waste into the gutters, and the fetid mass would run down the streets into the lake. On the façade of the nearest shop, a stone inscribed with an Arabic *tarikh*, or dedicatory poem, still marks the launching of the fountain:

> What the great Alexander did not bring,
> Djeladin Bey did – the water of eternal life.

Now the Chinar was boxed in by benches where locals sat in the shade, and boys cycled past with coffee trays on chains. Every day, I came down from the gated town to drink from the fountain, repeatedly explain to a shopkeeper who said we were distant cousins that I didn't know how he could obtain a Bulgarian (read EU) passport, and have Turkish coffee at a restaurant that backed onto Ohrid's last functioning dervish lodge.

One afternoon, I met the lodge's caretaker. She was the widow of the last *sheik*, or head dervish, and her son owned the restaurant. Her name was Slavche, a diminutive of Slava. She was a tall woman with a fine-boned face who moved with the air of one who knew her stature. It was not the time for deep conversation – it was Ramazan and they were fasting – but she did ask: 'Whose are you?'

At the table was another woman. Her husband had put on his white Albanian *keche*, or skull cap, and gone into the mosque to pray with a handful of other men. I mentioned the family name.

'Oh,' Slavche said, and smiled. 'The darling Tatjana! I see her as if it were yesterday. My son adored her. She was his teacher.'

She took my hand, her face shook, and tears rolled down her cheeks.

'I remember the day we buried her. The whole town came to see her off. It was a scorching day. The sun was shining and she was lying in that coffin. Her mother broke out in eczema. A remarkable woman, her mother.'

Now all three of us were crying. The other woman hadn't known Tatjana or her mother, she was crying for company. I suddenly realised that I'd never met Tatjana either. Later I learned that Slavche's younger son who had been Tatjana's student had died in a car accident. Slavche never mentioned her own loss, not now or later when I returned for her story. Her friend at the table was a Christian from a nearby village who had married an Albanian Muslim; to escape family opprobrium, they had moved here. Perhaps she had something of her own to cry about.

Watching the comings and goings in the charshia was a tradition. Men in keches, men on battered bicycles carrying humble groceries (a loaf of bread, three eggs in a plastic bag), elderly men with faded rolled-up umbrellas and old-fashioned trousers, young women in the painted-on jeans that are perpetually in vogue in the provinces of southern Europe, and Muslim women in headscarves. Some moved around with their overfed sons or grandsons, in whose demeanour you could glimpse that Oriental mix of henpecked and despotic. This wasn't a Muslim phenomenon, it was an Eastern phenomenon, and down in the charshia the East was as ever-present as up in the gated town.

Their habits were the same. Only their styles were slightly different.

Not many Muslims had ever lived in the gated town other than grandees in their sarays; the residents of Imaret, the former Islamic complex at the top of the hill; and the rulers in the kalé. In the early decades (the late 1300s) of the Ottoman conquest, those among the town's Christians who could afford it emigrated en masse to Venice. Many who stayed took Islam. The newly Islamicised became known as *ben Allah*, sons of Allah. Some say that the remainers saw themselves as guardians of the relics of Clement, 'our golden one', buried up at his monastic grounds at Plaoshnik Hill which was to become Imaret. And so the new arrivals and new converts took the lower parts of town, by the Chinar, where they built mosques and dervish monasteries, where the Via Egnatia passed, where the markets sprawled in the mud, where later the rag-tag armies of this *pasha* or that *bey* would block the view of the Lake as the Ottoman Empire began its long agony.

Meanwhile, being Ohridian became synonymous with having gardens. Muslims and Christians alike owned extensive orchards, vegetable plots and vineyards. The monk Naum is credited with introducing viticulture to the Lake, though it's hard to believe that vines weren't grown here earlier. There's a local saying about the Lake's hinterland: so fertile, it could birth a human. The old

Christians stayed in their gated town and tried not to mix with outsiders, especially not people from the outlying villages, seen as deeply inferior. Whose are you? Your name gave your origins away. Snobbery will be the last thing to die here.

Many of the men were merchants, traders, drovers and dealers who travelled for extended periods to Berat in Albania, Elbasan and Durrës (Durazzo), Venice, Salonica and Istanbul, Dubrovnik and Trieste, and later in the years of national revival to Leipzig and Vienna, Paris and Moscow. They'd leave the family in the hands of the oldest woman. These matriarchs were known as *kiramanas*, matrons in Greek. Many of the men secretly took other wives in other towns and villages, and had other families while away on business. Polygamy was open for Muslims, furtive for Christians. Perhaps that is why the gated town developed a matriarchal system of surnames: the women made sure they left their mark.

Whose are you?

I'm the daughter of Angelina.

So that girl would become Angelichina. The absence of the men made the women more powerful within families and communities.

Up in the gated town, people kept an eye on each other from behind twitching curtains, whispering, shuffling around at night to check up on the neighbour's tree, the one that cast a shadow, or the neighbour's wall, the one he was building illegally. I met siblings who lived in the same house but hadn't spoken for years, for reasons long forgotten but not forgiven. There was even a word to describe women who listen, then spin gossip: *portirka*, from the word *porta*, or doorway.

Just how attached this community were to their customs can be gauged by the fact that well into the twentieth century, when most Christian town women in the region wore modern European dress, here many stuck to traditional costume: an embroidered shirt, a thick black woollen belt wound around the midriff where you could tuck various objects and money; a heavy woollen skirt with an additional apron-like layer, and long embroidered arm warmers worn under wide sleeves, medieval style. How women managed to walk the steep lanes in this get-up is beyond me.

But there's more. The women of the gated town also wore the 'varosh veil', a thin white scarf that covered the forehead down to the eyes, and a black face cover indistinguishable from the Islamic veil. A town chronicler of the early 1800s wrote that 'women were not supposed to go to church, or anywhere else for that matter'; their only outings were on Monday, market day, and Sunday, bath day.

Down in the charshia of the lower town, people watched each other openly over the rumbling of voices and water fountains, the spinning of chickens on grills, the tumble of dice in backgammon sessions. Homeless dogs sunned themselves on the pavement and were treated as public pets. The only thing that interrupted this calm was the local madman.

Every day after lunch, he conducted his routine. He was a short man and wore his shirt open at the top, with tufts of black hair poking out. He bounced up and down the charshia with a grin and a radio blasting songs in different languages, and sang along with the lyrics, punctuating them with shouted swearwords. In Macedonian, then in Albanian, then perhaps in Serbian, Turkish and Bulgarian. The next day, the order was different, but the routine was always multilingual. People tolerated him with smiles.

'And anyway,' said the waiter at Neim's Restaurant, 'is he mad or do the rest of us hide it better?' The waiter was a tall, grey-eyed Albanian who had returned to Ohrid after twenty years in Zagreb, to look after aged parents. He preferred Zagreb, but—

'Fate,' he shrugged, as he served my order – a homely dish called *tavche gravche*, an Ohridian diminutive for beans in a clay pot. 'Balkan fate. You can't run away from family.'

'I know,' I said.

The restaurant was named after the owner, Neim – pronounced 'name', so that the running joke was to ask him in English 'What's your name?' and he'd say 'Name' – and it was the last establishment of the charshia, past the Evropa Bureau de Change and the Shogun barber's, and before the start of the new town, which wasn't in fact new.

When I asked the waiter how life was for the ethnic Albanians here, what with the current political deadlock, he said:

'We have always lived in peace. But who knows?' And his jaw hardened fatalistically. He relaxed when he asked what family I belonged to, and heard the recognisable surnames.

Neim, a stocky, charismatic local Turk, had gone to school with someone in our family.

'And of course, I remember Tatjana,' he said. 'How could I forget her?'

We watched the resident homeless dog eat the remnants of a meat dish on the pavement, but not the rice.

Back in the gated town, St Sophia sat in a small square lined with cafes and the remains of other churches. I came here every day to look for the monk of ten years ago. But instead of him, by the rose bushes sat a freelance guide with a paisley cravat and liver spots, who assured me that no such monk had been here.

'No, he was here,' I said, 'we sat on this bench. I still have his CD of chants sung by nuns.'

'Anything is possible,' he said. 'But this church has been a museum since before I was born, and before that it was a munitions depot for the Turkish army and then an arms shop. From about the mid-nineteenth century on. I'm even older than I look.'

And smiling flirtatiously, he took me around the grounds. There was far more depth than spread here. History was experienced horizontally, but read vertically: one lot of ruins sat upon another, and only the top layers were visible to the naked eye.

A couple of centuries after the Barbarian invasions, earthquakes, and Justinian's Plague in the sixth century, the town was resurrected and set up as a religious centre by the Bulgarian tsar,

Boris I. Over the next few generations it enjoyed a Golden Age of Slavonic literacy and learning, in which missionaries and writers from Bulgaria, like Clement and Naum and their followers, were instrumental. The two were disciples of the remarkable monks Cyril and Methodius, creators of the Glagolitic script. The brothers were commissioned by a Moravian prince to create a specifically Slavonic liturgy which eventually emancipated all the Slavs from the Greek and Latin scriptures (and therefore from ecumenical control). This is how the Glagolitic script was born. It was superseded by the Cyrillic alphabet, which was developed in the Preslav Literary School in Bulgaria, propagated across the southern Balkans by missionaries like Clement and Naum, and is now used in Europe and Asia by two hundred and fifty million people: at the westernmost end, the Macedonians and the Montenegrins; at the easternmost, the Mongolians.

The early enlightenment-seeking monks endured ascetic decades of wandering and persecution by the Latin Church before they settled on these shores. Among a population steeped in paganism, it was early days yet for Christianity. Clement and Naum's mission was to convert the locals to the ways of Christ. They were largely successful, and an early Slavonic Enlightenment took place on the shores of the two lakes. Then the Byzantines took over, and Lake Ohrid continued to be known as the Balkan Jerusalem, reputed to have 365 churches – one for each day of the year.

St Sophia was the largest survivor. Its badly damaged frescoes had a gentle eccentricity. The Virgin is grim-faced, with Jesus in her belly, unborn but fully formed. In another, Sophia herself appears, small and Gothic in a corner, a phantom in a nightie. This represented the dream of Archbishop Gregorius at the time, whose lapidary inscription in Greek, dated 1313, still marks the façade of the church. In another scene the Virgin Mary is on her deathbed, and among those who appear to her is Jesus – but he is still a baby. Or was that her soul?

The thirteenth and fourteenth centuries were a time of artistic flowering in the Byzantine world, and the way Eastern Orthodoxy of that period merges everyday reality with biblical and fantastical scenes is reminiscent of surrealism and the dreaming mind. It was appropriate that my memory of the vanished monk should be set here, where several reality planes meet in the frescoes. I wondered where the fifteen drowned people, from the accident I had witnessed a decade earlier, were buried.

The lake is a *gathering point*, the monk had said.

Like its Istanbul namesake, St Sophia had long run its course as a religious hub. Between 1400 and 1913, when Macedonia was wrenched from Ottoman hands, it had functioned as a mosque, with a minaret. But in the 1660s, the Ottoman travel writer Evliya Çelebi reported seeing Christians being admitted to pray, for a small coin, while Muslims didn't use the temple at all. St Sophia had been the town's key conversion – the Ottomans customarily converted the biggest church into a mosque, or a *fatih*, a way of marking territory – but St Sophia the mosque had never taken off.

A local historian told me that an inlaid stone with a medieval Arabic inscription had been removed by the authorities. It said: *You who are of spirit and enter here will feel like a fish in water, but if you lack in spirit – like a caged bird you shall be.* In its place, they had installed a faux-antique marble slab showing the Vergina sunburst – the one from the flag.

Dear St Sophia, whose are you?

As if reading my mind, the guide turned to me: 'Whose are you, my dear?'

Ah yes, he nodded approvingly. His uncle had been a master tailor, like my great-grandfather Kosta; they'd have known each other through the guilds.

'And of course,' he said, 'I remember Tatjana and her mother.'

I asked his name.

'Mustafa Shain,' he said, and we shook hands. He was a Turk.

A Muslim who showed visitors around the Christian heritage of a town that still had nine working mosques – this was truly an Ohridian occurrence.

'A Rumeli Turk,' he specified with pride.

This was the self-designated pedigree of ethnic Turks in the Balkans and it stands for cosmopolitanism and a role in the Balkan mosaic. A Rumeli Turk is a European Turk. Rumelia is how the Byzantine world was referred to, prior to modernity. The entire Balkan peninsula under the Ottomans was known as the land of the Rumeli, European Christians.

Mustafa Shain and I stood at a glass well, the older foundations showing beneath.

'It's the way we are here,' he said, 'each tribe came and left a trace.'

We too were the living traces of those tribes.

During the first Serbian annexation of Macedonia (sarcastically called here 'Serbia: 1', as in a football match), his family changed their name to Shainich, to pacify the Serbs. Then, during the second Bulgarian annexation of Macedonia in the 1940s ('Bulgaria: 2'), they became Shainov, to pacify the Bulgarians. In the space of forty years, Ohrid was claimed and annexed by Serbia and Bulgaria twice each: that's four changes of hands since its liberation from the Ottomans.

Mustafa shrugged. He had lake-blue eyes. 'But we are all linked like a chain, and nothing can separate us, not even God. That is why we must embrace, not fight.'

And then, to my alarm, he embraced me with such passion that I did have to fight him off.

'Look here, you're one of us.' He straightened his paisley cravat after the embarrassing scuffle. 'You must let me take you out to dinner.'

Pulling myself away, I passed a group of women with covered heads. I thought they were Turks. That's why Mustafa was hovering by the church – to cater for the large numbers of Turkish tourists in Ohrid, who moved in groups, following a nostalgic, whitewashed historic itinerary of Ottoman sites. But then I heard the scarved women speaking Russian. Like the ultra-pious adherents of the Islamised new Turkey, the Russian ultra-Orthodox headscarves were a way of showing allegiance to the powers of the day. The Russians, like the Turks, always moved in groups.

I left them to Mustafa. Ohridian men were consummate chancers. They flirted until they dropped dead – I saw men so ill and old they could barely move, and still they tried it on. This was a southern, water-borne sensuality induced by sunshine and tourism, but also a release from small-town life. Winters were long and dull. Marrying your cousin had lifelong consequences, but a summer fling didn't. And flirtation was a form of compliment here, whether you wanted it or not.

Evliya Çelebi, an omnivorous sensualist, waxed lyrical about the lake's inhabitants:

'Because the climate is so pleasant, the men and women, boys and girls here are very handsome. All have silvery complexions, a high stature and wonderful looks. Their beauty is well known throughout the world. Many a visitor has left their heart here.'

You wonder what he got up to. And looking at Ohridians today, who are on the short side, I wonder what happened.

Unlike Evliya's, Edward Lear's sexuality was painfully repressed into his work and adventuring. And yet he was not immune to the sensuous allure of Ohrid. He spent several months travelling through Albania and Macedonia on horseback and wrote a compelling diary. 'Of many days passed in many lands, in wandering amid noble scenery, I can recall none more variously delightful and impressive than this has been.' In his Ohrid watercolours men loiter at corners, dressed in long woollen capes, fezzes, baggy Turkish shalvar trousers, or traditional white Macedonian or Albanian kilt-like fustanellas over trousers. The only women who appear are peasants with donkeys; the gated-town women and the Muslim women of the sarays are nowhere to be seen.

Lear was pelted with stones by Muslim women and children in Ohrid. *Shaitan, Shaitan!* they yelled at him, thinking he was Satan stealing the images from real places and people. The locals had never seen a street artist before. He ended up escorted by a bodyguard issued by the then Governor of Ohrid, Shereeff Bey (nephew of Djeladin Bey). Here's his visit to the Upper Saray in the kalé:

> The Bey himself, in a snuff-coloured robe, trimmed with fur, the white-turbaned Cogia, the scarlet-vested Gheghes; the purple and gold-brocaded Greek secretary, the troops of long-haired, full-skirted, glittering Albanian domestics, armed and belted – one and all looking at me with an imperturbable fixed glare . . . The Bey, after the ceremonies of pipes and coffee . . . expressed his willingness to send guards with me to the end of the world, if I pleased, declaring at the same time that the roads, however unfrequented, were perfectly safe.

As he and his *dragoman* (translator-guide) continued their intrepid way west into Albania, Lear bought himself a fez – to try and blend in and stop being taken for some 'profane magician'.

But even if all travellers' accounts – from the twelfth-century Arab writer Sharif Al-Idrissi, who reported that it took him three days to circumnavigate the lake, to Victorians like Lear – speak of Ohrid's compelling aura, by the time my great-grandparents were born and the English writer and illustrator Edith Durham arrived at the turn of the twentieth century, life was grim for everyone. Socially and politically, the lake was a festering backwater. Ottoman colonisation lasted longer in Macedonia and Albania than anywhere else on the peninsula. The ravages of a decayed autocracy resulted in civil collapse and the rule of banditry. The Turkish soldiers whose job it was to keep the population down and quash rebellions, were neglected by the High Porte in Istanbul, and so impoverished that they wore socks stolen from women and raw sheepskins over their threadbare uniforms.

In the lanes around St Sophia, where workshops sold traditional crafts, one stood out. The artist-jeweller was doing something bold: blending old filigree silver lacework with contemporary design. Her jewellery captured the Lake.

'Because the Lake is inside me,' she said, and she did have the bronzed, wind-swept look of someone who spent her days on the water. Her name was Marta and she lived with her mother in one of the handsome wood-clad houses that hoard their secrets in towering stacked-up floors above the street. A plaque on the house recalled a key chapter in the Struggle for Macedonia. The Turkish groups walked right past it with their guides: histories of struggle and strife didn't fit with their Ottoman nostalgia.

Here had lived Marko Bosnakov, son of wealthy traders and one of the 'Salonica conspirators'. Marta was his great-great-niece and thus indirectly associated with the legacy of the extra-ordinary Internal Macedonian Revolutionary Organisation (VMRO). Along with the original Irish Republican Army, they were Europe's earliest modern independence fighters to turn to terrorism. The history of the VMRO is as tortuously tangled as the Balkans themselves.

The journalist Henry Brailsford wrote that 'Macedonia, in 1903–4, was . . . a desert swept by a human hurricane. It is in these conditions that the Bulgarian insurgent movement [the VMRO] has grown up, a constructive organisation opposed to a negative and destroying force – a government within an anarchy.'

The anarchy was the late Ottoman Empire. Marko Bosnakov had become involved with the Organisation at the turn of the twentieth century, while studying in Salonica's Bulgarian College where the sons of prominent Ohridians were sent. The aim of the Organisation was to ignite a popular movement for the liberation of Macedonia from the Ottomans, and Salonica (Thessaloniki) was its metropolis. These men had no illusions and their motto reflected this: 'An end with horror is better than horror without end.' Later, a branch of the Organisation simplified it to 'Freedom or Death'. That had been the slogan of the Bulgarian national liberation movement a generation earlier – 'Svoboda ili Smrt' – mirroring the even earlier Greek liberation movement with its identical 'Eleftheria i Thanatos'.

The Organisation had many cells. Marko joined one founded by the gemidjias, or Boatmen of Salonica, who weren't actual boatmen but described themselves poetically in their manifesto as 'a group of people who have made a covenant with death by boarding a boat on a turbid sea. We'll either crash, or navigate out of the storm.' Their dedicated underground work of propaganda and national consciousness-building meant that within a decade of its inception in 1893, every village and town of Macedonia supported their credo: 'Macedonia for the Macedonians' (initially, this included Greeks and Turks, but things didn't turn out according to plan).

Among the plots they planned and carried out was an act of public terrorism in Salonica. The aim: to shock Europe into helping Macedonia to shake off the Ottomans. After painstakingly digging a tunnel under the city streets, carrying out the soil in handkerchiefs from a small grocery shop that Marko had hired from a wealthy local, and helped by other locals who were in on the conspiracy, they blew up an entire district, including the buildings of the Ottoman Bank. A French ship was set on fire, to give France a jolt too.

The Ottoman administration was shaken to its core, but Europe did not intervene. France expressed haughty disapproval of the Organisation's methods, though in principle it sympathised with the plight of the Macedonians; the only immediate result was that their plight worsened as terrible reprisals were inflicted on civilians. The Struggle for Macedonia was the most dramatic late chapter in the collapse of the Ottoman Empire, itself a process dubbed by the European Powers 'the Eastern Question'. But what was the answer?

Most of the conspirators blew themselves up and ten bystanders were killed in the explosions. Marko, the youngest of the lot, was captured and given a life sentence in the Libyan desert. He lived to thirty, long enough to hear of the liberation of Macedonia in the Balkan War of 1912. Just as amnesty was announced, he succumbed to malaria. His last wish was to rest in Ohrid, so friends cut off his head and buried his body in a desert oasis. As you do.

'But we don't know where the head is,' Marta said. 'We know they brought it to Ohrid. Perhaps it's in some churchyard here in the gated town.'

Marta was a true Ohridian. She spoke of unpleasant things with quiet dignity.

'Enough about that,' she said with passion. 'I hate politics!'

She'd had a relationship with an ethnic Turk and it had caused a scandal. Everybody here said they hated politics. 'Politics' had come to be equated with injustice and manipulation.

In photographs, Marko has the same slight look as Marta, his black, deep-set eyes shining with intelligence and intensity, like hers. Her latest collection she had called Storm on the Lake: four striking silver necklaces.

'There are four stages in a lake storm' – she touched the necklaces one after the other.

'One, calm. Only the fishermen know it's coming. The rest don't believe it.

'Two, imminence. All four winds appear and blow geometric patterns on the water.

'Three, here it comes. That's what people say when they see the storm coming and stand transfixed on the shore. There's nothing to be done.

'Four, it has passed. Now, the aftermath.'

Just then, church bells rang, slow, deep-voiced, archaic. I couldn't tell whether they were ringing in celebration or in doom.

★

'In the old days, the bells had a range of ringing patterns for different occasions. Slow for death, faster for a birth,' said my new friend Vlado Zhura, while his wife – also a distant relative – served the moist, layered Ohrid *torta* with the world's smallest coffee spoons.

'How can we forget Tatjana?' she said. 'Tatjana and her mother Velika.'

When people spoke of my aunt Tatjana and her mother, they were invoked together. Tatjana had been the apple of her mother's eye.

Vlado was the unofficial archivist of the gated town. A retired journalist of some renown, he was a well-spoken, stubby man with a cauliflower nose and affable personality. Due to poor health, he was confined to their shuttered house at the top of the old town, full of books in many languages. Their sons were my age and both lived here, with the parents. From their high balcony, the gated town looked ready to tumble into the lake.

'The highest bell in town was rung to help orient fishermen in heavy fog. Instead of a lighthouse. Or in case of fire, to alert the townsfolk. Same thing with the muezzin's call to prayer, it had a range of chants. When someone died, the name was said as part of the call to prayer. Did I mention that Djeladin Bey appointed exclusively Christians to the top jobs?'

Djeladin ruled for fifty years (1780–1831), Vlado told me, and is remembered for three things. One, his punishment of debtors. A boat trip to the middle of the lake would be arranged, where the charged were brought in cages. Those cages must be still at the bottom of the lake. Two, that his estates and Ohrid's top jobs were managed by Christians: the chief of police, the chief of carriage transport, the chief tax inspector, the chief of the Tailors' and Silk Embroiderers' Guild of which my ancestors were members. But above all, Djeladin was remembered for his Christian wife Tashula, brought to Ohrid as a slave from a massacre of rebels in the Macedonian town of Naoussa, and for whom he had built a private chapel here. Their only child died in infancy, and after his death Tashula lived a long, quiet life in the fishing community of Kaneo under the old town, and was still invoked in songs.

Vlado knew all the family histories of the gated town and I had come to ask about mine. But the Gardeners, my great-grandfather Kosta's lot, were not well recorded, unusual for an old family. It was supposed that at some point around the 1600s they had come from the Caucasus as gardeners.

'Some Ohridians did come from Armenia and Georgia,' Vlado's wife said.

'The bavchas of Ohrid and Struga were renowned throughout the empire,' Vlado said. 'Like the trout.'

My grandmother believed there was some 'exotic' mix in her father's line, and the possibility delighted her. In early adulthood, Anastassia and her two brothers looked like their father Kosta – olive skin, close-set black eyes, thin noses. They were children of the Balkan Orient that, by the time they were born in the 1920s, had officially packed up and left. But the Orient hadn't moved an inch, because the Orient had always been here: in the air, in the way people looked, ate, loved, and mourned.

Vlado Zhura sighed. He was diabetic but couldn't resist the layered Ohrid torta.

'Things are complicated here. There's always been pressure on us, one way or another. Take my grandmother Chrisanta, we called her Santa. When she walked home from her night shift as cleaner of the wagons on the new steam-train railway, she'd be stopped by police. They asked her name. But she couldn't always tell if they were Serbs or Bulgarians, and she only knew if she'd given the right name if they didn't slap her.'

Chrisanta's mother, Despina, hailed from Crete. They arrived with nothing and stayed poor.

'So poor that my grandfather Argir said: If all the water in the lake turned to milk, still there wouldn't be a spoonful for us.

And my father said: If all the water of the lake turned to ink, still I couldn't write that poverty down.'

But he did: Zhura senior wrote a spirited memoir, describing the life of a poor kid through the multiple nationalities of twentieth-century Ohrid. At primary school, he made his own writing pads from butcher's paper and his own pencils from graphite and bits of wood. In the mid-1930s, he was thrown out of high school for refusing to learn German. Then the Serbs closed the high schools of Macedonia, to keep kids dumb. And a few years later, when the Bulgarian state set up shop in Ohrid, he was nearly executed for being in the resistance. But there is a happy ending. He married a Communist from a rich family.

In a portrait of them from that time, in peaked partisan hats, they look radiant with the bright promise of Tito's Yugoslavia. And it did deliver – for them and their children. Within one generation, this family had gone from extreme poverty in a post-colonial backwater to being in the political and cultural elite of a new country. With his partisan distinction from the war, Vlado's father became chief of regional police, retired at forty-five, and enjoyed a life of privilege. Vlado's mother had been so devoted a Communist that she gave away all the family property to the state.

'We were not impressed,' Vlado said tartly. 'We had to buy this house ourselves.'

Here, you inherit property, you don't buy it. Your ancestors owe you a house, and you owe them your soul.

Vlado and his brother were first-generation, as the expression went – the first lot of Macedonian intellectuals under home governance, or almost. Vlado was aware of the politics of growth and of stagnation. The last twenty years had passed under the rubric of stagnation.

'I hate politics,' Vlado said. He had turned to the past, a safer place.

In his father's memoir is a telling episode recounted by Grandmother Santa. It was the early days of the Struggle for Macedonia, and the Organisation's outlaws were all over the mountains. One such komita, wanted by the Turkish authorities, was hiding in the gated town. When time was running out, just before the Turkish police burst into the house his hosts came up with a plan. What the police found was a dead woman lying on a high bed, with candles burning, flowers in her hands, and women wailing. They backed out respectfully. But under the 'dead' woman, hidden by thick rugs, lay the wanted komita.

To survive in Macedonia, you had to play dead. 'Not here.'

The Young Turks supported the komitas – they had a common enemy in the decaying High Porte. The Young Turk movement, which would beat out a modern nation-state from an obsolete empire, started here, in Macedonia. Mustafa Kemal Ataturk was born in Salonica and studied at the military academy of nearby Monastir (Bitola), named after its many monasteries. The complex ethnogenesis of each modern nation-state, large or small, in the Balkans was in some way reflected in a similar process by its neighbour. But 'to describe the ethnogenesis of Macedonia as "complex" is to understate egregiously its tortuous, labyrinthine obscurity,' warns Fred A. Reed in *Salonica Terminus*, an overlooked masterwork of contemporary political literature, and it's true: everything here was so connected and contradictory at the same time, that I was getting vertigo trying to follow the different strands before they became passionately entangled and descended into a heated power struggle, followed by disintegration. A familiar cycle.

Vlado smiled, and his whole face became florid, not just his nose.

'Whatever happens here is déjà-vu. That's why this lake has more patron saints and hermits' caves than Palestine. There's a lot to pray about. Not that it's helped.'

Vlado the child of sworn Communists was a sworn atheist.

★

Every time I stopped in a sleepy lane to catch my breath and take in the lake view, an old lady would materialise from behind a rosemary bush:

'Whose are you, girl?'

Something about the way I look must have given me away. Only twenty years ago you'd be invited up from the street for a cup of coffee and small crystal dishes of home-made jam, or *blago*, served with water. You would sit in shuttered salons and they would weigh you up and family-tree you, searching for some ancestral disgrace, some thread they could pull and unravel you back to where you are nothing. The gated town held on to the discreet charm of its bourgeoisie. Ohridians knew their town was very old, and this was their wealth. Despite recent knocks to their pride, their prejudice and starched linens were preserved in the shuttered houses above the Lake – like Marta's house, like the houses of my relatives.

I pictured Anastassia handling those irritating doll's-house spoons and thinking: One day I'll get out of this place. She found Ohrid's conservatism suffocating: a girl must be somebody's and the boys have the right to polygamy, you pander to your elders no matter how awful they are, and keeping up appearances is a full-time job.

Even now, inside the gated town you felt as if you were watched by the houses. The tap-tap of your steps on the cobble-stones was magnified by the lake. The silhouettes of night walkers moved against the great pink walls of St Sophia, lit up with pro-jectors at night, as in some shadow theatre. When I sat under my cherry tree at night, sensing the vast presence of the lake, I almost expected to see the outlines of my own mind projected on those walls, as in some open arena of the collective unconscious where everything is laid bare.

Ohrid is still a bastion of Eastern hedonism and puritanism. Together, these seeming opposites continue to prop up the Eastern patriarchy. In Anastassia's girlhood, Ohrid had several hammams, or public baths, and it was the custom to make a day-long visit there on Sundays, taking a packed lunch, and in the courtyard of the hammam you'd purchase chilled refreshments like *boza*, the fermented-millet drink beloved in the Balkans and an acquired taste for the rest of the world. You went in groups – the women separate from the men, though Christians and Muslims bathed together. You would then scuttle down the back lanes, hiding your flushed post-hammam face behind a shawl. A woman was never to walk down the charshia twice on the same day. To walk down the main street twice was to exhibit yourself.

I went to see the site of the old Gardeners' house where Grandmother Anastassia had lived in the 1940s and where her mother Ljubitsa had lived with her daughter-in-law, the twins and Tatjana later. The spot was next to the former central hammam (in use as late as 1959), and though it's on the flat, the Lake looms big and blue at the end of the street.

Then the Yugoslav state 'estranged' the house from the family, as the official term went – under Communism, owners were literally estranged from their property, family members from each other, nations from their neighbours *and* from their recent histories – bulldozed the whole block and built a shopping arcade called 'Amam', a warren of shabby little shops which were, ironically, as Oriental in nature as the hammam had been, but minus the charm. Fragments of the old baths, built from rose marble, were preserved inside a dingy disco club.

It was here, my twin aunts told me, in her bedroom, that my great-grandmother Ljubitsa would pray to St Petka-Paraskeva. Ljubitsa lived with a sense of unfulfilled potential, a queen deprived of a crown. Her intense mental energy had been sucked into the petty politics of family. A sense of enclosure dominated her life.

'Ohridians. They shut themselves in dark rooms and worry about death and their reputation,' said Gotse Zhura.

Gotse Zhura was an expert on religious art and also Vlado

Zhura's brother. Like Vlado, he was a bit of a legend. They lived on separate levels of the same house and kept their distance. By claiming archival expertise in different parts of the Lake, they'd negotiated their sibling rivalry: Vlado covered the town's families, and Gotse had the Lake's frescoes.

He was a short, robust man of Dionysian energy. As a boy, he'd got into a fight and lost the sight of one eye. The resulting squint gave you the feeling that he was looking at you *and* something beside you, perhaps your shadow.

'Ohridians,' he said, 'are like an Indian caste. Fossilised.'

True, he was one of them, but he'd rebelled. He had encouraged his daughter to study abroad, even if it pained him to see her so rarely.

'Ohridians are turned away from the Lake,' he said. 'All they see is the past. As they age, their grip on their children tightens. Their favourite topic? Illness.'

It sounded familiar.

We had driven to Imaret-Plaoshnik at the top of the hill, even though it was just three hundred metres from his house. After a lifetime of climbing rope ladders to cave niches, Gotse had injured himself and couldn't walk. Like his brother, he was confined to the house, and unlike his brother, he'd been drinking to anaesthetise his pain. We'd been drinking together, in fact, from a bottle of home-made plum rakia.

He used to come every morning to meditate on Clement's Hill, Plaoshnik.

'Though I'm an atheist and a Communist,' he said. 'Even after forty years of hanging out in cave churches.'

In his younger years he'd take an old gun and a knife, and camp in lakeside caves, like the hermits – waking at dawn, swimming, fishing. To get the vibe.

'Each hermit dwelling has its own vibe.'

Everything here led to something else, he said, everything was connected.

'You know Chelnitsa?'

Chelnitsa, or the Front Church, was a curious place, named after its position right next to the Front Gate of the old town. The gate had been walled up in the thirteenth century, after a Byzantine ruler of Macedonia and Thessaly, one Theodore Komnenos Doukas, was crowned here. According to tradition, the gate through which a ruler passed en route to his coronation had to be walled up – so that no other ruler would follow him. A doomed wish for permanence. The Komnenos dynasty ruled the lakes, without kindness, for a century.

'There's a tunnel under that church that pops out in the cave church above St Petka Monastery. Though I've never walked it myself.'

That was a long way – the monastery was high in the Petrino Mountain above the lake.

'Over the ages, whenever something was partly destroyed, a secret sign was left, a *nishan*.' A Turkish word. 'When you explore sites, you look for the nishan.'

This is how he excavated old churches, including one buried inside his wife's family house by St Sophia. It is now a gallery with a fountain. The family's name was a nishan in itself: Shandanov, meaning candelabra, indicates the proximity of a church, and the family had always known about the remains in the basement.

At Imaret-Plaoshnik, the swallows were singing. We sat down on a ruined basilica wall, Gotse wincing with pain at each move.

'Fuck pain,' he said, 'I won't let it get me down. Not when I have this!'

The glittering Lake stretched out like a carpet of infinity. Gotse pointed with his cane at the marble *turbe*, or tomb, where one Yusuf Sinan and his brother were buried in 1493.

'The oldest surviving Islamic site in town,' Gotse said.

Yusuf had been one of Ohrid's enlightened beys. Imaret, the former Islamic complex here, was his bequest: a public kitchen-shelter for the poor, regardless of creed. Mansions of Muslim and

Christian grandees had stood here, gardens, vineyards, a Muslim cemetery. All that remained of Imaret was the name.

Across from the tomb was a three-naved church: Clement's ninth-century monastery of St Panteleimon, built on the ruins of a fourth-century Roman basilica, destroyed and rebuilt as a mosque in the fourteenth, and rebuilt to resemble its original shape within my lifetime. But what *was* the original shape? A seam of lead ran across the walls like a wave, showing the tideline of epochs. The original shape was out of view.

'Ironically,' Gotse said, 'Clement never actually lived here.'

But actuality didn't matter to the people of the Lake. Continuity did, and Clement was a symbol of continuity. For Gotse, this spot was the most sacred place in Europe.

'And sacred places belong to nobody,' he said. He had turned his back on the small-minded old town and dedicated his life to the Lake. He knew he belonged to the Lake, not the other way round. We all did. Gotse Zhura died by the Lake in the spring of the following year, but while we sat on the hill, the spectral blue of water, mountain and sky presented a picture of the world at peace so sublime, so immortal, that we both offered thanks.

Lake Ohrid

Age: 1–3 million years

Depth: 300m maximum; average 15m

Altitude: 695m

Highest peak in the area: Galicica Mountain, 2,270m

Catchment area: 2,600 km2

Islands: none

First known name: Lacus Lychnitis (Lake of Light)

ACROSS THE LAKE

It was early morning and the water was transparent like a membrane, newly born. My guide was a young woman called Ivanka who happened to be a cousin of Tino, my cousin and Tatjana's son. I had booked the boat trip without knowing this – yet again, I had landed in the lap of distant relatives.

The faces of the gated town had begun to feel too familiar after a week. There were streets I had started to avoid, and I was keen to get out on the water. The eastern shore in particular interested me. I wanted to find out how my great-grandfather had escaped in 1929 by making the lake crossing myself. Had he crossed the whole length of the lake to the Albanian shore in the south? He had been with a friend. In the era before the motorboat, they would have rowed thirty kilometres.

'Anything's possible if you're desperate enough,' said Ivanka's dad in answer to my question. He was a placid man with kind eyes, and the boat was his. I asked him if he remembered my aunt Tatjana, his sister-in-law.

'How can I not?' he said simply, and wanted to say more, much more, but couldn't find the words. Besides, I was a stranger to him. 'Tino grew up with us, after her death.'

His own girls had set up the first hiking tour company in Ohrid.

'Dad encouraged us all the way,' said Ivanka, and unfolded a camping table. We breakfasted on succulent tomatoes, sheep's feta, *burek* (stuffed pastry), and triple drams of 'breakfast rakia' made from grapes – golden and smooth, only forty per cent, said the dad.

'When my sister and I trained as mountain rangers, we were the only girls out of a hundred!' Ivanka said. 'They hadn't expected women so we had to do the same press-ups as the men. But we did it. Dad always believed in us.'

Dad was not one to take credit, but he did his bit for the business, with the boat. Of course, the business was family-run. If you were to succeed at anything here, you did it as a family.

'It's a super-conservative culture,' Ivanka said. 'My sister and I are exceptions – doing something active, daring to dream, not just marry and have kids.' Getting out on the lake with the wind in your hair helped you dream, I felt it already.

We passed the forested peninsula of Goritsa, once Tito's summer estate. It was still the property of the president of the republic, occasionally in use.

'We went in to see the villa, once,' said Ivanka. 'It's like a museum. Tito's portraits are still on the wall. Creepy.'

The few shore miles after that were lined with aged Yugoslav-era hotels whose names provided a chronological rewind of the country's self-image, from Communism back to antiquity: 'the Granite', 'the Cement', 'the Metropol', 'the Philip of Macedon', 'the Dessaretae'. Above them perched the Lake's monasteries. The most mysteriously named among them was St Stefan Panzir of 'the Chain Mail', after an army of soldiers in chain mail who perished on that spot just south of the Egnatian Way. But who were they? Nobody knew for certain.

One reasonable guess, based on oral histories, is that the battle foreshadowed the First Crusade and the rising tide of bellicosity in Western Christendom against the East. The Islamic East and the Christian East, both. The Normans invaded Albania from the Adriatic during the years 1080–85, and were defeated here by the Byzantines, the then defenders of Lychnidos, whose archbishop had taken refuge with hermits in the cliffs. And what made the

Byzantine army so strong? The huge numbers of Turkic mercenaries and other Orientals and 'barbarians' in its ranks.

The more I learned about this region, the more it struck me that the south-west Balkans, and the Balkan peninsula as a whole, were an arena both of marriage and of war not only between Christianity, Islam and Judaism, but also between the Occident and the Orient, and therein lay their complexity and their trouble. The Orient had given birth to Judaism, Christianity, Islam, Hinduism; and before that, the earliest practices of Asian Shamanism. It was in the Orient's nature to contain all of these simultaneously, across time: to be polyglot. Not so with the Occident, or not to such an extent.

We learn from the medieval epic *La Chanson de Roland* and also from Al Idrisi's *Book of Roger* (twelfth century), that the Byzantine army had soldiers of twenty-seven ethnicities and faiths, including Turks, Persians, assorted Slavs, Armenians, Pechenegs, Avars, Hungarians, and 'Strymonians' (from the region of the River Struma, or Strymonas). As late as the end of the thirteenth century, when the armies of Charles of Anjou continued to assault the peninsula via the Egnatian Way, Byzantium and Bulgaria repelled them with the help of Turkic and other Asiatic soldiers. It was the ambiguous, many-faced, multi-theistic East pitted against the more singular righteousness of the West – and against one another, as in the case of Bulgaria and Byzantium. These internal Christian wars ultimately opened the way for the Ottoman Turks to enter the European stage.

I looked at Ivanka and her dad, all three of us born of this peninsula's baggy, natural cosmopolitanism, understanding each other perfectly, yet artificially estranged from each other by divisive internal politics.

We rejoined a wild coast. As the hotels disappeared, the limestone mountain grew. I could see the odd hermit niche, and even a rope ladder hanging halfway down the cliff. It had been a while since anyone had climbed there. Perhaps Gotse Zhura had been the last.

'In the distant past, the lake was higher,' said the dad.

Some of the caves now out of reach could have been reached by boat even just a hundred and fifty years ago. If we went far enough back in time, the lake would become a sea. Geological relics of its existence have been found as far as the Debar Lake, sixty kilometres to the north. It had been one giant body of water, inside the Dessaret basin, a tectonic depression formed three to five million years ago. It gave me vertigo to think that the time we have been here (forty-six thousand years for humans, less for *sapiens*) is but a blink in the life of the lake. And here I was, trying to understand the emotional life of just a hundred lacustrine years.

I asked how deep it was where we were.

'If you can see through, then it's no more than twenty-three metres,' the dad said.

The reason for this extreme transparency is the multitude of sublacustic springs that feed the lake, including the ones that come all the way from Prespa.

'This lake is Europe's largest natural reservoir of clean water,' said Ivanka. 'The greatest threats are pollution and over-urbanisation.'

A natural scientist told me that the lake's retention period, meaning the time it takes to fully renew its water, is seventy-five to eighty years. That's a lifetime! It was almost a miracle that the lake had retained its cleanliness, clean enough to drink, when all else around it – the state, the economy, the climate – had been eroding. The engine was too noisy for us to talk, so Ivanka and I lay on the hard boat benches and soaked in the morning sun, while her dad steered us south. The lake sparkled, full of sky. But the jagged tops of the mountain, where a white paraglider hovered like an albatross, looked hostile to humans. I was sure that Kosta had done this crossing by night. He had been one of countless lake escapees between the two world wars.

'Many didn't make it,' the dad said. 'They were eaten by the fish.'

'Or the *samovilas* tricked them to the middle of the lake,' said Ivanka, smiling.

'We have no business in the middle of the lake,' the dad said, not smiling.

One of the lake's folk legends involved the Slavic *vila* or samovila, the shape-shifting entity that takes the form of a woman, like a nymph who moves very quickly above ground and usually appears at full moon, in forests and other liminal time–spaces. I'd never before heard of lake nymphs, though.

'This lake has its own samovilas,' said Ivanka. 'They sing to the fishermen, songs without words. Until they drown.'

'There is a song from the 1920s, when many men escaped across the lake,' said the dad, and sang the first lines:

'Ohrid, Ohrid, ubav mil
ti za mene ray si bil.'

Ohrid, Ohrid, gentle, wise,
lost to me, like paradise.

The song was actually written by another ancestor of mine who also escaped to Albania. It was the song of the Ohridian exiles.

The dad smiled in a conciliatory way. Like many lake people I met, he was not keen on turbulence.

But Kosta had been. My great-grandfather Kosta, of the Gardeners, had been one of Ohrid's most eligible and outspoken young men, well known in the charshia. So outspoken that on one occasion he walked up and down by the Chinar, clutching his birth certificate and shouting: 'Look here! Look at this *ferman*. It says by signature of the Sultan that Kosta Bahchevandjiev was born in 1890 a Bulgarian! Who is the shitface to contradict me?'

In the only portrait of him I have, he must be around thirty years old. He looks so intense, with his acquiline nose and fierce black eyes, that he almost burns a hole in the photo. When he rowed across the lake in 1929, he was running from the consequences of this patriotic episode, or similar. But many of the men who escaped were young and single, like the author of the song, whereas Kosta was married with three children.

There were no surviving letters or stories, not a scrap of memory passed down from the four years after Kosta's escape. It was a black hole in the family history.

At the dawn of the twentieth century, before any of this came to pass, Kosta was studying at the School of Fine Tailoring in Salonica. After the First World War, in which he fought on the Bulgarian side, he moved to Sofia and set up a business. That is where he met Ljubitsa, a young woman from the Zarichinov-Karadimchev family in Ohrid.

Why were these two young Ohridians living so far from their beautiful lake?

Because the Struggle for Macedonia was not over. The Greek expression for it – *Makedonikos agonas* – reminds me that agony (*agonia*) is inevitably the result of violent contest (*agon*). They are practically the same word. The Struggle for Macedonia was, at various times, at the heart of domestic politics in Bulgaria, Greece and Serbia, and shaped the course of both world wars in the Balkans. When the 'Macedonian Question' first emerged in the late nineteenth century, Macedonia was a large province of the Ottoman Empire, itself dubbed 'the sick man of Europe' by Tsar Nicholas I of Russia.

Macedonia's main commercial city was Salonica, its administrative and military capital Monastir (Bitola). Its eastern boundary was Pirin Mountain, and its western boundary Lake Ohrid. In the north, it reached Üsküp (Skopje) where the province of Kosovo began. Macedonia and Albania remained under Ottoman rule long after all other peoples in the Balkans had won their independence. Those who finally wrenched Macedonia from the Ottomans in the First Balkan War of 1912 – Bulgaria, Serbia, and Greece – were fighting over it in the Second Balkan War the following year.

By then the new, successfully decolonised and rapidly modernising Balkan nation-states were vocal about their historic precedence – and hence their territorial claims to Macedonia. But what about the Macedonians – that is, the *many-coloured blossom* of humanity that inhabited the territory of Macedonia? Memoirists, chroniclers and travellers describe how Muslims, Christians and Jews had lived in relative harmony for centuries.

'These poor people have the unenviable privilege of being claimed by three different nationalities,' wrote the French officer and chronicler Edmond Bouchié de Belle shortly after the Balkan War of 1913 had poured salt into the Macedonian wound, leading to the devastating battles for Macedonia in the First World War, which cost him his life too. 'And each nationality used all available means of propaganda: the church, the school, even the bomb.'

The three million people of Macedonia spoke a Babylon of languages: Ladino (Judaeo-Spanish), Greek, Bulgarian and regional Slavic dialects, Albanian, Turkish, Aromanian, Armenian and Romani. The dominance of each language or dialect changed from district to district, and awkwardly, village to village. Salonica was a major Sephardic city. Aegean Macedonia had a majority of Bulgarian or Slavic speakers in the villages (both Christian and Muslim), but a strong Greek-speaking merchant class in the towns. This densely woven pattern could not be separated into individual threads, and therein lay the 'Question'.

The main religions were Eastern Orthodox Christianity, Islam and Judaism. Social allegiance was determined by faith, and to a lesser degree by language. There were Orthodox Bulgaro-Macedonians, Orthodox Greeks, Bulgarian-speaking Pomaks and Torbeshes (Muslims), Muslim and Christian Albanians, Turks, Armenians, Jews, and Aromanian Vlachs who were typically Christian but on occasion Muslim. There were even Turkish-speaking Christians – the Gagauz, whose descendants still live in the Balkans, including in Romania. No combination of language, faith, costume and visage was too outlandish in Ottoman Macedonia – the *salade macédoine* had a colourfulness impressive even by Ottoman standards.

This cosmopolitan abundance was a legacy of the land's intermingled ancient civilisations, the settling of Sephardic Jews in Ottoman Europe after their expulsion from Spain, and other movements of people over the last two thousand years, not least the numerous Slavs who had interbred with the autochthonous inhabitants of the ancient world – Thracians, Illyrians, Macedonians and Romoi, or Romans (as Greeks referred to themselves in the Byzantine era and beyond). It was to prove a nightmarish kind of abundance.

Macedonia had been a prominent civilisation at the time of the Macedons of Philip and his son Alexander in the third to fourth century BC. But Macedonia of the late nineteenth century and Macedonia of antiquity overlapped only partially on the map. The geographical contours of Macedonia had shifted over time.

In his deeply observed chronicle *Macedonia* (1906), the most valuable source on the region from that time, Henry Brailsford describes a village above Lake Prespa where two brothers lived. One said he felt Greek. The other felt Bulgarian. How can one mother give birth to sons of different identities?

Identity – or rather, the pressing and sudden need for it – was at the heart of the Macedonian Question. The mother is not quoted on how *she* felt. She probably wasn't too fussed as long as her sons were not recruited into some guerrilla band and killed before they reached thirty, as was the common fate of Macedonian men. In another village on the boundary between Albania and Macedonia, the Scottish writer John Foster Fraser asked an innkeeper:

'What are you?'

'Well, sir,' replied the man, 'I find it best to be Greek.'

'There was a Greek band in the neighbouring hills,' Fraser notes drily.

Like Kosta's and Ljubitsa's families, many of Macedonia's Slavic speakers at the time identified as Bulgarian, if they identified at all, though a separate Macedonian identity would emerge. They belonged to the Bulgarian Exarchy, which had wrestled power back from the Greek Patriarchy in Constantinople in 1870. The Greek Patriarchy and the Bulgarian Exarchy waged a merciless war over hearts and minds, resulting in many dead bodies. Entire villages in Macedonia would give different answers to the emissaries of the governments that courted or threatened them, sometimes all within one week. And the whole time, they lived in fear for their lives, in case they gave the wrong answer. Like Vlado's great-grandmother going home in the dark.

Identity as tyranny: that's what the Macedonian Question became, over time. Fraser writes:

> What amounted to civil war began. Greek 'bands' adopted the methods of the Bulgarian 'bands'. Greek-speaking villages which had adopted the Bulgarian Church were obliged to renounce their religion and become Greeks proper, or have their houses burnt, or worse. The villagers, who would like to be left in peace, yielded, and instead of Bulgarians became Greeks. When the Greek 'band' withdrew, down came the Bulgarian 'band' to reconvert the village and make the inhabitants Bulgarian again. Thereupon the Greek 'band' cut a few throats and fired a few houses just to remind the peasants they must be Greeks or be killed . . . The bishops and priests of the Greek Church in particular not only countenanced but urged crime as a means of compelling Bulgarian Macedonians to proclaim themselves Greeks.

Travelling across Mount Athos in Greece a few years after Kosta rowed across the lake, the English travel writer Patrick Leigh Fermor 'fell in' with a lone walker from Macedonia. He 'didn't seem quite certain whether he was Greek or Bulgarian', Fermor writes. 'He was a melancholy, bearded chap.'

To not *seem quite certain* could have deadly consequences. To this day, the nations once involved in the Macedonian Question cannot agree on a single version of the past, or even on compatible versions, which is why each writes their own sanitised version, and in each the protagonist nation has the last word on victimhood. When you consider these versions closely, they all contain truths as well as lies in the shape of omissions, evasions and self-deceptions. In some cases, these form the very backbone of the cleansed national narrative. The Scottish writer Neal Ascherson has called this syndrome of selective national memory the 'biscuit-factory line of history' – one that favours homogeneity over ambiguity.

To be uncertain could kill you, but to be certain was equally dangerous when the winds changed so frequently. When my great-grandmother Ljubitsa was nineteen and freshly graduated from the Bulgarian high school in Ohrid, she was sent to Sofia with her younger sister Tsareva (from *tsar*, 'the kingly one' – because one had standards!). It was an unsettled time. It was *always* an unsettled time, but this particular time was newly into the First World War. Every day, explosions thundered in the hills above the lake.

For these conservative girls who had been embedded in the bosom of family, to find themselves in the big smoke with just distant relatives to fall back on must have been a shock. Ljubitsa, smart and with a solid education, found work as a clerk, and her sister enrolled in a high school – education was high priority in the Zarichinov family, even for girls. In Sofia, Ljubitsa started going out with an officer. There was a ring, later returned or perhaps thrown in the lake. For, even from across the border, the Zarichinov family were keeping an eye on their girls. Soon, Ljubitsa's future was decided. She was to marry a fellow Ohridian from a suitable family, who just happened to be living in Sofia too.

Ljubitsa and Kosta married in 1920 and their first two children were born in Sofia. Mitko inherited his mother's cautious pridefulness and Anastassia inherited her father's combustible temper. Sofia of the 1920s was a bustling, cosmopolitan, on-the-make city, halfway between the languid Orient and the industrious West, teeming with crooks and poseurs, clandestine Communists and mutually murderous agents of the hydra-like Internal Macedonian Revolutionary Organisation (VMRO) – the offspring of the Struggle for Macedonia – tobacco barons and tubercular ladies of leisure, foreign consuls, and traumatised exiles from the Balkan Wars, the First World War, and the Armenian Genocide in Turkey.

And everyone needed a good suit – which is how Kosta found himself running a bespoke-tailoring business. Ljubitsa helped. He had twenty young apprentices, the most senior known in the trade guilds as *kalfa*, master-apprentice. Thirty years later when my mother was a girl, when Sofia had been levelled by Soviet-inspired architects and the old town with its Oriental bazaars bulldozed to make room for a later version of the twentieth century, her mother took her to a lane where a tailor called Asparukh still had his workshop. He was Kosta's head kalfa, who had held his baby daughter Anastassia in his arms.

The family lived very well for a few years, but Ohrid was calling. Ljubitsa's sister Tsareva also married an Ohrid man in Sofia called Dimitraki (or Taki) who, after serving in the First World War on the Bulgarian side and losing the use of one hand, went silent – post-traumatic shock. Unlike her sister, Tsareva opted to remain in Sofia. She enjoyed being free to walk down the same street twice. But Ljubitsa missed Ohrid.

Back in Ohrid, Kosta and Ljubitsa found themselves in the midst of 'Serbia: 2'. Anastassia and her brothers went to the Serbian school, the only school now, and soon spoke Serbian. This was an era of political and cultural repression. The authorities closed down all but five high schools in southern Macedonia – for education breeds independent thought. Two generations of Macedonians were deprived of higher education. The Secret Police were at every corner and the once rich lake district became the poorest corner of Yugoslavia. Yugoslavia ended in violence – as it had begun.

In *Footnotes on My Town* a local writer, Nikola Janev, wrote: 'between 1914 and 1941 Ohrid was dying, physically and spiritually. Every day an old house collapsed and ivy invaded the ruins. The little intelligentsia we had was mowed down: the vast part remained in Bulgaria, a smaller number were dispersed within the Kingdom of Yugoslavia, and the remaining few somehow stayed close to home.'

Kosta was constitutionally incapable of toeing the line. Some people are like that: they would rather call you a shitface and be shot than goose-step. My grandmother Anastassia was like that, she got it from him. Kosta's brothers had already cut their losses and emigrated to Romania. In countless local histories of that time, I found the sentence: *He escaped across the lake*, often followed by *and was never heard from again*.

'Trpejca,' Ivanka said, rising from the hard bench. I too wrenched myself from the dreamy lull of engine, water and sunshine.

Trpejca, pronounced Ter-pey-tsa, sat on a piece of rocky coast jutting into the water. The houses were embedded in the hill like semi-precious stones.

'Welcome to Saint-Tropez,' said a short man with badly burnt fair skin we'd accosted at the beach for a quick coffee at his small restaurant, St Tropez. He was an uncle of Nate's, cousin Tino's wife. Trpejca-Tropez with its pristine sand and nearby cave churches had welcomed holidaymakers for decades in the era of Yugoslavia, but that was followed by a slump during the Yugoslav Wars and Macedonia's own civil war.

'Now it's back to business, thank God,' the uncle at St Tropez said. 'Our village has been here a long time. The lake even longer. And nationalities are recent. There was no distinction between us and the Albanians or Bulgarians, for most of the lake's history. We're the same people.'

Surprised by this statement of solidarity, I nearly hugged him. His straw-fair hair and light eyes were a feature of the people of Trpejca, which they joked about themselves. I knew this because Nate had told me. With her copper hair and freckly skin, she looked Celtic.

'It might be the Italians left some seed behind,' she'd said with her Gioconda-like smile, 'We always say there's something in the mix that isn't from here.'

In the nineteenth century, Trpejca was known for its women who rowed like men: an older woman would sit at the prow of the ancient boat, and two younger women rowed.

Seeing the traditional lake boats, *chuns*, in a museum, was a shock – they look prehistoric but were in use well into the 1950s. With its coffin-like squareness and high sides, the chun was the very likeness of Charon's boat that takes your soul across the Styx. It made the same ancient impression on writers over the centuries: the chun had remained unchanged since Roman times, and its prototype came from the Illyrians. Which makes the Ohrid chun seriously old. It was in these vessels that the women of Trpejca took logs to Ohrid town, to supplement their fishing income.

For centuries, fishing had been the livelihood in lakeside villages like this one. The *pastrmka*, the famed trout of Ohrid, was carted all the way to Istanbul.

'There used to be twenty fishermen here,' the uncle said. 'Now there's one.' Trout had dwindled as a result of overfishing, resulting in a ban, while the other famous Ohrid species, the eel, had dwindled as a result of damming. Its story is unbelievable.

'But true,' said the dad. We were back on the noisy-engined boat.

The young eels travel east, all the way from the Sargasso Sea in the Atlantic, via rivers and underground streams, to this lake and none other. When they reach maturity, they travel back to the Atlantic to mate. Nobody knows just how they make this epic journey, and the place in the Sargasso where they drop their eggs hasn't been located. The damming of the River Drim in the late 1950s put an end to this mysterious pilgrimage. For the first twenty or so years, the eels remembered the ancestral migration route, and faithfully tried to retrace it – they'd throw themselves en masse into the maw of the hydroelectric beast, resulting in massacres, time after time. But a few individuals would make it across and continue the laborious cycle. Ancestral habits die hard.

An ecologist told me that the eels have all but disappeared; but nobody cares, since it is the trout that fetch a good price on their way to restaurant plates. Attempts were made to bring in some baby eels from Greece to rejuvenate the population, but EU regulations about livestock got in the way, since Ohrid is not part of the EU.

Suddenly, the rocky inlet of Zaum appeared. We had reached the deepest part of the lake and now disembarked at the small beach. There was a church encased in scaffolding. Extensive living quarters had been recently built in place of the long-ruined monastery.

'For the needs of the church,' said the caretaker neutrally, but it was clear: church officials had fenced off this inlet – which was public ground – and claimed it as their own. So that clerics could come to eat, drink, and cool their gout-swollen feet at the beach. Or the building would be turned into a hotel, the revenues of which would fill the pockets of the Church. We had to pay to use the grounds. Feudal behaviour was a recurring motif.

'We planted these trees in the 1970s when we camped here,' said the dad. Willows and chestnuts spread their thick shades over the courtyard. The public improvements were all made by locals.

A karst peak called Big Shadow rose vertically above the monastery to over three thousand feet. The water in the shallows was so clear it was almost illusory, but only thirty metres out, the shoreline suddenly dropped into an underwater abyss with a depth of 280 metres.

'The mountain is reflected in the lake,' said the dad. 'The higher the mountain, the deeper the water.'

A place of perfect echoes. I swam out. Diving in, I could see long soft reeds, ten, twenty metres down, attached to the sandy bottom. They reached for my legs and wrapped themselves around me like long hair. I wriggled out of their slimy grip, and losing my nerve, quickly swam back to the shore. A legend was told about a woman who decided to measure the depth of the lake here at Zaum. She spent years weaving a long rope from silk, and one day came here by boat and dropped it over the side. But the weather suddenly turned. She barely managed to row herself back to the inlet, vowing to build a church here if only the lake would let her go. Humans had no business in the deepest part of the lake.

The church, built in a cross-shape, was just metres from the water. Its valuable frescoes were badly damaged; it was in an abandoned state of renovation, full of bird droppings.

'It's been a hiding-place forever,' said the caretaker behind me, in the dank darkness, as if reading my thoughts about Kosta. ''Cause of the difficult access. It was abandoned for years.'

The Ohridian nobleman who commissioned it was of Herzegovinan descent, and named the church Virgin Mary of Zaum, after his birthplace near a lake. Zaum's was supposedly a sister monastery to Naum's down the coast – even their names rhymed. Here was the earliest surviving image of the monk Naum, healer of the insane.

The frescoes were painted sixty years after the building's construction, and the faces had that heart-stopping, expressive liveliness characteristic of the humanism of Balkan Byzantine art in the thirteenth and fourteenth centuries. Anna in a vestment of deep red was shown breastfeeding Mary, displaying the only naked breast on show in the whole of Eastern Orthodoxy, said the caretaker. Generations of graffiti scratchers had left the frescoes in a state of devastation.

'The graffiti are in five languages,' he said. 'Macedonian, Bulgarian, Serbian, Albanian and Greek.'

The symbolism was deeply Macedonian: all the self-proclaimed lovers of this lake had taken turns at vandalising it. The locals were the worst. One had used some blunt instrument to scratch his sorry existence in huge letters, scraping the rich blue pigment between Anna and another saint, stopping just short of the naked breast.

Many of the saints had been blinded. Traditionally, this was blamed on 'the Turks', but the truth is more varied. Aside from plain vandalism by both Christians and Muslims, there was also superstition. Balkan peasants believed that by scraping the eyes off the miracle-making saints and applying or even ingesting the paste made from the scrapings, their ailments would be cured. The feet too were dug out, for healing disability. The paste was often made and sold by the Orthodox clergy, never ones to miss a business opportunity. The result: blind and hobbled saints all around the lakes' shores. It was an unsettling sight.

Surprisingly, the hermit cave in the Big Shadow above was inhabited until as late as 1937. The resident monk was called Kalist. It is not known when he left or died. I pictured Kosta hiding in the bat-infested church with his mate, with nothing but the shirts on their backs and these faces looking down at them with no eyes. Had Kalist come down his rope ladder to say hello to the fugitives or to give them a dish of berries?

Back in the boat, we set off into the deep, to where the woman with the silk rope had sought forbidden knowledge.

'It's here!' the dad shouted.

You could see the line where it went from light blue to impenetrable darkness. Beneath us were nearly three hundred metres of black water.

'See, it's water like any other,' the dad said.

Water like any other, but nobody ever swam here. It was to do with the winds.

There were two types of strong wind here, the dad said, aside from the obvious directional ones like northerly and southerly: the *mokra* or wet one, and the *strmets* or steep one. There was also the treacherous underwater wind, the *podvalnitsa*, product of the lake's internal weather and which was activated at random. And finally, there was the Sahara wind that blew in from Africa and covered cars and boats in a gritty, moist layer, like fine mud.

There were many stories of people drowning at Zaum. The most dramatic was about a party of Serb officers who'd visited Naum Monastery and, in a drunken brawl, arguing over the existence of 'miracles', shot at an icon of St Naum. On the way back to Ohrid, the weather suddenly changed at Zaum. All drowned except the boatman. Ohrid town mourned them, even though they were 'the Serbs'. The moral of the story seemed to be that you disrespect St Naum at your peril.

On the other side of the Zaum cliffs, we pulled in to see one more cave church that could have served as an overnight hiding-place.

'St Nicholas,' said the dad. 'Protector of fishermen.'

The church nestled in the rock face at one end of a long sandy beach. An old camping ground was nearby, and a giant dump of plastic bottles uncollected since last summer. I climbed the broken steps into the exposed niche. The smoke of a thousand fires had blackened the frescoes here, and the rain of six centuries had washed away most of them, but the pigments had preserved something of their saturated richness – dark red and blue – and the figures appeared ghostly on the rock face. The heads of the two myrrh-bearing women were gone, only the wine-red and aubergine of their gowns was left, like a stain of memory. The two central scenes could only just be made out: *The Angel at the Empty Tomb* and *Jesus's Harrowing of Hell*. Bumblebees and crickets buzzed in the foliage behind. The earth had been dug up by something.

'Wild pigs,' said Ivanka.

We walked along the waterline while her dad rested in the boat. A thick tideline of detritus had washed up – shampoo bottles, shoes, broken toys, plastic wire for fishing rods, the waste of the human world that didn't belong here.

'They send us this from the Albanian side,' said a man who suddenly popped out of the bushes with a fishing rod and a joint.

His name was Angelo and Ivanka knew him. He had deep lines down his cheeks, tattoos on his arms, and restless eyes.

'I'm from the village up here.' He gestured to the hills above the beach. It was the last before St Naum Monastery. 'A village of mean people. Though there's hardly anyone left.'

He offered the joint around.

'You from the old country then,' he said sarcastically. 'Oh yeah, I got a Bulgarian passport. All I had to do was answer the question Do you feel Bulgarian?' He cackled.

The three of us walked back to the boat. I looked at the labels on the plastic bottles and tins washed up on the lake shore: they were all in Cyrillic. They were not from the Albanian side after all.

It is easier that the shadow rest with the other, not with the self.

At the mouth of a small tributary that snaked into the thick overgrowth beyond the shore, the carcass of a cow lay tangled in shrubs, black with flies.

'This cow is all ours, mind you,' Angelo said, and disappeared back into the bushes.

It was not possible to go all the way to Pogradec in Albania, because of the water border. I knew this already, but the sting of it surprised me. By the time we were at the mouth of the mighty springs of Naum that rushed icily into the lake, the monastery rising above, we were only a few hundred metres from Albanian territory.

'We can't.' The dad shook his head.

'There *have* been attempts to open the water border,' Ivanka said.

The water border didn't need opening, because it wasn't there. That's what stung about it. Music from a beach restaurant on the Albanian side carried across the water. The checkpoint was only five hundred metres up the road. But I hadn't brought my passport.

Deciding on the spot to walk back to Ohrid, I reassured Ivanka and her dad that I'd be fine, and we said goodbye. From the springs of Naum I watched their boat dissolve into the sunshine.

Walking back to Ohrid took me seven hours. No other walkers crossed my path, only the odd car and some Dutch cyclists. The road was so steep in places, they had to push their bikes uphill.

Kosta had escaped across the lake, but returned to Ohrid by road many years later. I too would return to Ohrid by road, even if I couldn't retrace his whole journey across the lake. To do that, I'd have to do it clandestinely, at night. Like him. Once he'd reached the Albanian side, Kosta made his way to the Adriatic coast, and from there to Italy. From Italy, he followed an eastern route through Austria, Hungary, Romania, to his final destination across the Danube: Sofia. It took him two years. He didn't see his wife and children for four.

The last people left who'd known Kosta were my aunts – Tatjana's twin sisters. They were his granddaughters, and I resolved to talk to them. A pattern was emerging – of absent men and women left behind, unbending women who dislocated themselves and their *loved ones* out of shape trying to right what had gone wrong with the family, the world, life itself. We hold in our energy system people we have never met. Kosta's restless rebellion runs hot in my blood, and the prideful, furious sorrow of Ljubitsa weighs down my bones at times. I have carried these people all my life.

The road followed the lower part of the Galicica Mountain, rising and falling. Past a wartime Italian bunker with a view, sprayed with graffiti. The buzz of bumblebees and the scent of wild herbs everywhere. Colours intensified in the afternoon heat and the lake took on a peacocky blue. The mountains across the lake were wrapped in white vapours, like Biljana's linens.

Wouldn't it have been simpler all round if Kosta had ended up at the bottom of the lake? My grandparents wouldn't have met. My mother, my sister and I wouldn't exist, someone else would. The Pain wouldn't be a member of the family, everything would be different.

Or perhaps not at all different. It may be that we are simply the human form that particular forces assume, generation after generation. I looked at my dusty sandalled feet. Perhaps their road trips were epigenetically determined.

It may be that the epic journey of the unborn is already written in the ciphers drawn by winds on the lake, as if by cosmic calligraphers. Drawn and ceaselessly redrawn, because the winds come from so many directions that they override each other in a polyglot conversation that will not end, not until the lake dries up and the wind no longer moans and laughs like the samovila of the ballads – with a human voice.

Girl of the waves
On a rock by the sea.
Men come and go
but he doesn't appear.

'Birds, you're my hope.
You travel over land and sea.
Did you see him?
Did you see him? Did you see him?'

Albanian Tosk song

ONE THOUSAND
SEVEN HUNDRED YEARS

Tanas Spassé had said to meet him by the Struga bridge where the boats are moored and the lake's reeds reach four metres in height. In the breeze of early summer, the silky reeds whispered. Trout and carp squeeze themselves through the reeds to help release their eggs. I was taking another break from Ohrid town. I wanted to see the west coast and try, again, to cross into Albania by water.

From the Struga bridge, you could see the Black Drim River rush out of the lake in a thick jet of champagne, to make its way northwards, carving canyons into several mountain ranges before it hit the coastal plains of the Adriatic.

Rebecca West observed that nature worship is 'the basic religion' in Macedonia, 'with its special preference for water'. Given all this water, it's not surprising. Here is a river so determined to follow its own course once it springs out of the flank of the Galicica Mountain, at the southern tip of the lake, that if you draw a horizontal line to cut the lake in two halves, like a pear, you have Struga bridge at the northern tip and Drilon at the bottom tip, in Albania, where the river springs rush into the lake. People said you could see the river inside the lake from the air.

It seems counter-intuitive for a river to run *out* of a lake, rather than into it, so much so that Evliya Çelebi noted excitedly, and wrongly, that 'a water like a life potion pours down from the plain and discharges into the Ohrid Lake'. He had stood in the same spot as me. An '8000 step long road . . . paved with white cobblestones' led to Ohrid town, passing through vineyards and orchards, he noted. He was walking the original Egnatian Way. The orchards are still here, though I didn't count the steps.

It was morning and the surface of the lake was still. Tanas Spassé was in his boat lacquered in red and black, though the choice of colours didn't immediately strike me as symbolic. Tanas's name was given to me by my cousin's husband, a doctor. I'd mentioned that I wanted to meet people whose lives straddled both sides of the lake. Tanas was his patient, he had chronic back pain.

Tanas made a living taking tourists on lake rides.

'On the Struga side,' he specified, meaning the west side. 'I rarely go to the east side. Same with the boats in Ohrid, they keep to their side.'

I stepped into the boat. I was beginning to grasp the ways of lake living: it was all about how close you are to a particular stretch of the shore. That's your patch, that's where your life will be. The rules were respected by all.

'Except Albanian poachers coming to steal fishing nets,' Tanas said.

What, with the fish in them?

'*Komplet*,' he grinned briefly, and started the engine.

He wasn't a smiley guy. A stubby, weather-beaten man of seventy, at first glance he looked no different from the other leathery fishermen and boatmen – peaked hat, hands thickened from rope-pulling. But at second glance, something *was* different about him – he didn't have the extrovert way of the others. His body language was that of someone who is not fully at home in this life of leisurely boat rides.

'I was born in Pogradec in 1948,' he said. 'I lived in Albania until 1992. I have an Albanian pension.'

Tanas was the son of Macedonians from different sides of the lake border. His mother Zorka was from a Struga family of textile merchants. In the 1930s, around the time of Kosta's escape and for similar reasons, Zorka's father escaped to Albania and hid with a family in the fishing village of Lin. After her father's return home to Struga, the two families kept in touch, and ten years later, Zorka and the Lin family's son, Sandro, married and made their home in Pogradec, Albania. Zorka brought a rich town-girl's dowry: furs, heavy kilims, embroidered linens.

In one black-and-white photograph Tanas had brought to show me, she wears high heels, lipstick, and a full-length fur coat made of small animals, a defiant look in her eyes. Her father had studied in Paris and had built a house in Struga for her and her future family. This house is for Zorka, he kept saying, long after he lost hope of ever seeing her again.

The Albanian side's in-laws were happy; the Macedonian less so, which was to do with social snobbery, not with the sides of the border, for the border was not yet hard. As word spread of its imminent closure by the Hoxha regime, Zorka ignored her parents' pleas to return to Struga. By the time Tanas was born, Sandro was working for the Sigurimi (the Albanian Directorate of State Security, meaning the Secret Police), and already in trouble for criticising the dictums of Communist Chief Enver Hoxha. Word reached the couple that they were coming for him soon. In Albania, Bulgaria, Romania and Yugoslavia of the late 1940s, when you heard that *they were coming for you*, you knew your time was up. The decision was made overnight. Sandro urged his wife and his mother to come with him across the border, on a motor-bike – but how could two women with a toddler and a baby cross the wild mountains on a motorbike?

'You go, save yourself, we'll manage here,' Zorka said. Her words must have haunted her.

'He escaped alone overnight, from Pogradec to Lin, and across into Radozhda,' Tanas said. Radozhda was a Macedonian fishing village, a mirror image of Lin.

'On the Yugoslav side, he handed himself in and they interro-gated him,' Tanas continued, over the roar of the engine. 'In case he was a spy.'

Quickly identified as a promising candidate, Sandro was recruited by Tito's Secret Police and landed a job with the Yugoslav Ministry of Internal Affairs. The state gave him an apartment in Belgrade where he was trained, then an apartment in the elite neighbourhood of Skopje where my great-uncles also lived until the earthquake of 1963 destroyed their homes, and where Sandro would spend the next forty years in comfort – material comfort, at least. He got together with another woman, a Bulgarian who worked in Yugoslav television. She too was probably a spy. I know from my grandmother at Radio Sofia that many who worked in the media at the time were spies, for either the Yugoslavs or the Bulgarians, or both.

'But they never married and she knew that, if his family ever turned up – that's us!' Tanas smiled – 'Well, she would have to disappear.'

Would she? Forty-two years is a long time.

'It is,' Tanas agreed. 'But my dad kept his word. He never stopped thinking about us.'

Something painful passed over his face: the possibility that his father had, in fact, stopped thinking about them, as he got on with his life.

'I didn't have a single photo of my dad. I didn't know how he looked until I met him.'

In a photograph Tanas showed me, it's the 1980s. Sandro and his girlfriend are in an Ohrid restaurant with friends – glamorous in summer dresses and suits, drinking wine. He looks worldly and she has kind eyes. As an apparatchik and a television researcher, they would have travelled all over the world, and all of this is there on their faces.

'She became my friend,' Tanas said, and carefully put the photograph back in its plastic pouch. 'A very fine woman.'

Back in Pogradec in 1949, the Sigurimi arrived to search the family home in the wake of Sandro's escape. Every item was to be confiscated by the state, along with the house. From now on

Zorka, her mother-in-law and her two kids would be branded as 'enemies of the people'. A friend of Sandro's was in the search group. He secretly told Zorka to hide her kilims with friends and sell them later, which is what she did. The kilims of her Struga dowry weighed twenty kilograms each and went to local families, Tanas said. He was one year old at the time.

In another photo, Zorka stands against a background of lake reeds, her two small sons in front of her, all three looking hungry and hunted, wearing the garb of poor peasants. The boys are wearing rags on their feet instead of shoes. The two women and two children were loaded onto an open-backed lorry and driven west in the shadow of what was once the Via Egnatia, via Elbasan, then south, over the frozen white mountains of central Albania.

'It was January,' Tanas said.

Once they arrived in Berat, where 'enemies of the people', all of them women and children, were brought from around the country, they were sent further south and lodged in a former Italian army camp. Though 'lodged' is not the word; they were shoved into the stables.

'Like horses,' Tanas said.

The women's task was to go up the frozen mountain to fetch wood for the town's stoves. Not for themselves – they had no heating in the stables. Many kids died of hunger and exposure. In the communal cauldrons, there was never meat, sometimes vegetables, but there were always worms. And the kids ate the worms.

'You know the worst thing?' Tanas glanced over the water, which had become choppy. 'When a child died, the family hid the corpse, to get its rations.'

What astonishes me, though, is that the Sigurimi hadn't given up on the 'traitors' in their ranks. They came up with a plan to lure Sandro back across the border: Tanas and his brother and grandmother were packed off to Pogradec, back to the lake. For two years, Zorka was separated from her children. For two years, Granny Persephone, whose mythical name is incongruous amid this blighted landscape, laboured on a construction site by the lake, while the two boys grew stunted with hunger. The malnourished child is present in Tanas's short stature.

'We had no bread. There was a Young Pioneers' summer camp on the lake. When the kids were gone, my brother and I would sweep the building, looking for leftovers. If we found old bread, Granny sun-dried it for winter.'

Sometimes, old friends of their father's would secretly bring them sugar, but it was risky to help enemies of the people. Sandro, now working for the Yugoslav Secret Police, got word that his children were near the border, but didn't take the bait; knowing that the Sigurimi would be waiting for him, he sent three others instead in a wooden boat, a chun, to reconnoitre. One of them was a young cousin from Lin, and later, his bullet-riddled body was displayed in Lin's main square as a lesson to potential traitors and infiltrators. The second man was an Albanian spy; his fate is unknown. The third jumped into the coastal reeds and swam back to Yugoslav waters to tell the tale. Sandro didn't get to see his children or his mother.

Eventually, Zorka was reunited with Persephone and the boys. They were resettled in a well-organised concentration camp for enemies of the people in the outskirts of the fertile district of Lushnjë, only a mountain range away from their beloved lake, and only miles from the beach lagoons of the Adriatic, from where you could see the coast of Italy.

'They did give her a chance,' Tanas said of his mother. 'They kept urging her to divorce my father, sign a statement that condemned him, and remarry. But she couldn't. To you, he might be an enemy, but to me he was a good man, she said, and that was that.'

Tanas and his brother grew up in the camp.

'They had a grading system. They somehow worked out the degree to which you were an enemy of the people. We were high up. Once marked, that was it. Not like in a prison, where you can shorten your sentence with good behaviour. In Lushnjë, it was already too late.'

Granny Persephone would never see the lake or her son again.

Back in Lin, freshly cut off from its mirror image Radozhda, Sandro's remaining family didn't cope well with the new order. Tanas showed me a photo of Sandro's uncle Boris, the village priest, in a robe and wearing a long beard, beside a church. This is the last photograph before *they* (the Sigurimi) arrived, Tanas said. They cut off his beard and burnt down the church. Border villages like this were treated with particular harshness.

'And Uncle Boris – they called him Bise – Bise shut himself in his bedroom and never left the house again. That's where he died. Two years ago, I went to Lushnjë and dug up Granny Persephone's bones, and brought them back to Lin. Next to her brother. That was her wish, to return to the lake.'

Ironically, the dictator Enver Hoxha was from a religious family that at some point had had a hodja, or Muslim preacher, in its ranks; hence the family name.

'I don't know about Hoxha,' Tanas said, 'but the whole nation was secretly praying. My mother prayed to St Petka, for us and for the whole nation.'

Which nation?

'Albania,' he said. 'Where the worst suffering was.'

He had pointed the boat inland, and we were approaching a monastery complex built into the rugged karst hills, full of hermits' niches.

'People come for the Black Madonna,' Tanas said, 'and the curative spring.'

A skinny, odd-looking man approached the bay at the foot of the tiled monastery terrace where we hovered with the engine silenced, and waved his arms in the air, beckoning us. We waved back. Something was wrong with him.

'Oh, him,' Tanas said, looking at the man. 'I didn't expect to see *him* here.'

The man had a souvenir stall in Struga, and a reputation.

'He isn't a religious type,' Tanas said. 'But people change. He's looking much skinnier these days.'

A female Orthodox chant rose from the monastery grounds just then, deeply Oriental, and we sat for a moment, listening. The skinny man had put it on especially for us. I wanted to climb to the tiled terrace and see the Black Madonna, but the weather was turning.

'Things can change in minutes on this lake.' Tanas started the engine again, heading on towards the border, and resumed his story. 'There were many others in the same boat. We made friends. There were displaced families from all over. In Lushnjë town itself, there were normal people. Hardcore Communists too, exemplary cadres.' He said it without sarcasm, matter-of-factly, the way he said everything.

In an ironic mix of savage politics and gentle geography, the district of Lushnjë became known as the concentration camp capital of Albania, but for centuries it had been known as the country's garden and bread-basket: orchards continued to thrive, even as factories were being built by slave labour. The inmates, like Tanas's family, were allowed to move within a radius of ten kilometres of the camp.

'I started working in construction. I helped build the plastics factory. I remember the Chinese engineer . . . The textile factory was also Chinese-owned,' Tanas said. The Chinese laughed when Tanas and his mates used the communal water fountain to wash and drink. The Chinese didn't drink water, he said, only tea. And everybody was on Chinese bicycles. By the time Tanas was an adult with a bicycle, Mao's China was the only country with which Albania had close relations.

'Lots of young Albanians came to work in the new factories voluntarily. And also lots of deportees. Intellectuals were interned with their families. There was an engineer who was a plumber. An agronomist who was a labourer.'

Tanas was allowed to finish high school but was denied his diploma – that way, he would remain officially uneducated, and only eligible as a labourer. He became a mason.

All adults were required to report to the police twice a day. Like criminals.

'The worst time was when I got toothache. I asked for written permission to visit the dentist in town. But the dentist wasn't there. I couldn't sleep from the pain. When I asked the Party commissar for another permission to leave the camp, he exploded. If that dentist still isn't there today, I'll order him to pull out all your teeth! he shouted. So you stop creeping about like a spy! I begged him not to do it. I was terrified.'

For the first time since the morning, Tanas looked upset – here, in the boat, was the sixteen-year-old boy.

'That's how it was. They could do anything to you. And two out of three were spies.'

A joke was doing the rounds. Three men are walking in single file to the factory. The middle one breaks the silence: 'You know, the guy behind me is here for me, and I'm here for you.'

'It's not that they were bad people, the stooges, it's just that under pressure, people change,' Tanas said.

There were monthly film screenings in the town cinema. Attendance was compulsory. After the screening, the ceremonial pillorying would begin. Party functionaries would pick on young people, at random, and pull them up onto the stage for 'ideological criticism' – in other words, public humiliation, Maoist style. They had to repent for imaginary transgressions.

'One day, they picked on my friend. We grew up together. We worked on the same construction projects. But when the Party commissar started shouting at him, he answered back.'

Tanas looked away and cleared his throat.

'They sent him to a labour camp. For agitation against the state. Ten years.' He popped a lozenge in his mouth. He had a cold. 'And after that, just when he was due to be released, we heard they'd given him another ten years. I was married by then.'

His friend had been sent to the notorious Spaç mountain prison in the north, described by its survivors as 'a symbol of the Communist inferno', and a ruin today. Inmates were worked literally to death in an old copper mine. As I write this, the surviving former inmates have finally won a long battle to receive pensions for their decades of forced labour at Spaç. Perversely, although records existed of their imprisonment there, no records of their labour were kept by the Communist state. For twenty-five years, the post-Communist state had exploited this to strip these men of their meagre pensions.

But Tanas's friend was not among the survivors.

The water was an unearthly turquoise here because the north-west of the lake is much shallower than the rest of the rim. But it was difficult to enjoy the water's colour while listening to what Tanas was telling me.

Spaç was the worst of fifty prisons under Hoxha. Forty-three thousand people were imprisoned there, many of them on charges similar to those given to Tanas's friend, or for joining a book club, making a private joke about the regime, or reading a book that was deemed either pro-Western or pro-Soviet – for the Hoxha regime had also fallen out with the USSR. In 1973, the year Tanas's daughter and I were born, the inmates at Spaç staged a revolt. It was crushed, the leaders were executed, and an additional communal sentence was slapped on the rest: one thousand seven hundred years.

One thousand seven hundred years.

But one thousand seven hundred years was not a sentence. It was the regime's message to its subjects, all of whom were in effect prisoners: Abandon all hope.

'I was lucky,' Tanas said. 'You see, if you were in your mid-twenties or late twenties and still unmarried, you became suspicious. You became even more vulnerable to accusations of

treason. They encouraged you to get married early, settle down.'
So that you had more to lose than just your own life. Tanas was
fortunate to marry for love, he said, and the first real smile of
the day lit up his face.

Later, at the pier back in Struga, his wife would come to
meet him, worried that he'd been out on the breezy lake with a
sore throat; she brought him a jumper and took him home. She
was a short woman with a warm Levantine face. Her name was
Elena and she was from the Greek community in Albania who,
like Tanas's family, had found themselves locked behind the Iron
Curtain overnight. Her family were butchers who for generations
had traded with Corfu, which is where they had originally come
from.

Tanas showed me another photo from his plastic pouch. A
young man in a soldier's uniform, with an open, guileless face,
sits on a rock by a sunny sea. Across the water in the very near
distance – land.

'Corfu,' Tanas said. The young soldier is him, serving compulsory military service in Saranda, a small peninsula on the southern
coast near the land border with Greece. Two years.

'As a listed enemy of the people, I had no right to carry arms.
There were lots of guys like me. So *they* came up with a job for us.
The slogan was: Let's turn the mountains into fields!'

I didn't understand.

'Sure you don't understand. Because it doesn't make sense.
We spent a year in the mountains, cutting down trees. Beautiful
old forests. Then, out of the trees, we made steps, to go up the
mountain. Vertical. The world's longest mountain stairwell. And
on the cleared flanks of the mountain, they made us plant citrus
trees. To turn the mountain into an orange grove. But it wasn't a
success.'

He said it in a slightly apologetic tone, as if it was somehow
those young men's fault that the stone mountain could not be
turned into an orange grove, that they had perhaps believed they

could do it — so that they could carry on with the senseless task. The Sisyphean stairwell was still there, I imagined. He shrugged. He hadn't been back to check.

But I kept looking at the photo of the young man. Once on holiday in Corfu, I had heard of Albanians who had swum or paddled across; many died of exposure or drowned. I'd heard of old women on floating tyres, fighting against the current.

'Weren't you tempted to swim across?' I asked Tanas.

There was a moment's hesitation.

'No, not me. I couldn't do that to my mother.'

Something about this caused him discomfort. What about here at the lake, weren't there any successful escapes?

'There was a case . . .' He trailed off. 'A family from Pogradec, friends of my father. Sixteen people in a boat. They made it to Naum Monastery.'

That family emigrated to Australia and returned after the fall of the regime. They bought a tobacco factory and owned hotels now, on the lakeside. Tanas's face looked pained. He turned off the engine.

'This is the border zone,' he said.

There was nothing to show there was a border here — just water for as far as you could see. And the houses of a pretty village on a rocky outcrop of the shore, swaddled in vineyards, a swimmable distance across. Lin, his father's village. We were five hundred metres from the water border. Tanas told me this was as far as we could go. If I wanted to see Albania, I'd have to go by road — over the forested mountain, through the Chafassan checkpoint.

I was sorely disappointed. I'd thought that we would visit Lin, drop in and see the rebuilt church where his uncle Boris-Bise used to preach, and Granny Persephone's old house. I thought the border was only a token, a nod to the past, not an actively policed zone.

'How would anyone know if we just keep going to Lin?' I asked. 'How does anybody know where the border is anyway?'

'Oh, *they* know,' he pointed to a building on the shore. 'I'd be fined and lose my licence.'

They were the Macedonian border police. There used to be no police here, just forest, Tanas said, but then the border trafficking started. During the Kosovo War in the late 1990s, Kosovars were smuggled from Lin to Struga, and then on to Skopje. Weapons too. And women were sold as prostitutes. Big bucks, Tanas said, big crimes. So they built the border patrol house.

'Now it's mostly drugs. And boats. You see lots of stolen boats in Pogradec,' he said, and stroked the side of the boat. 'It needs a lick of paint.'

Red and black are the colours of the Albanian national flag, it only struck me now. But also of VMRO, the Internal Macedonian Revolutionary Organisation, which is still the name of a political party here, and another one in Bulgaria too. I didn't know how to ask which of the two Tanas had in mind, with his choice of colours. But I asked him about his parents' reunion in 1991. The border had been partially opened, and Zorka had obtained permission to visit what would soon cease to be Yugoslavia, to see her sister and her husband Sandro. Her parents were dead. Her sister had been writing to her all these decades, in coded language, so as not to excite the Albanian censors, who studied all correspondence from abroad.

A crossing point was then partially open on the other side of the lake, at St Naum. Zorka walked from Pogradec, alone, with a small overnight bag. There were others in similar circumstances: this was a day on which people would be let through, for twenty-four hours, to be reunited with long-lost family.

Zorka's welcoming party on this side consisted of her sister and Sandro, now in his seventies. The sister had brought a bunch of flowers, which she put in Sandro's hands. But Sandro was uneasy. When the crowd from Albania crossed into Macedonian territory, he did not recognise Zorka. Which one is it, which one do I give the flowers to? he kept asking his sister-in-law.

Perhaps he was looking for a younger woman, the woman he remembered.

She recognised *him*, though. The man good enough for her. The man she wouldn't divorce. I think of that woman, a quiet heroine, who in the bloom of her life had become a prisoner but remained loyal to her own truth. The sisters recognised each other instantly.

'There were many women in her situation, in Albania,' Tanas said. 'Who'd had to become mother and father, woman and man in one.'

It was an awkward reunion for Zorka and Sandro. She quickly returned to Albania; and two years later, Tanas, his brother and their families all arrived in Skopje and moved into Sandro's flat.

'Thirteen of us,' Tanas grinned. Thirteen people who turned up from Enver Hoxha's Gulag hinterlands, after decades of physical and psychological hardship. Sandro's Bulgarian girlfriend made herself scarce, and so did Sandro, who joined her in the countryside. That's when Tanas knew it was time for them to find their own feet. They returned here, to the lake, where they had been born.

'Where we belong,' he said.

The Struga house that had been built for Zorka by her father had been occupied by relatives after the father's death. Tanas and his family started from scratch, found jobs, built a house, learned the language, and tried to blend in. Tanas, then in his forties, continued to do the only thing he knew – masonry. But back pain eventually stopped him.

'The lake's in my blood. I bought a boat and here I am. I enjoy myself now. To make up for lost time.'

Though he only went back to Albania once, to collect Granny Persephone's bones, he kept a little bit of that country in his black-and-red boat.

His wife Elena's family had been forbidden to speak Greek, and Tanas's mother and grandmother didn't dare speak Macedonian to Tanas and his brother. Elena and Tanas speak Albanian to each other to this day – the language of their misfortune, and also of their fortune. The pettiness of the Greek–Macedonian dispute was revealed when you saw them together: a Greek and a Macedonian who spoke Albanian, who had married for love in a time of tyranny.

I asked Tanas if his mother had regrets about that decision she made, back in 1947, to leave her family in Struga and settle with Sandro in Pogradec.

'It was meant to be,' he shrugged. What is the use of regret? he seemed to say.

Perhaps his mother's prayers to Petka had helped her.

'What makes me really happy is that the kids travel,' Tanas said. 'When I was young, all I could do was learn the capitals of the world. Now my daughter goes there. And she calls me. Dad, guess where I am.' His voice went hoarse and he popped another lozenge.

His son and daughter were both living abroad.

'That way, they're free,' Tanas said. 'Here you can't be free.'

The southerly rushed in from Albania and the waves slammed into the boat, solid like concrete. Not another boat in sight. We were far from land. Why can't we be free here, now? I wanted to yell at the great emptiness of water.

But Tanas had made his peace, I was the agitated one. He started the engine.

'Put your jacket on,' he said, 'it'll be a rough ride.' Then he smiled, though not with his eyes.

'Don't worry,' he said, 'We'll make it.'

I knew this rock well. I had lived under the shadow of it all my life. All our Western thought is founded on this repulsive pretence that pain is the proper price of any good thing.

Here it could be seen how the meaning of the Crucifixion had been hidden from us, though it was written clear. A supremely good man was born on earth, a man who was without cruelty, who could have taught mankind to live in perpetual happiness; and because we are infatuated with this idea of sacrifice, of shedding innocent blood to secure innocent advantages, we found nothing better to do with this passport to deliverance than destroy him. There is that in the universe, half inside and half outside our minds, which is wholly adorable; and this it was that men killed when they crucified Jesus Christ. Our shame would be absolute, were it not that the crime we intended cannot in fact be committed.

It is not possible to kill goodness. There is always more of it, it does not take flight from our accursed earth, it perpetually asks us to take what we need from it.

Rebecca West, 1941

THE KEEPER OF THE
BLACK MADONNA

'I'll leave you alone with her,' the keeper said, laughing away my protestations that I wasn't here to ask for help, I just wanted to see the icon.

'It doesn't matter,' he said. 'She doesn't discriminate.'

The flagstoned terrace of the monastery was ablaze with morning sunshine. He'd been sweeping it with a long-handled broom. He was radiant – about the brilliance of the day, about being here. His tall, gaunt body was in perpetual motion – brushing blossoms from a bench, watering flower beds, unlocking the souvenir shop, waving his arms to point out parts of the monastery complex with its handsome mansions reserved for the clergy whenever they deigned to visit, showing me the 'curative' mineral spring in the rock that was especially good for the eyes; and leading me up the newly built staircase into the hermit niches where the Black Madonna had been painted, he said, by a monk who lived in darkness and so everything appeared dark to him.

'But don't take my word for it,' he laughed, and the apple in his skinny neck moved. 'I'm no expert. I'm just a fool glad to be alive.'

I had returned to the monastic cells hewn into the rock, as curious about the Black Madonna as I was about the odd-looking keeper who had beckoned from the shore. His name was Clement, Clemé for short, after the protector-saint 'our golden one'.

'I knew you'd come back,' he grinned, with his missing front teeth bar one, a grin so unselfconscious that you were won over. He had recognised me from Tanas's boat some days before.

'I look like an imbecile but I have a memory for faces.'

His face was lopsided and one of his eyes was filled with blood – the effect of a stroke that had nearly killed him four months before, though he was only my age.

'You've come before the season, so you can have the place to yourself. But come September – well!' The monastery's festival day fell in September. People came from all over to ask the Black Madonna for help.

'Every monastery specialises in something,' he said. 'Naum specialises in mental disorders. The Black Madonna is for infertility and illness. Jovan of Bigor up in Debar is for addictions. Drugs, gambling, sex. And believe me, I've covered the spectrum. Now, here you have to crawl, if you don't mind losing your dignity.'

I crawled inside the hermit's niche. It was just wide enough for a person to lie down, but the ceiling was high, at least.

The karst shore of this western side of the lake must have struck the monks of early medieval times as especially welcoming, with its natural niches, fertile hilly hinterland and proximity to water. Generation after generation had lived here in blissful silence, in the dim light of candles they made themselves, like everything else they needed. The niches had been plain for several centuries, until artists started painting them in the thirteenth century.

Just up from the niches was a small chapel, richly frescoed with lifelike characters. Here was Clement with his teachers, the brothers Cyril and Methodius, holding a script of early Glagolitic – the alphabet that would be adopted by the entire Slavonic world and then vanish, to be replaced by Cyrillic. Here too was the pagan healer and seer Panteleimon who never took payment, holding the tools of his practice. He was converted to Christ's ways by the defaced figure next to him, guessed to be Hermolus, which got them both killed in 304. This 'church' was cacophonous with epochs: from Jesus to the ninth-century Clement. The artists ranged from the sixteenth to nineteenth century. Two of them had left their names: Jovan and Angel. At the other end of the beach was another cave church, where the healers Cosma and Damian were depicted. Many of the monks themselves had been healers.

'I don't mind telling you,' Clemé said when we went down the steps again, ''cause you'll be wondering what a vagabond like me is doing in this place.'

He'd been in a coma for a week after the stroke, and in that time he had a dream.

'I saw many faces, painted-like, a sort of voiceless chorus. Among them was this familiar face, a woman's face with a halo. She was looking at me with such understanding, I could have wept if I hadn't been in a coma.'

He knew this was his last chance. When he came round, ignoring the doctors' advice he checked himself out of hospital and walked the few miles to the monastery.

'I came to the Black Madonna and kissed her. Then I went straight to the abbot and said, I want to work as a volunteer. He took me on. After a month, he offered me a job. A monastery is always short of hands. You say you're not a Christian, but it doesn't matter what you are 'cause this is a place of wonder. I wasn't a believer either, I was a cynic, a waster and a goner, oh yeah.'

A few months before his stroke, his mother had been struck down too. She was paralysed down one side and bedridden. After his coma-induced dream, he begged her – she also wasn't a believer – to come and visit the Black Madonna.

'By then, she could move with crutches. And what happened? She stood before the icon, and when she went to go, the crutches fell out of her hands, as if wrenched by a force. I picked them up for her. But once again, they fell out of her hands. And she walked. Like a healthy person. Last week, I had a brain scan. The doctor didn't believe his eyes – no trace of damage. Now go on, tell me that miracles don't exist!'

Just then two young unshaven men in leather jackets came through the monastery gates, one pushing the other in a wheelchair. They came to the spring. Clemé and I moved away, to give them privacy.

'You asked who comes here. Those who suffer come here. And because there is suffering every minute of every day, the visitors never stop.'

In the garden he tended were two graves: sister Efrossinja and sister Irina.

'The last nuns,' Clemé said. 'I knew sister Irina. She was a tiny but great woman. She dug her own grave, right here, and knew when she would die, to the day.'

Until after her death, in the monastic tradition, the complex had been self-sufficient for hundreds of years – with its own herds of goats, chickens, vegetable gardens and extensive vineyards. Wine, bread and honey were produced in a large farm building by the beach, fallen into disuse after the deaths of the last nuns.

Beyond the farm building was a beach thick with giant reeds and overlooked by two hotels that appeared abandoned but weren't. A row of milky-skinned Dutch lay inert in chaises longues, like patients in a sanatorium. In the courtyards of those hotels remnants of the Via Egnatia had been found by passing archaeologists, but when I went up to look for them later, I was told by a waiter who'd worked there for forty years despite his small wages – because he couldn't live away from the lake – that the last of the Via had been dug up when a hospital was built. Though it was never used as a hospital.

'Because nothing finds its true purpose in this country, ideas and people get wasted. And I'm still here,' the waiter smiled philosophically, 'serving breakfast to the Dutch and watching them burn every summer.'

Where the hillside hotels stood now, there had once been vineyards, and this is where a great-great-great-great-uncle of mine, a bibulous monk called Kiril, had spent his life tending the vines. When he ran out of string, he'd tie them up with threads from his hemp robe.

Clemé had chores to do so he left me with the Black Madonna, which – the harried-looking abbot with his hair in a bun and long black robes told me – had *not* been painted in the rock niches above. Her origins were uncertain, but she had been brought to the lake by a monk from Mount Athos. The unknown artist had worked in the Russian iconographic tradition. She was one of several hundred 'Black Madonnas' in Europe. Most were painted during the early Renaissance in Italy. Some were associated with 'miracles'. This one, the story went, had been thrown into the lake three times 'in chains' – by German or Italian soldiers. And each time, she freed herself of the chains and floated back to the same spot on the beach.

There *was* something about this icon. I was drawn to it, but unable to say why. Against the white background inscribed in Greek, the figures were black in both skin and dress, except for the scarlet robe of Jesus and the white edge of the mother's shawl. The abbot told me that the icon had darkened over time, after many dips in the lake and centuries of exposure to smoky votive candles. The glass over it was already smeared with the finger- and lip-prints of the morning's visitors; it was Clemé's task to wipe the glass clean at the end of each day. Later, I returned to the monastery and Clemé asked the abbot for a day off.

Clemé had begun a degree in geodesy, but come the 1990s, an era of quick business opportunities, he ditched his studies and got into retail. Until his stroke this year, he'd travel to Sofia and Istanbul to buy clothes in bulk, and had a permanent stall by the Struga bridge where the River Drim emerged ebulliently from the lake, cascading over the locks.

'Welcome to the men's beach. On the other side is the ladies' beach,' Clemé said.

The cafes along the ladies' beach were run by Macedonians

and those on the men's by Albanians, but with names like Vanilla Sky and Malibu you couldn't tell which was which, and all were frequented by a mixed clientele.

'Because business knows no ethnicity,' said Clemé.

We had coffee in a cafe run by an Albanian family, traditionally keepers of boza shops, the pan-Balkan drink of fermented millet, and from the way the podgy waiter shook hands with Clemé I could tell the extent of his change, post stroke. The same happened when we walked along the river stalls where he used to sell his imported clothes. The stall holders' expressions, when they saw Clemé, ranged from protective on the faces of the women, to sadness on the men's. A stall holder told me Clemé had had a beard, did weights, and had a night job as a bouncer. The women loved him – he winked at Clemé – didn't they, eh? Clemé laughed it away. He didn't seem to miss it.

One Turkish craftsman hadn't seen Clemé since before his stroke. His own father had been a farrier, and his grandfather a tobacconist selling ivory-inlaid tobacco boxes. Struga, like Ohrid, had an illustrious merchant and craftsman tradition, now reduced to trinkets. Evliya Çelebi wrote about the spectacular Struga fair, visited by ten thousand people from all over the Balkans, who bivouacked in the environs for days, resulting in massive parties.

'The town houses of old Struga were a beauty to behold,' said the craftsman. 'The destruction began in Tito's time, with these hotels along the lake. You have come sixty years too late, my dear.'

Struga had natural beauty on its side, but was much reduced. Communist-era hotels in various stages of decrepitude lined the lake. One of them was still called Hotel Belgrade. Some of the beautiful town houses still stood in the narrow lanes of the old town, their dilapidated wood-clad upper storeys jutting out. The fin-de-siècle façades of public buildings recalled a once hopeful era. Clemé ran into an acquaintance – a Gypsy man who made hand-woven rope in the old style, for boats and livestock. He had a coil of it, a remnant of another age, around his chest.

Men line-fished along the riverside promenade, shaded by lime trees. Groups of teenagers circulated by the beach – Clemé could tell the Muslim Albanians from the Macedonians through subtle differences in dress and mannerism, but I couldn't.

With its line of minaret-studded villages stretching along the western shore and overlooked by the hills of Kara Orman, or Black Forest, Struga carried a Balkan-Oriental feel. But vestiges of its cultural aspirations were everywhere. At first, the bronze busts along the river puzzled me.

'Poets,' Clemé said, 'like you.'

Here was the Russian poet Sergei Esenin, who had been first enthused then bitterly disillusioned with the Bolshevik Revolution, and wrote his farewell poem in his own blood before committing suicide. Next to him was the Polish Romantic poet Adam Mickiewicz, who died of cholera in Istanbul while preparing to join a Polish–Russian army of volunteers against Turkey in the second Crimean War. The two poets kept company with fez-wearing literary and public figures from the national revival movements: Dervish Hima Ibrahim, a thinker, publisher and politician and one of the founders of the Albanian movement for independence, exiled from the lake; and Ibrahim Temo, an Albanian supporter of the Young Turk Revolution, who died in exile in Romania.

Equally typical of the times was that a person of literary genius like the younger Miladinov brother, Konstantin, born and raised here, would pen his best-loved poem in faraway Moscow and die in a typhus-riddled Istanbul jail – betrayed to the Ottoman authorities by a Greek Orthodox clergyman and accused of being an 'enemy of the sultan'. Like the Russian poets in the first half of the twentieth century, he and his brother were literally killed for poetry. It was a time when advocating, writing and publishing in a language or an identity other than the prescribed one landed you with exile or death. What these exceptional Eastern men shared is that their youth coincided with the death throes of an old colonial order before a new one could be born. They were looking to Europe – to the West – with hope and faith.

We visited the house of Konstantin and Dimitar Miladinov in the old town, where I saw the original cover of the book from my childhood: *Bulgarian Folk Songs*.

> Give me wings and I shall soar
> back to our lands, our shores

Strolling in Struga's shabby East-meets-West streets with Clemé, I understood that the poem 'Longing for the South' strikes an archetypal note not only in its conjuring of the essence of place, but in its invocation of place as a state of mind. Here, the South was equated with the Lake, with the original home, and with the true self.

There is a recurring motif of *el sur* in Argentine literature and music – and Argentine culture, like the culture of the Balkans, is one of fusions and tensions. One of tango's earliest songs is 'Vuelvo al Sur', 'I Return to the South'. The South is the indigenous American continent before it was colonised by Europe. In his story 'The South', Jorge Luis Borges tells of a conservative Buenos Aires man of European ancestry who fantasises all his life about a hacienda in the South – the spaciousness of the untamed, native, precolonial Pampa appeals to him through the pages of books – but when he finally makes the long train journey there, the untamed South greets him in the form of hostile, drunken gauchos in a grubby pub who challenge him to a knife fight he will instantly lose. He is surprised that he is ready to meet his own ironic, Borgesian, modernist death in 'the South'. It is the price he must pay for his romantic delusions, for the part he has played in colonising the South, and for being self-colonised.

In the Romantic longing I have inherited, the South is paradise lost, the missing link which, once regained, will make us whole. This South runs in my veins, its salty-sweet blood pumps through my heart. But run-down, regressive Struga and Clemé with his missing front teeth reminded me that the South is also riddled with oppression and unfulfilled potential. That's why its native thinkers and revolutionaries were looking to the West with such hope, before they died young.

'Me, I don't think of here as south or north, west or east. It's just where I've always been and where I'll die,' Clemé said.

We walked by the river. It was afternoon, and elderly Albanian men with worry-beads and white keches on their heads came out to promenade; the few who'd been to Mecca wore black keches. Married Albanian women in headscarves and sometimes the long mantles of Islam walked separately from the men, like gaggles of chatty crows.

'Here, I feel at home,' Clemé went on. 'You know how many job offers I've had abroad? But I love it here, by the lake.'

Struga had become more Islamised in the past twenty years. This was a result of the Kosovo War. Prostitution, drugs-, arms- and people-smuggling had enriched some Albanian men from conservative outlying villages. 'Peace-keeping soldiers came across the border into Struga for the weekend,' Clemé said, 'and you can guess the rest.'

Old Strugan families, by contrast, had become impoverished and forced to sell their properties to drug-rich Albanians from the villages. The face of the town was changing: from cultural hub to backwater, from a majority Christian Macedonian town to majority Muslim Albanian. The current mayor was Albanian. Albanian taxis and Macedonian taxis had separate stands. The Albanian ones were cheaper.

The Albanians and the Macedonians, the Turks and the Roma, had lived together yet apart for centuries here, symbolically divided by the river – the Muslims on the eastern side. Respectful cohabitation had been the norm. This is why I was surprised to see a massive new double-minareted mosque at the edge of town, placed with territorial aggression right beside the Christian cemetery and its small church – 'out of sheer bloody-mindedness', Clemé said, laughing. The mosque had been built recently in the ostentatious Wahabi style; it struck a dissonant note against the local domestic, everyday Islam of single-minaret mosques, markets and mercy. These new symbols of autocratic Arabic Islam were no friends of the older, humanist, Balkan Islam. Repeatedly, I heard worried words to this effect from locals, both Muslims and Christians.

'But the thing is,' Clemé said. 'Hardly anyone goes to that mosque. People don't love it. It's empty. And the other funny thing? When there's a Christian funeral, it's always timed at mid-day, to clash with the call to prayer. So the church bells collide with the muezzin. Out of sheer bloody-mindedness.'

We laughed, but I knew and he knew that this is how wars begin.

During Macedonia's 'insurgency', in effect a brief civil war, Clemé had joined a paramilitary group. They camped near Tetovo in the north where the conflict had been most inflamed. Forty-eight young men like him camped in a house, each telling of 'a house burnt by Albanians or some other crime committed against them, each with a mind for revenge', he said; and out of that band thirteen were killed.

'They were good guys.' His face darkened. 'My friends.'

'But you have Albanian friends too!'

''Course I do! But my friends here are not like those guys up north. Those guys were from Kosovo. Not our own Albanians. And anyway it was war. Let's talk about happier things,' he said.

I wondered what he really did 'up north'.

We visited the largest mosque in town, where Albanian men in keches sat in the courtyard, smoking. The mufti, a small man with unhappy grey eyes, led us inside to show us the space – a rare honour for a woman, Clemé said. A man and a young boy were praying. The mufti warmed to my questions, told me eagerly that 'us Muslims and you Christians' have much in common and it is

only bad politics that divide us; and ended up delivering a mono-
logue – Clemé sneaked outside, but I was stuck – on the dangers
of sexual perversion, and how the end of civilisation would be
brought about by homosexuals.

'Even the Bible says so!' he concluded, his face flushed with
the passion of one who would like some sex but none was on
offer, ever, and let me out of the door reluctantly. Clemé saw the
expression on my face and laughed with his single tooth.

'I'll tell you why I joined the war,' Clemé said suddenly as we
walked by the river.

Two men waded in, waist-deep, with nets, to collect the algae
that had come in from the lake.

'I had an uncle,' Clemé said. 'When my mother got pregnant out of wedlock, the man who got her pregnant – my father
– disappeared and her parents disowned her. But my uncle, he
always helped her.'

In 2000, the uncle, who was a social worker, was shot dead
with a hunting rifle by a local who didn't want social workers
visiting the family. Clemé's mother was devastated.

'You could say that was the first killing of our war,' he said.
That's why he'd joined. Because his blood was boiling. He wanted
revenge for his mother's loss. The killer had been an Albanian.

'First I wanted to kill him, then I wanted to kill Albanians,
then I didn't care.'

And did you, did you kill? I asked him.

He looked at the river.

'I fired one hundred rounds from my Kalashnikov. Put it this
way: if I killed someone, I didn't see his face.'

That's why he never married, he said. Because he'd been
wedded to the idea of revenge. I met his mother. She was a blurry,
slow-moving woman who was making preserves for winter, and
gave me a jar of peppers. Clemé had been the apple of her eye.

'She gave up everything to have me,' Clemé said. 'She could

have aborted me. But she gave life to a good-for-nothing instead,' he said.

I wondered how his mother felt about his part in the war. They seemed an accident-prone lot, as if violence had always been present among them. During the war, Clemé had fallen off a motorbike and sustained a head injury, and it was an aneurysm from the accident that led to the stroke.

And the man who killed the uncle with a hunting rifle?

'He was killed too,' Clemé said. 'But by then I no longer wanted revenge.'

I returned to the monastery months later, on the designated night in September, to witness the procession of people who came with offerings. Some came with nothing but their wrinkles.

Dozens of long wax candles were lit on the monastery terrace, in sandpits, giving the scene an archaic feel. A village couple had brought their granddaughter who was unwell, and a live sacrificial lamb, trussed on the stony ground, its glassy eyes stunned with fright. The older people crossed themselves multiple times, from right to left in the Eastern Orthodox manner, and some bowed to the floor. Inside the church, the Black Madonna was kissed by hundreds of lips, so that if you hadn't brought an illness with you, you were certain to pick one up.

The poverty of ordinary Macedonians was plain to see. Women from the surrounding villages brought a loaf of bread, apples from their garden, a few eggs, tied up in festive embroidered cloths. Women and men with rounded shoulders and children in nylon tracksuits filed respectfully past the splendidly robed, cold-eyed priests who had come down from Skopje. Later, they'd collect the gifts and the money with their bejewelled hands, distribute it among themselves, pile it up in their expensive cars and drive back to the capital. Like the feudal lords they were – worthy descendants of the patriarchs of Byzantium.

Meanwhile, childless couples came asking for children, couples with sick children came asking for health, couples with healthy children came asking for peace, the peace they'd had before the children – or had they? No, they hadn't, they'd been frantically praying for children then. What we have is not enough: a fundamental human condition was summed up in the queue of supplicants.

Here were women with cigarette-ashen faces and men heavy with unemployment. The overindulged asked for moderation and the skinny for abundance. The youths in leather jackets and skinny jeans came on fairy-lit boats from Ohrid. A rock musician and his dreadlocked family in cowboy boots came as celebrity guests of the clergy. Women in blurry leopard prints and fake Gucci bags came, and diaspora Macedonians from Australia in angora sweaters and real Gucci bags brought the easy confidence of wealth. There were fake blondes with piled-up hair and platform shoes and dapper Roma guys in shiny suits and dazzling smiles. Muslim Albanian women in flower-printed headscarves bought worry-bead bracelets and mini-icons of the Black Madonna. People queued up for the rock spring with bottles. The musical Orthodox recitatives went on for four hours, in church Slavonic, and aromatic incense coiled around the inside of the crowded church, which nevertheless began to smell like a stable.

Gospodi pomiluy, gospodi pomiluy, gospodi pomiluy. God have mercy on us, intoned the hundreds of lips that had kissed the Black Madonna. Many of the women wore the familiar mask of ancient tragedy.

May your progeny be as countless as all the earth's sands, pronounced the archbishop with greasy lips. A curse disguised as a blessing. 'The fertility for which women were asking the gods everywhere in the dark night over Macedonia was not as simple a gift as they supposed,' wrote Rebecca West in *Black Lamb and Grey Falcon: A Journey through Yugoslavia*, in 1941, after she witnessed the paganistic rites that Christian and Muslim women were performing on the night of St George. Here, Christian women were sleeping on top of a carved cross on the stone floor of a chapel, and Muslim women were hugging a seven-foot-tall phallic stone in a dervish *tekke*, their faces covered by black veils. 'They were begging for the proper conduct of a period of nine months and a chance to ripen its fruits. They would obtain the bloodstained eternity of human history.'

Eighty years later, the invocation was the same. Nothing had changed. As if time had telescoped into a single moment. We, the living of today, are the answers to those women's prayers of eighty years ago. Our birth did not bring them lasting happiness.

Trauma demands repetition, wrote the child psychoanalyst Selma Fraiberg. 'Repetition, repetition, repetition.' This was palpable here, tonight. Life without transcendence is a shuffling of ghosts, a wound ritually repeated. All of us duly born and named after ancestors, waiting for our turn to be processed. Sigmund Freud, who had named his own children after ancestors, observed that this act made the children into phantoms, or revenants. *Re-venant*: one who returns. I had returned to the lake for my grandmother, even though it was my sister who was named after her. My sister had children instead – that is *her* form of ancestral return.

Meanwhile, Clemé was in charge of the souvenir stalls all night, doing brisk business and chatting in Albanian with the women in headscarves. He was glad to see me and immediately appointed me as his sales assistant, and I found myself dodging questions about saints and counting out change for the banknotes people gave me in exchange for the bracelets, icons, 'blessed' water, and 'monastery wine' that wasn't made at the monastery. By now, the trussed lamb had disappeared into the bowels of the complex.

When it was time to say goodbye to Clemé the next day, he gave me a print reproduction of the Black Madonna crafted by him into a small icon. And a crumpled photograph.

'Will you keep this for me?' he said casually. 'It was part of my life but I'm ashamed of it. People say I'm touched now, but I was crazier then.'

Although the photo made me shudder, I took it. Later, I destroyed it. In the photo, a younger, beefier Clemé in camouflage gear stands in a room lined with mattresses and sleeping bags, posters of bare-breasted women on the walls. He holds a Kalashnikov and grins.

Clemé had been dumb as a child, he'd told me. Thinking he was retarded, the Yugoslav authorities took him away from his mother by force and placed him in a home. Living in that home made sure he didn't say a word until he was eight.

Without meeting him, I wouldn't have allowed for the possibility that the Black Madonna might be a conduit, if not for a 'miracle' then for personal transformation, which is the same. I also understood why those soldiers had thrown the icon in the lake, repeatedly.

In most Eastern depictions of the Virgin Mary, the child is stylised, separate from her and looking at the viewer, formal in the knowledge of his exalted destiny. In the Black Madonna of the Lake, the child's face is pressed to hers, his hand clutching her robe; and both mother and child wear expressions of such stark premonition of what is to come, of the violent world of humans that can be avoided only in this moment of hope captured by an unknown hand – yet their gaze says 'There is time yet, you can do things differently' – that to keep looking, you have to confront something within yourself.

Swaying between joy and sorrow
you are the prey of the transient.
Love's infinite garden holds other fruit
besides laughter and tears
forever fresh and green without
spring without autumn.

Rumi, thirteenth century

ROADS

'My memory's not what it was,' said Slavche. 'It's all jumbled up, the weddings and the funerals.'

Slavche and I were sipping tea from tulip-shaped glasses in the family restaurant by the tekke. Her fine-boned face was drawn but she was as poised as ever. Observing Ohridians, Rebecca West wrote: 'Here in Ochrid [sic] the conspicuous personages are slender old ladies with shapely heads, feline spines . . . fine hands and feet, and a composure that sharply rather than placidly repulses recognition of all in life that is not noble. A more aristocratic type can hardly be conceived.'

That was Slavche, and my great-grandmother Ljubitsa. In fact, Slavche reminded me of Ljubitsa. But Slavche, without physically going anywhere, had diverged from the life prescribed for her: she had converted to Islam. Through my afternoon teas with her, I began to discover an extraordinary mystical Sufi tradition. Although this particular tekke dated from the 1600s, I was surprised to learn that Sufism had entered the Balkans *before* the Ottomans. It emerged from the Islamic Golden Age during the eighth to fourteenth century, and has outlived it by many hundreds of years.

The story of Balkan Sufism begins in the mid-thirteenth century with a peripatetic figure called Sari Saltik. His legend, told in cultures ranging from Albania to Persia, is worthy of *A Thousand and One Nights*. *Sari* means 'yellow': he was said to have a blond beard. Saltik was a disciple and companion of Hadj Bektash, founder of Bektashism, the first Sufi movement. Like many holy figures of the East, Saltik appeared with a halo, and transcended time and space. He first travelled from Uzbekistan to Cape Kaliakra on the Black Sea in Bulgaria with a hundred Turkic families. Some see their arrival as the beginning of Turkic migration into Europe, but by then, other Turkic peoples had already settled by the Black Sea and beyond: Bulgars, Pechenegs and Tatars.

Saltik's gift of ubiquity meant that he was seen all over the Balkans, sometimes simultaneously in two places, and posthumously: from Kaliakra to Corfu, from Durrës to Ohrid. And everywhere he passed, his legacy of 'turning evil into good' was perpetuated. In an echo of Balkan folkloric tropes about supernatural heroes like Krali Marko who stride over valleys, his 'footsteps' are found in sacred sites and by curative springs. When death approached, Saltik requested that seven coffins be prepared for him, and so he has seven known resting places where he has been worshipped as both a Muslim and a Christian saint ever since. One of his resting places is St Naum Monastery, where for centuries he has been conflated with Naum himself.

Saltik was a persuasive proselytiser of Bektashism, which differed radically from mainstream Sunni Islam. Subsequent Sufi orders, both Shia and Sunni, followed the Bektashi principle: they incorporated aspects of Eastern Christianity, Tibetan Buddhism, Cabbalism, Gnosticism and Asian shamanism. It was these generously eclectic qualities that were key to the spread and endurance of Sufi Islam in the Balkans. Furthermore, Sufism – its philosophy, aesthetics and architecture – shaped the towns of the Ottoman Balkans.

Ohrid once had half a dozen dervish lodges belonging to different orders. Slavche and her surviving son were keepers of the last tekke. It is laid out in the harmonious Islamic tradition: a circle of handsome houses built around an internal courtyard which contains the mosque, a rose garden and a small cemetery. This blend of public and private reflects the traditional function

of the tekke. The homely mosque was built in 1590, long before
the tekke itself was founded in 1720 by a dervish named Mehmed.
Mehmed belonged to the Khalvati *tariqa*, or order, of dervishes.
Tariqa means 'road' in Arabic – the road of the seeker – and there
are twelve Sufi 'roads'. The Khalvati road had three branches, and
this one is indigenous to the western Balkans.

'Anyway, twelve is a magic number in Sufism,' Slavche said.
'Twelve imams, twelve letters in the declaration of faith, twelve
lines of poems.'

And she recited: 'Swaying between joy and sorrow, you are the
prey of the transient', from a poem by Jalal ad-Din Balkhi-Rumi,
the thirteenth-century Persian mystic after whom the Mevlevi
order with its ecstatic whirling prayer was named. *Mevlevi* meant
'my master'.

Several centuries after Rumi, Mehmed and his party had travelled a long road to Ohrid. He and his wife and two daughters,
and other dervishes, set off from Khorasan – literally, 'where the
sun rises' – in Persia. It is not known how many years they spent
on the road, but they arrived in Macedonia in 1667. Mehmed set
up other Khalvati tekkes in the region and Khalvatism became the
most widespread Sufi order in Kosovo, Macedonia and Bosnia.
He died and is buried right here.

'We don't know where his *khalvet* is, though,' said Erol. Erol
was Slavche's surviving son and had joined us at the table. He was
a middle-aged man in a crisp pink shirt and with a hollowed-out
posture, as if suffering from a chest condition. He had his mother's delicate build.

'Khalvet is a space for prayer,' Erol explained. *Khalva* meant
'retreat' in Arabic. 'Which is the basis of Khalvatism. Meditation,
self-scrutiny and fasting. It's more introspective than other orders.'

'Somewhere along Mehmed's road from Khorasan to Ohrid,'
Slavche said, 'there is a dedicated Chinar, or plane tree. That's his
khalvet. Like our Chinar here, planted by another holy man.' She
pointed to Clement's tree.

'Movement was a way of life for dervishes,' Erol said. 'Wandering was a way of attaining knowledge beyond the material world.' A precept of dervishism is renouncing possessions, surrendering to the Road.

'There were gatherings along the way, adventures, wondrous encounters, and symbolic manifestations. That's Sufism, it's dynamic. Or was,' Slavche said, interrupting her son, who raised his eyes in irritation.

'One of the duties of the tekke was to shelter travellers,' he said, and she started drumming with her fingers on the table.

They were like a married couple. They'd never lived apart. He rose from the table abruptly and went to fetch something. Slavche sighed.

'He should come back,' she said. 'My memory is not what it was.'

But her memory was excellent. Slavche was raised in a family of Vlachs, or Aromanians, who had come from Albania as traders. In the troubled 1930s her mother's sisters emigrated to Romania, and missed Ohrid all their lives.

'Ohrid, Ohrid, gentle, wise, lost to me like paradise,' she sang. 'You know the song?'

When Slavche met her future husband Kadri, she was still at high school. An attraction developed, but there was a catch: he was a Muslim; and not only that, he was the sheik, the head dervish of the tekke.

'It was a scandal. We were pitted against the town. To defy convention in Ohrid – can you imagine? My family severed relations with me for six years. But they got over it. Because nothing could break my bond with Kadri. I adopted Islam as my own faith.'

Her Islamic name was Hidaet, meaning One Who Gives. 'But it was Kadri who was the giving one,' she said.

My aunts confirmed that Sheik Abdul-Kadri, the last initiated head dervish of the tekke in an uninterrupted line since the 1660s, was a progressive, well-read man with a fine sense of humour, much loved by the town. He had died twenty years ago. In this land of heterodox couplings of all kinds, mixed marriages weren't uncommon, and neither were religious conversions. Interfaith relations only began to deteriorate in the second half of the nineteenth century, with the rise of national movements and the revolutionary komita bands. The complicated politics at the end of empire brought a climate of conspiracy and mistrust. Mixed couples and Muslim communities became a target for persecution and murder by the komiti; these atrocities have been whitewashed from official history. A culture of paranoia took root. This is why it was a scandal when Slavche married Kadri in Socialist Yugoslavia.

Once committed to the relationship, Slavche-Hidaet had to learn not only the tenets of Islam, not only the intricacies of this particular Road, but also the Turkish language. She and Erol spoke a mixture of Turkish and Macedonian. But the Turkish spoken here had lots of Macedonian words in it already, just as Macedonian is heavily infused with Turkish words. The Turkish spoken by locals is frozen in time; Erol told me that he understood Turkish speakers in Azerbaijan better than those in modern Turkey.

'*Turlu-tava*,' Slavche said. *Turlu* is 'mixed', and *tava* is 'tray'. 'You know that dish?'

No, I said, I know *imam bayaldi*.

'Turlu-tava is like imam bayaldi, but even more mixed,' Slavche said.

While we sat talking through the afternoon, locals stepped into the restaurant to greet Slavche and Erol. The only way I could tell Muslims from non-Muslims was the Turkish phrases used by the Muslims.

What became of the position of head dervish after Kadri? I asked her.

'I'll tell you what. Various wannabes presented themselves. Two of them who assumed tekke duties died. One right inside the tekke, he just keeled over. And the current one,' she said with cool relish, 'I said to him, You know, it's your turn now.'

Erol had returned from the tekke.

'My generation was born under Communism,' he said. 'We are disadvantaged in matters of spirituality. And Sufism is about spirituality, not dogma.'

He was next in line to be head dervish.

'I'm teaching myself Ottoman Turkish. I feel duty-bound,' Erol said.

The tekke contained archives four hundred years old, and hundreds of untranslated books, many in Ottoman Turkish, a language nobody understands except Ottomanists.

I asked if a woman could join a dervish order today.

'Yes,' he said. 'There are women dervishes in Struga. But they don't assume public duties.'

Why not?

Erol took off his glasses. 'Because women are privileged. Their power is private.'

His mother didn't disagree, but I couldn't tell whether she agreed.

I was amazed to discover that there were entire Bektashi sisterhoods in the early days of Sufism. In fact, a woman became the first direct successor of Hadj Bektashi. Kadandjak Ana lived in Cappadocia as an ascetic and exhibited supernatural abilities – turning herself into a bird, becoming invisible, and appearing in her future parents' dreams. In the world of Sufi mystics, time is not linear, all is symbol.

'To become a dervish,' Erol went on, 'you have to earn spiritual credit through prayer and contemplation. You practise for three or four years under a qualified dervish until you have a dream.'

Your teacher must dream of you at the same time. And to become a sheik, you must have special powers – prophecy, dream work, the ability to heal. These powers are developed through devotion to the inner life, and prayer – not the customary five times a day, but six. You must pray that extra sixth time, pronounce the ninety-nine names of Allah (Sari Saltik lived for ninety-nine years, allegedly). That's why worry-bead strings traditionally have ninety-nine beads, Erol said.

The practice of whirling, or 'prayer on your feet', for which dervishes are known in the West, was solely a peculiarity of the Mevlevi order – the spontaneous creation of Rumi. Walking through a market one day, he heard music, and in the melody he heard *la elaha ella'llah* – there is one God and Allah is his name – and in a state of exaltation he started whirling. In a separate episode, while listening to his teacher playing the reed flute, he was seized with a desire to whirl. Sufi devotional music, and the Mevlevi tradition in particular, have two key instruments: the flute and the lute. The Mevlevi dervishes could dance only when the flute was played – a shamanistic practice similar to fire-walking to the sound of drums and to other meditative altered states accompanied by music.

What strikes me here is that the reed flute was seen in Sufism as the instrument of the soul and also of deracination – for it sings forever of the native reedbed whence it was cut. The reed flute, *kaval* or *kawali* in Persian, features in the last line of the poem 'Longing for the South', and in many other Balkan songs and poems – for it was the instrument of the mountain shepherds, and the mountains and their rivers and lakes are where much of Balkan folklore originates. For the shepherds, poets and mystics of the East, the kaval has been the chosen instrument of the soul.

> There [by the lake] I'd sit, I'd play my *kaval* a while.
> The sun would set, I'd sweetly die.

'The last prophet of this dervish line was Sheik Zekiriya, our great-grandfather,' Slavche said. When you are born into a tekke, you have a moral obligation: you must never abandon the house.

'Sheik Zekiriya warned his brothers against selling their share of the tekke,' she went on. Erol had gone off again. He was a restless man. 'But it fell on deaf ears. One brother emigrated to Turkey, suffered total loss and died in poverty.'

The other brother moved to Turkey too, and his wife and children were to follow. Sheik Zekiriya dreamt of turbulent waters and warned them not to travel by sea, only by land, but they boarded a ship at Salonica, the ship sank before reaching the Bosphorus, and the family didn't survive. That brother went mad with grief and spent his last years in a Turkish asylum.

'One of the duties of the tekke was towards the mentally ill,' Erol said – he was back – and began to unfurl a long scroll, intricately inscribed in Ottoman Turkish with coloured calligraphic inks. It looked like a genealogy with thousands of branches.

'Nine metres long,' he said. 'The original was brought by Pir Mehmed.'

Mehmed had carried a ferman, or authorisation, from the sultan, allowing him to spread the teaching of Khalvatism in the Balkans; and here it was, followed by the compiled records of successive administrations. The process by which the tekkes were perpetuated was impressively democratic: each ferman was issued only after a number of citizens of high standing from the multi-denominational community had written in its support. It detailed the activities of the tekke as they were at the time of each ferman: distributing ashure (barley pudding) to the poor; teaching boys in its madrasa; hatip, or charitable donations; sheltering travellers, and the 'insane and melancholy' until they were recovered. The sheik was expected to have a special quality called baraka, a spiritual mana associated with wise men: by being in his presence, you felt better.

'He listened to people's problems without judgement. The tekke was a refuge from worldly worries,' Slavche said.

She had baraka.

'Christians visited the tekkes and Muslims the monasteries. At festivals, we still exchange gifts of food,' Erol added, trying hard not to interrupt his mother.

Another peculiarity of the tekke, shared with monasteries and other Christian and pagan holy sites, was to do with what Erol called a very old tradition. He showed me inside. The tekke was decorated with ink drawings of the ninety-nine names of Allah, and lined with sheep and goat skins, like some tents of the steppes. Here, people of any faith or none could leave a piece of clothing overnight. If they collected it and washed it the next day, they would be cured of their affliction.

This creative integration of shamanism, in addition to drinking alcohol, allowing women in, believing that music, poetry and even erotic ecstasy were direct channels to God, is what puritanical mainstream Islam objected to. Then and now.

Erol showed me accessories left behind by dervishes over the generations: a seal ring, a collection of exquisite wizard-like wands and staffs with carved heads whose jaws had secret compartments – in a way, a dervish *was* a wizard – and silver cigarette holders inscribed in French, an ink-stamp bearing the Ottoman coat-of-arms, a long silk shawl. The colourful Khalvati flag of the tekke was the original one brought from Persia. Wandering dervishes carried three symbolic objects wherever they went: a bag, a flag and a carved staff. Such dervishes were known as fakirs, from the Arabic for 'poor', but the figure of the fakir came to be associated above all with magic.

Slavche rose from the table; she was retiring for the afternoon. But before she went, she gave me an envelope, to open later. She put her long hand on mine:

'It's a fine thing that you've returned to the Lake. Because no matter where one goes in one's wanderings, you and I know: the Balkans are the heart and soul of this funny old world.'

And she added, quoting Rumi: 'Love's infinite garden holds other fruit besides laughter and tears.'

Erol and his family lived in the sheik's house behind the

restaurant, but Slavche had retreated to a corner of the complex, where she had a small studio. These were not the lodgings of a queen, but she liked her independence, had her own bookshelves, a single bed and, as she put it, peace.

After his mother had gone, Erol and I carried on talking.

'There is a saying in dervishism, which keeps us grounded, so we don't take ourselves too seriously,' he said. 'While there's enough space on earth, there's no need to glorify anybody to the heavens. This is the core of dervishism. It is earth-bound and encourages individual thought and expression, rather than group-think and blind devotion. But—'

He took his glasses off. His eyelids were inflamed.

'It guts me to watch the decline of values. Religion has become about money and party politics. How can you call your-self faithful, when you're driving a new car but your neighbour is hungry? How can you boast about going to Mecca three times when your friend is freezing? True Islam is humane.'

Rumi speaks of the ego as the greatest enemy on the Road.

'Where there is ego, there is no God. We live in a world of ego.' Erol's voice was catching with emotion.

This is what was eating him up.

The madman of the charshia came and went with his radio, bouncing along with his shirt open to reveal his black hairy chest. By now, I saw him as quite sane. He was performing a public service – every day at an appointed hour he became mad, so that the rest of Ohrid didn't have to. The wandering dervishes had once performed this role of holy madmen – with their shirts open at the chest, their large-buckled belts and sceptres topped with carved animal heads, they often appeared unhinged. But they were conduits for collective energies, archetypes who enacted what was taboo. Travellers write of seeing dervishes throughout the Balkans perform uncanny feats: standing immobile at cem-eteries for weeks like living statues, going into trances, appearing and disappearing at unlikely speed, and curing incurable ailments with herbal potions and numerological and Quranic incantations. Just like the anchorite monks and the yogis of Asia.

It was time to go. I had consumed juicy meatballs, salads and coffees for which Erol didn't let me pay.

'You do realise,' Erol said as a parting shot, 'that Europe wants us to be slaves?'

Oh, no, I thought. Here comes a rant I've heard before.

'That we have lived here peacefully for centuries and survived all manner of upheavals, thanks to the lake. Thanks to the lake, the world comes to us and keeps us worldly,' he went on, passionately. 'But Europe wants us to be poor, divided and ignorant. That's why we've had nothing but bad governance. It's all orchestrated by the great powers.'

In his late years as an unwilling Yugoslav, my great-grandfather Kosta hummed a sad song. He had given up the struggle, only the lament remained. My mother remembers the song:

> From the top of Pirin Mountain
> I hear a sorrowful voice –
> Macedonia is weeping.
> Be damned, oh Europe,
> Babylonian whore.
> You want us to be slaves.

Erol spoke in the voice of Kosta.

'Here in the Balkans,' he went on, 'we have another problem: accelerated change. In just twenty years, we've been expected to catch up with what the West has achieved in three hundred years.'

In just twenty years, the little republic had experienced post-Communist shock, mass emigration, autocracy and civil near-collapse. It was about to experience an emotionally fraught name change too, dictated by 'Europe' in the guise of Greece.

'It's a lot,' I agreed.

'And we're only human,' he said, and smiled for the first time that day.

Erol was trying to carry the tekke, his father, his dead brother, and the lake's Sufi legacy. It was a heavy load.

The Turkish community of Ohrid was dramatically reduced. Waves of emigration had shrunk their ranks: during the discreet purge of Yugoslavia's Muslims between 1954 and 1967, seventy per cent of the town's Turks emigrated to Turkey, and when I had coffee with the son of the town's oldest Turkish family – the Ohrizade family, from the Persian for 'son', *zade*, and so 'sons of Ohrid', who had arrived with the Seljuk Turk colonists in the late fourteenth century – he told me that all his relatives in Turkey mourned for Ohrid for the rest of their lives. 'Ohrid, Ohrid, gentle, wise . . .' Did I know that song? His family were traders. He sold lighting, his grandfather had manufactured and sold cartwheels, then they had a logging business because Macedonia is rich in forests, he said, then tea, and finally – sulphur, mined at Kosel nearby and exported to Istanbul. And of course, they'd had extensive orchards, though no longer.

Traditionally, much of Ohrid's wealth lay in its fertile land. Evliya Çelebi wrote of the the lavish orchards, the twenty-six fruit compotes he sampled. Wealthier Muslim families had had orchard estates just outside Ohrid in 'beys' villages'. One such estate village survived: Orman. My curiosity was further piqued by a town chronicler who wrote in the early twentieth century: 'Many an aga's garden, vineyard, entire estates, went to mistresses, taverna chanteuses and other amours. This is how the last of aga fortunes went out, like candles burnt to a stub in the heat of the agrarian reforms and la dolce vita, leaving nothing for their descendants.'

A walking distance from Ohrid, Orman was a giant orchard fed by a river that emptied into the lake. A fully preserved Roman bridge crossed the river. Boris, or Borche, was waiting for me by his grandfather's house. He was a friend of a friend, an excitable man of Erol's age who had dedicated his life to organic fruit cultivation.

'Orman has a microclimate,' he said, 'because of the arc of the rising sun.'

We sat in the garden with his old Auntie Rouska, and ate cherries from a bowl, so plump and sweet they nearly brought tears to my eyes.

'The cherries of Orman have been voted the best in Europe!' Borche said, and it was a fact – the cherries had a certified geographic location and had won prizes.

'Life was better during Yugoslavia,' said Auntie Rouska.

'Auntie, please,' said Borche, and to me: 'She's deaf.'

'And better yet in the agas' time,' Auntie Rouska went on.

'My great-grandfather and my grandfather were employed at an estate here,' Borche said, trying to steer the conversation. 'They grew wheat, rye, potatoes, and produced dairy, which they also sold in the gated town.'

Borche had left his life in the city to run his own organic orchard and farm, with a cousin. It was a family business, of course; everything was kept in the family and now he wanted his son to get involved.

'I want to prove that it's possible to produce quality fruit with minimal treatment,' he said. 'Because that's the future.'

'The agas were fine people. Better than us,' said Auntie Rouska. 'Generous. Each house had three bulls. Usually gifts from the agas.'

'Auntie, please,' Borche said.

'This land we're on,' Rouska went on, 'was a gift from one aga. A woman in our family was his lover.'

Borche tried to explain, but choked on a cherry.

'The tower over there' – the aunt pointed at a turreted house lost in greenery – 'is part of an old estate. The aga's daughter owns it. She's married to a Macedonian, lovely couple. They come in summer.'

'Yes, the agas came in summer with their families,' Borche said. 'But most of the time it was just the estate gardeners and farmers here.'

'We worked hard,' said Auntie Rouska, 'beating butter in cauldrons, cutting the rye with scythes. But it was a balanced, seasonal life. The agas took fifty per cent and left us the rest. Sometimes more.'

'During the war,' Borche said, 'some men were working in the fields. The Germans thought they were partisans, rounded them up and lined them up for execution, fifteen of them. In the field over there.'

Borche's grandfather had just returned from a German prisoner-of-war camp where he'd been interned as a resistance fighter. Before that, he'd served with the Bulgarian army. In the process, he'd learned German. 'And it was thanks to his German that these men's lives were saved. He explained this was an aga's estate and not a partisans' hideout. The Germans let them go.'

After the war, brutal nationalisation began. People watched their fields, orchards and vineyards become cooperatives. Many emigrated to Turkey.

'You didn't know who you were working for,' said Auntie Rouska. 'Or why.'

'Come.' Borche got up restlessly. 'I'll show you the orchards.'

'Come see a sight, a rabbit in a turban, a wolf in a dress,' Auntie Rouska recited by way of farewell.

It was an old song from Orman but she had forgotten the tune.

The orchards were heavy with fruit – plump cherries that could send you into a sensual frenzy, Evliya Çelebi style; and there were also figs, hazelnuts of the Nutella sort – but no apples.

'Oh, the apples.' Borche stopped in his tracks. 'Oversupply killed them. The prices plummeted, we kept making losses. I'm a third-generation apple grower. It broke my heart to uproot the old apple trees.' Among the old apple trees had been one that gave a thousand kilos of fruit per season.

'But in their place, we planted lovely cherry trees.' Borche filled a bag with cherries for me. He was not one to dwell on the past – he was too excited about next season.

I didn't want to leave this orchard where everything tasted so good. The original landlords were gone but the workers had stayed and bought them out: from feudalism to capitalism, via Socialism.

Back in the gated town, I sat under the weeping willows of Sarayishte beach to watch the orange sunset, and opened the envelope Slavche had given me. A black-and-white photo was inside, of her younger son in shorts. His teacher Tatjana, my aunt, is behind him, hands on his shoulders, their faces radiant with the lake's light behind them. They stand in the ruins of the Lower Saray, once a gorgeous mansion built by forced labour for Djeladin Bey, and now a stage for summer concerts.

During the Yugoslav Wars, when the virus of ethno-religious nationalism spread here, and when even in tolerant Ohrid minds and windows were closed, as she put it, Slavche was framed and tried for 'Albanian separatism'. I wondered if that ordeal had contributed to her husband's early death and her son's fatal accident. She was acquitted, but the grotesque trial unfolded over many months, during which she was jailed. It was a dreadful time, she said, but they allowed books inside. In her cell, she read Churchill's autobiography and that kept the black dog away, she said, an attitude which contrasted with her son's bitter disillusion with 'Europe'. After all, it was Churchill who memorably said that the Balkans produce more history than they can consume, seemingly unaware of his own country's contribution to this excess. One way or another, Slavche had preserved her sanity, grace, and faith in life. She had, in the wider sense, remained on the Road. She was not a fakir, but her spiritual resilience was almost a miracle in itself.

Sandals on, I waded into the transparent water. The land is

riven with the anguish and contradictions of linear roads, but the lake contains multitudes. It cannot be imprisoned by chronology. The lake is where all roads end. The boats seemed to float on air. I plunged my arms into the lake, *forever fresh and green without spring without autumn.*

The valley where we lived lay under two old mountains. Great powerful waters flowed from both. In spring, when the weather opened up, the earth and the sky shone with the light of those waters. In the gardens, in the furrows, the water was everywhere.

And across the valley was the lake, itself like a sun.

Zhivko Chingo, 1961

THE POETRY AND THE HUNGER

Two thousand feet above the lake, within earshot of a waterfall, is the Monastery of St Petka. It is built into a cliff and looks down on a lush precipice – figs, cherries, plums, almonds, a jungle of sweetness all the way to the water's edge.

The steepest section of the Via Egnatia climbed through here on its way east, and even the name of the village below the monastery is traced to the days of the trade route, when travellers stopped to taste the famous food of an innkeeper, one Vele. Vele would feed, or *goshtava*, the guests, or *gosti*, and the name stuck: Velgoshti. But to me, this is the Village of Cherries. I have never seen so many cherry trees.

The Village of Cherries is symbolic of the lake's fortunes through the twentieth century. It had the first komitas in the lake district and even some local Turks joined them. Which didn't stop the komitas from cutting the throats of two village women for having relationships with Turks. The aftermath of the Ilinden Uprising in 1903 brought fresh violence in the form of mercenaries, not all of whom were Muslims. The end of the Balkan Wars in 1913 awarded the lake to Serbia, at which point seventy-five men were lined up in the square and every fifth was shot. Among them was a returning émigré; he'd just sailed back from America, to be shot on his first morning home.

The monastery was above it all, literally. It radiated peace, like the face of Petka carved in the stone. Petka was ubiquitous, like Sari Saltik. I'd seen so many churches dedicated to her across the Balkans that I had to look her up.

Petkana-Paraskeva of the Balkans was born in the second half of the tenth century on the Marmara Sea – on a Friday (*petak* in Slavic, *paraskevi* in Greek). After witnessing atrocity as a child, Petkana went blind. By the time she regained her sight, she had spent so long with her gaze turned inwards that she was set on a path of contemplation. Having spent five years of silence in a monastery, she set off on foot from Constantinople with a group of pilgrims, but following a vision she split off from the group and walked across the Jordanian desert alone. She lived as a cave hermit for forty years. A Berber woman befriended her and brought her food and news of the world. The news was more of the same: children were born, grew up, and fought terrible wars. Returning to her native town Epivates to die, Petkana was buried as a stranger – outside the city walls – but in the centuries to come, her remains became much travelled, as various Balkan rulers claimed them even though she had never set foot on their side of the Bosphorus. By being invoked across the entire peninsula, she could be said to have achieved the peace she aspired for – by imaginatively uniting a collection of peoples divided by the same brutish politics she turned her back on, in search of the bigger picture.

What I like about her is that she is not a distressful martyr. She lived a silent life and died a natural death. The arc of her story is typical of the canon of Oriental ascetics.

My twin aunts and I had been driven up to Petka's monastery by the husband of one of them, a retired bon-vivant who went along with the twins' whims. He had a routine of his own: at dusk, he cycled from the Turkish neighbourhood where they lived to the lake front where he threw bread to the swans.

'Me, I'm a messenger.' He winked at me. 'I run errands.'

'You'd be bored without us,' the twins said.

'What would you do without us?' the twins said.

'Your life would have no meaning,' said the twins affection-ately. And he agreed.

The twins were a duet. Identical in face and inseparable in deed, my aunts agreed on everything and formed a unified front, though they had an ongoing discussion about which one was the dominant personality. I liked being with the three of them, there was always fun to be had and little of the heaviness I asso-ciated with this feminine line. The only drama was the weather, discussions of what to wear in case the wind changed and caused 'draughts' from which you could 'catch your death', and whether to take snacks on our expeditions or wait until lunchtime.

Each week, the four of us drove up to a monastery above the lake, for coffee. Each of these monasteries was overlooked in space and preceded in time by anchorite caves dating from the ninth and tenth centuries, and cave churches elaborately painted in the thirteenth and fourteenth. This week, it was St Petka.

From the monastery courtyard, the lake looked like a crater filled with blue light. A stone bore a humble plaque dedicated to the locally born writer Zhivko Chingo, and quoted a line from *The Great Water*, his coming-of-age novel set in a postwar orphanage on the lake, though the lake is never seen by the imprisoned children, only sensed beyond the walls.

'The only thing which is truly yours is that which you give away,' the plaque said.

My aunts were not poetic types. They had inherited some stur-dier, down-to-earth streak in the family. Every other week, with quiet loyalty, they'd visit the town cemetery to refresh the flowers and candles at the graves of their mother, their sister Tatjana and grandmother Ljubitsa. The men's graves too – their grandfather Kosta, their uncle, and their estranged father.

The women's graves were apart from the men's. 'That's because when Kosta died, Ljubitsa said to us: For God's sake don't bury me next to him. I've had enough of him in this life,' said Snezhana.

'He was possessive,' said Biljana. 'In the early days, he'd check her shoes to see if she'd been out without his permission.'

'But in later years, he lightened up. He liked to provoke,' said Snezhana. 'He was a daredevil.'

'But with Ljubitsa it fell on deaf ears. She was dead serious,' Biljana said. 'Everything was taken literally. Two and two . . .'

'Was four,' Snezhana said.

'She cleaned a great deal,' Biljana said.

'Cleanliness, morality, education . . .' Snezhana said.

'And early marriage,' Biljana said. 'To avoid disrepute. Those things were set in stone.'

'Tatjana had a romance with a lovely man,' Snezhana said. 'But . . .'

'Grandma put pressure on her,' Biljana said. 'Always on her case.'

'She said, You are to marry and start a family by twenty-three,' Snezhana said.

'And she did,' Biljana said. 'She married at twenty-three.'

'She married the wrong guy,' Snezhana said.

'He was not right for her,' Biljana said.

'Tatjana sang in a choir and had a degree in English Literature. She named the boys after English writers. She was broad-minded.'

'She had friends all over the world. We stayed in touch with some of them.'

'But with time, we lost touch.'

Ljubitsa had married Kosta at twenty-three.

'She didn't want him,' Snezhana said.

'He asked for her hand three times,' Biljana said.

'It was only under pressure that she said yes,' Snezhana said.

My grandmother had married at twenty-three. My mother? Married at twenty-three.

The twins had married in their mid-twenties, just as their sister was dying. They had grown up in an all-female household, with their mother and grandmother, both immaculate home-makers. Ljubitsa kept her granddaughters on a short leash. To avoid further disrepute.

'What about those four years after Kosta's escape?' I asked.

The twins shrugged. 'She didn't talk about that,' Biljana said.

'She prayed to Petka a lot,' Snezhana said. 'She came up here to pray.'

'Then one day, she smashed the icon of Petka against the wall. And took a job at the printing press,' Biljana said.

'She loved the printed word,' Snezhana said. 'She read the papers religiously. And always had a book.'

'Grandad Kosta too,' Biljana said.

'They read the papers together and talked politics.'

In Macedonia, you never ran out of political talk.

That night in 1929 when Kosta vanished across the lake, Ljubitsa became an abandoned wife with three children to feed. And where were her well-bred family in her hour of need? Once a woman was married, she was no longer the responsibility of her family but of her husband. Too bad if the husband was gone. But one of her brothers did show her kindness by buying her a sewing machine. So at night, she sewed and embroidered. She was also reduced to renting out part of the creaky old house. I picture that proud daughter of the gated town walking down the charshia, but never twice in one day. Her social standing had collapsed but she did keep her children fed and educated.

Four years later, when they joined Kosta in Sofia, he was suffering from severe burnout. It was the Great Depression, there was no work.

Every evening, the reunited family would sit around the table in their rented rooms in the neighbourhood of Banishora, between two streets called Ohrid and Struga. This was where the *banished* lived – Macedonians like them, exiled from the Yugoslavia of King Alexander; and refugees from Aegean Macedonia in northern Greece, where the government of General Metaxas was carrying out a brutal campaign of hellenisation. Unsavoury VMRO agents with bulges in their leather coats circulated around these struggling households, collecting 'voluntary' donations for the Organisation.

In these reduced circumstances, it was more vital than ever to keep up standards. The family would sit around the table, always perfectly laid by Ljubitsa with dinner plates, cutlery and napkins, but there was nothing on those plates. They were broke, and too proud to ask relatives for help. Why the fuss with the plates, then? Because Ljubitsa was keen to make sure the landlady next door heard the clatter of plates at dinner time. She was assumed to be eavesdropping, Ohridian fashion, and Ljubitsa didn't want her to think them poor.

Kosta was keen for his children to relearn standard Bulgarian, so they wouldn't be mocked at school for speaking their Ohrid dialect. So they sat with the empty plates in front of them, with nothing but the books on the shelves – of course, there were always books – and recited poems to cover up the rumbling of their stomachs.

Give me wings . . .

Hunger stays with you, they say. Those months, possibly years, of hunger when all they had for breakfast was sunflower seeds may be the reason why Grandmother Anastassia and her younger brother – who during one family reunion made a hundred pancakes for us before dawn – became compulsive overeaters and ruined their health. Their hunger could not be sated: for food, for beautiful things, for attention, for love.

The Banishora neighbourhood is still there, and though the handsome town houses are replaced by apartment buildings, the leafy streets have kept their names: Ohrid, Struga, and Skopje, Strumitsa and Salonica, Kukush (Kilkis), Kostur (Kastoria) and Voden (Edessa), Prilep and Bitola. The ghost of geographic Macedonia was here, with its huddled towns partitioned among three countries, its rivers and mountains, its unearthly lakes and fevered dreams.

Ljubitsa had brought her sewing machine to Sofia and started making clothes to order. As a Macedonian refugee, she felt shunned by the Bulgarians proper, but she was also so aware of her diminished standing that she wouldn't socialise with better-off fellow Macedonians either. One self-permitted comfort was to visit the two St Petka churches in Sofia – until one day, she threw an icon at the wall in rage. Again.

Kosta drank on an empty stomach. A speculative investment he had made in some copper mines had failed. He tried to set up a tailoring business again. With hindsight, Anastassia said, even then she could see her father's fundamental problem: he was long-sighted, never comfortable with the small-scale world of stitching and pattern-cutting. And restless as ever. Across Europe and the Balkans, markets were unstable, governments repressive, and in the streets of Sofia urban warfare raged between the two main factions of the Organisation (the federalists and the autonomists) and the smaller factions. One generation and several wars after its 'constructive' inception, plagued by internal splits and external power games, the Organisation had lost any vestige of youthful idealism and had turned into a hydra of terror. A mafia-like state-within-the-state.

Kosta was an urban Socialist, opposed to the repressive royalist regime which forced the left underground and routinely murdered opponents. As a Bulgarian nationalist, he must have supported the federalist faction of the VMRO, though I don't know how involved he became and when he stopped feeling sympathetic – but stop he did. Later in life, he voiced outrage at their infamous execution 'methods', which they carried out on enemies and on each other, in revenge for some perceived failure of loyalty.

The children, meanwhile, had to help make ends meet, and Anastassia and her brothers worked folding and stacking news-papers at a large printing press – which doesn't sound so bad to me, but to her it was mortifying. Or rather, it was mortifying to her mother. They were now *officially* poor – so much so that they received social welfare in the form of free fabric for clothes. Aside from her school uniform, Anastassia had just one dress, of navy-blue wool. When the time came for her graduation ball, her girlfriends were excited about their outfits. She kept quiet. Aren't you going to the ball? Ljubitsa asked one evening.

No, said Anastassia, I don't feel like it. The truth was, she had no dress. You *will* have a dress, said her mother, and transformed the navy-blue dress into a ball gown by cutting up a yellow silk blouse and sewing bits of the yellow silk onto the plain dress. Anastassia had an outfit for the graduation ball. For all the drama it represented to mother and daughter, her sartorial deficiency was no barrier to male attention. One day, wearing her one and only navy-blue dress before it was turned into a gown, Anastassia jumped over a puddle while out in the streets of the Banished. A tall lanky guy with blue eyes watched her from the other side with a smile. A smile I'd get to know as his granddaughter: evasive not seductive, sarcastic not chivalrous, a non-committal smile.

'You'll ruin your dress,' my future grandfather said, not looking at the dress.

Alexander lived nearby, also in rented lodgings, and was studying accounting. He came from a farming family in the north, where the people were pragmatic, unromantic, not at all like the tormented Macedonians. Soon, he was called up.

In 1943–4, Sofia was heavily bombed by the US and British Air Forces, as punitive action for the country's role in giving Nazi Germany passage into Greece. No military targets were hit but three thousand civilians were maimed or killed. The bombings began in 1942, and so, as soon as Anastassia graduated from high school, the Gardeners packed up and returned to the lake.

They returned to Ohrid in high spirits: the town council was under a Bulgarian flag; the mayor was from a well-known local

Bulgarian family, and the new letters and words introduced by the Serbs were excised. Children went to Bulgarian schools again. Meanwhile, the creaky old house by the hammam had been occupied by tenants, and the family lodged with a Turkish land-lady in a house on the lake front. Her name was Nadzie and she took a shine to Anastassia, who was given special privileges that she didn't show her own sons. For example, while she allowed Anastassia to walk barefoot in the kilim-padded rooms, her sons moved around on their knees, a way of both protecting the carpets and showing respect for their elders. After years of privation, there was no more hunger, but a revolving roster of delicious cooking. Ljubitsa made sure to cover up any plates containing pork. And when there was a Turkish wedding in town, Nadzie would bring along Ljubitsa and her daughter as special guests. Once Kosta had given his permission, of course.

It was during this time that some well-wisher reported to Kosta that his daughter had been seen walking down the charshia *twice*. That evening, there was a scene. Don't ever shame our family like this again, he yelled, and hit her with the hot hair curler she was using. She was nineteen.

You'd think that after what the family had been through, he might have adopted a broader perspective and forgiven his daugh-ter's mild rebelliousness, which she had inherited from him after all – but no. Returning to Ohrid, he fell back into the tribe. His daughter never forgave him. On his gravestone, the dedication is 'from his grateful sons'. No daughter, no wife.

It was around this time that Ljubitsa passed on to her daughter a family motto she had received from her own mother. The motto was 'Perfection or death'. It was said to come from a great-uncle, the poet, polyglot and scholar Grigor Prlichev who had won Greece's top poetry competition for an epic poem written in Greek. Rejecting the relative glamour of life in free Greece, he had returned to still-colonised Ohrid with the much-quoted words, 'There is a great need for me to go home.' His poem-requiem

'Summer 1767' became the first hymn of Ohrid – a lament for the crushing of the Ohrid archbishopric by the Greek Patriarchy.

This was all well and good, but 'Perfection or death' are three words that freeze the heart. A self-curse, really. It was no doubt suited to the revivalist, revolutionary spirit of the times, but not to times of peace. Not to private life where perfection is elusive while death is certain. This doctrine, whose embodiment Ljubitsa was, is responsible for much generational struggle in this family.

I had wanted to speak with my aunts about their grandmother Ljubitsa, but they only knew one side of her – the Ohridian side, and nothing of her Sofia side. It was the same with Kosta. By the time the twins knew him, he had been neutralised. He was burnt out by the struggle, the Bulgarian–Macedonian cause was lost, and he had to let his two sons and their children get on with being successful Yugoslavs.

It is my mother alone who remembers Ljubitsa in her Sofia guise. After Kosta's death, Ljubitsa would visit her daughter and granddaughter in Sofia. She brought along her other grand-daughter Tatjana as her escort – and my mother felt that Ljubitsa was not *her* grandmother but Tatjana's. Tatjana was confident and gathered admirers everywhere, while my mother was made of more delicate stuff. In contrast to the glow that surrounded Tatjana, my mother was in the shadow. Literally – she has never liked the sun on her skin, she is not of the South.

I met my great-grandmother Ljubitsa once: a petite woman with cold, intelligent eyes. She washed and cleaned obsessively. My one female cousin, a sunny neurologist in Ohrid, said that there was something going on with cleanliness as moral virtue in our family, extended into an unhappy scrutiny that was passed down to the girls: finding fault with everything, as if life was pre-soiled. Out, out, damned spot! There isn't a single photograph of Ljubitsa smiling.

Like many ambitious women in a patriarchy where they don't have full expression in society but absolute power in the family, Ljubitsa inhabited the destructive shadow archetype of the mother-queen: needing everyone to remain small and needy, looking up to her and infusing her with importance (after all her sacrifices, it's the least they could do). Like a poisoned mantle, this psychological imprint was taken on by my grandmother and then by my mother, and sometimes I feel it creeping up behind me too, ready to enshroud me and make me mean.

This female burden of bitterness is our collective patriarchal inheritance. It is described with uncanny perceptiveness by Rebecca West on a visit to a Bosnian friend's house where she sees a photograph of her friend's late mother: 'This woman, sitting with a white cloth about her head, in a rigid armament of stuffs, exercised the enormous authority and suffered the enormous grief of the Madonnas. She was the officer of earth, she had brought her children into its broad prison, and her face showed how well she knew what bitter bread they would eat in captivity.'

A famous literary character associated with the Lakes is the matriarch Sultana, portrayed in a quartet of classic novels set in the national revival period, by the Bulgarian writer Dimitar Talev (*Ilinden*, *The Iron Oil Lamp*, *Bells of Prespa*, *I Hear Your Voices*). In her claustrophobic domestic kingdom, the perfectionist Sultana reigns over her *loved ones* by means of power games and sheer force: 'She was like a hammer beating the same anvil, year after year.' Her husband, the stoic Stoyan, accuses her of being 'like a whip behind my back, a studded whip that lashes me with each step.' At one point, Sultana's 'sinfully beautiful' daughter Katerina, having fallen in love with the wrong man, is induced by her mother into a forced abortion, which ends up killing her.

Sultana tragically embodies the tyranny of the obsolete system from which her family, community and nation seek emancipation so desperately. Sultana is the private dimension of the political, patriarchy internalised.

Ljubitsa was Sultana. From the day Kosta escaped across the lake, Ljubitsa wore black for the rest of her life. It was her power suit. She would sit at the head of family tables, cast a critical eye over the proceedings, and make the food stick in the throats of her *loved ones*. The food that she'd cooked to perfection but could not enjoy. When our lot began to be born in the 1970s – first Tatjana's son, then me, then Tatjana's second son Tino, my sister, and so on – Ljubitsa wrote letters to her daughter Anastassia in Sofia:

'Now that everyone is busy with their own affairs and has abandoned me, I turn to you in my hour of need. Perhaps you and your husband can find a doctor in Sofia who can help me with my illness.'

The letters go on eloquently about the illness, quoting from books and reflecting on the disappointing nature of people, especially *loved ones*:

'My sister Tsareva may call me a "burden" if she wishes to. But of course she does not suffer from my terrible illness.'

It is only once that the illness is named: loneliness. Having spent her life ensconced at the core of households, she felt devoid of purpose, perhaps depressed. Until the end she complained that Tatjana was ignoring her, that Tatjana wasn't visiting her, clearly too busy with her own affairs.

'I'm angry with her. I'll go to my grave angry!' Ljubitsa said to the twins.

'And we couldn't bear to tell her,' Biljana said. 'Tatjana was the apple of her eye.'

'She went to her grave without knowing,' Snezhana said. Luminous Tatjana died the same year as her grandmother. In ancient tragedies, it is the most beloved that must be sacrificed to appease some faceless, perpetually angry god.

And what about her relationship with Kosta? I asked.

'She didn't want him. That's what it was.'

'And he wanted her,' the twins said.

'They were too different, temperamentally,' the twins said.

This made me wonder whether — when Anastassia said that deep down, her mother didn't love her father, that he was hoping for a scrap of attention that never came — whether that was the result of those years of poetry on an empty stomach. Or had it been like this from the beginning? Whether Ljubitsa, duly married at twenty-three, never got over that officer whose ring she returned or threw in the lake, an unpaid self-debt of happiness. Thereafter, it was up to her *loved ones* to make her happy.

And Kosta clearly couldn't do it. I saw him differently now, getting into that boat and rowing to Albania, to wander hungry and disconsolate the streets of Europe, that *Babylonian whore*, with just the tailored suit on his back.

Inside the St Petka Church, the inscriptions on the ceiling had been corrected: letters considered as Bulgarian had been whitewashed and replaced with Serbian ones — the я of the first had been replaced with the diphthong *ja* of the second. This kind of 'correction' distressed my grandmother on visits to the lake; she called it state-sponsored vandalism.

She was right at the time, but we could have done with less righteousness in this family, and less distress. Craning my neck to look at the church's ceiling, I suddenly saw that the distress was not personal, though it felt so. In reality, it belonged to this entire land. The righteousness and the distress were ever morphing, cunningly assuming different shapes within families and societies, the better to keep us dependent, not free to just be. Beneath the genuine warmth of rare family reunions by the lake — once every ten to twenty years — there was an undertow. The last time I saw my Great-uncle Slavejko, in the last year of the twentieth century, we sat in their apartment and while his wife served Bosnian pastry, Greek olives, Macedonian tomatoes and Bulgarian wine, he said to me:

'Your grandmother Anastassia was an idealist. She remained a

Bulgaroman. Just like our parents. But they were wrong. We are of pure Macedonian pedigree, an ancient race.'

'Well, who cares?' I said, keen not to enter petty disputes over patrimony. 'We are family, you can't draw a line like that.'

But he could. With a straight face, Uncle explained the line to me: this most genial of men who had sobbed like a child for his lost sister, and made for us one hundred pancakes before dawn. 'It's like this,' he said. 'Bulgars are descended from Asiatics, and we are descendants of the Macedons. You're children of Genghis Khan and we're children of Alexander the Great. See the difference?'

He was referring to the fact that the original semi-nomadic Bulgars had migrated into the Volga and Pontic (Black Sea) regions, and then west into the Balkans from central Asia. They were Asiatics: they spoke an Oghur-Turkic language, worshipped the god of thunder Tangra and practised shamanism, and established powerful khanates – the origins of the Bulgarian state. Uncle was a physicist, but he was interested in history and we both knew that since the Macedonian Empire had ended in the second century BC, a great deal had happened in these lands, a great many peoples had come and gone, been settled, displaced, resettled, purged, renamed, converted, deconverted, reconverted, married and divorced. In *Who Are the Macedonians?* Hugh Poulton tracks in some detail the workings of this nation's ethnogenesis, a product of the dramatic 'natural and unnatural demographic change' in these lands in the past one hundred years, and of more recent nation-building policies during, and post, Tito.

The twentieth century was about to close, and in the Balkans it closed under the sign of Sarajevo's siege, the massacres, mass rapes and concentration camps of Bosnia and Kosovo, the American bombing of Belgrade, and millions of visible and invisible wounds that would take generations to heal. The healing had not even begun. And still Uncle wanted to keep shredding our Balkan tapestry into smaller, more pitiful pieces. We sat and ate baklava, although he was diabetic and I was on a diet (perfection or death).

At least we agreed that baklava was Turkish. Mistaking my silence for self-doubt, he reassured me.

'Don't worry, dear child,' he said. 'You too are Macedonian, you take after your grandmother.'

I really had no problem being Bulgarian *and* Macedonian, Balkan *and* European, and most recently Antipodean, I wanted to say to Uncle. But all this was draining me, and I bolstered myself with another piece of baklava.

The Yugoslav Wars had obsessed me, even though I was living in the Antipodes and none of my relatives fought or died in it. I even planned to join a humanitarian organisation in Bosnia. At the time, I had a Croatian boyfriend in Auckland, an exile who'd left to avoid drafting. He was a gentle, dispossessed soul. I was drawn to his pain, of course. 'Don't go,' he said, 'this is war, not a movie.' I heard him, but I was still compelled to read every book on the war that I could lay my hands on. The horror was unfathomable, yet the extreme passions behind it felt familiar.

Why? Kiwi friends asked me. It has nothing to do with you. But it did – with me, and with them too, in a way. Because the Balkans, that's us.

In the end, Uncle and I laughed, spreading pastry flakes over the table. We had genuine affection, and this was a precious time together. It was the last time I saw him. He died of coronary congestion. The blood clot that had killed his mother Ljubitsa by travelling to her brain twice (with meaningful timing, she had her first stroke while visiting her *loved ones* in Sofia) travelled to his heart. His older brother died of cardiac arrest. Slavejko's younger son, who lives in Portugal, nearly died of deep-vein thrombosis as a young man, and my mother's illness is vascular. They all had extremely high blood pressure. My sister and I have severe circulation problems.

Every family has its disease and sometimes, the symbolism is hard to miss: with us, it was as if a shard from some past wreckage kept getting stuck in the system, obstructing the flow.

★

My aunts, the sweet husband and I lit candles for our dead under the clear gaze of Petka. We shared our dead, and that meant something.

In some iconography, St Petka is depicted holding a pair of eyes on a plate, like fried eggs, to warn against wilful blindness. Blindness and blinding were a major lake motif. In *The Great Water*, one distressing scene involves an enraged physical-education teacher at the orphanage, who tries to blind a boy with a chisel after the boy defaces her bust of Stalin.

'Petka is believed to cure ailments,' the sweet husband said, and winked at us.

'They say,' Biljana said, 'that when they first started building the monastery, it kept falling down at night.'

'A small icon of Petka placed in the cave church kept disappearing every night,' said Biljana.

'And they'd find it in the same spot in the morning. Here,' said Snezhana.

'Until they realised Petka was guiding them. She wanted the church here,' Biljana said.

There was a tunnel between the cave church and the monastery, two kilometres long. Not only this – the tunnel continued downhill into Ohrid town, an underground road that was likely part of the ancient town, and popped out at Chelnitsa, the Front Church, next to the walled-up gate.

Edith Durham's formulation a hundred years ago – 'the burden of the Balkans' – still rings true. The past is a burden of multiplicities here, but only because reductive dogma has prevailed too often. The walled-up gate now struck me as symbolic of all dogma: in the attempt to shore up one's own power for evermore, one blocks the natural flow of change. The walled-up gate was like the arrested clock.

My grandmother held on to her multiple identity in a world that rewarded subscribers to a single one. She had also tried, fiercely, to hold on to everything she touched: her wartime romance, her daughter, her family, her youth. That was her burden, our burden. We could not let go of anything, especially not our idea of how things should be but are not, and our disappointment over time becomes a mournful distinction, to wear like a war medal or a black veil. Yet Zhivko Chingo was right: the only thing that is truly yours is that which you give away.

We drove down the steep road, past the exuberant waterfall, past the trees heavy with fruit that no one was picking. The fecundity was oppressive.

Vlado and Gotse Zhura's great-grandmother Despina, the one who came from Crete in poverty, had told a story that strikes with its Tantalus motif, so symbolic of the Macedonian predicament:

Once, Despina and her friend decided to come cherry picking up here. It's an hour on foot from the old town. Despina awoke at dawn. She hurried to the Upper Gate where her friend was waiting. Her friend rushed ahead with unnatural speed, up to the cherry trees. Just as Despina reached out to pick the first cherry, cockerels crowed. Despina came round, and saw where she really was: not in the Village of Cherries, but on the Kaneo cliffs above the lake. One more step and she'd plummet and break her head on the rocks below. Drenched in sweat, she walked straight to the friend's house. Sorry, the friend said, I overslept. Despina realised she'd been tricked by samovilas, those shape-shifters who operate at full moon and, if you can't tell reality from illusion, the moon from the sun, trick you into an early grave.

But how to tell reality from illusion here, where the statues of each regime were on the rubbish heap of the next? And then at the bottom of the lake.

'It is a land made for the exhibition of mysteries, this Macedonia. Here is made manifest a chief element in human disappointment, the discrepancy between our lives and their framework,' wrote Rebecca West in 1937. 'The earth is a stage exquisitely set;

too often destiny will not let us act on it, or forces us to perform a hideous melodrama.'

In this land so giving it could birth a human, generation after generation have been forced to emigrate, to sit with empty plates and be homesick for 'our places', to be looked down upon as 'others' with names too difficult to pronounce and histories too complex to grasp, and carry their hunger on to the next generation, and the next. A hideous melodrama indeed.

'See you next week,' the twins said. I looked forward to it. I felt at home with them.

'And put on some socks, you'll catch your death,' the twins said.

We were back by the jetty where I'd met the suitor.

I walked by the water. The lake had gone choppy and splashed onto the promenade, as if grown in volume. The previous day, I'd heard a story from a lonely old man in another village above the lake that had touched a raw nerve, and I couldn't stop thinking about it. He'd invited me into his garden for a tipple of home brew and told me that his old neighbours, the few that remained in the village, were still Bulgarian-identifying.

'But not me,' he said. 'I'm Macedonian. You know what I can't stand? When someone tries to tell me what I am.'

He spat on the ground. We drank to that and he said:

'Since you're interested in family stories, here's one.' He didn't specify whether it was his own family.

It was the eve of the First World War. A young man was due to be drafted and sent to the Macedonian Front. His mother was undone by the prospect. She had already lost a child in the recent Balkan Wars. In the night, she dragged a massive anvil to where her son slept on the floor, and with inhuman strength lifted it up and dropped it on his foot. Drafting was avoided, he remained by his mother's side, and dragged his crushed foot around for the rest of his life.

'This was the grandfather,' said the man, and poured himself another glass. 'But here's the thing. All the children in the family were born with defects of the legs.'

When he rose to see me off, I saw that he had a hobble himself, as if one foot was heavier than the other. I had heard a similar family story from a woman my age in Sofia. Mothers were maiming their sons all over the Balkans, to stop them being maimed in the Balkan Wars.

A hundred years ago, Henry Brailsford made the observation that in Macedonia 'fear is more than an emotion. It is a physical disease, the malady of the country, the ailment that comes of tyranny . . . Looking back upon my wanderings among them,' he writes of the people, 'a procession of ruined minds comes before the memory – a woman who had barked like a dog since the day her village was burnt; a maiden who became an imbecile because her mother buried her in a hole under the floor to save her from the soldiers'.

During the Ottoman centuries a regular 'blood tax', or *devshirme*, was exacted from Balkan Christian families – in the form of taking boys from their families – but though the Ottomans were gone, the blood tax had continued, forcing people into a form of insanity.

What struck a nerve was that the violence had over time become turned inwards at *loved ones*. At the self. Some Christian girls had their faces cut up by relatives – crosses slashed into their cheeks or foreheads – to stop them being taken by Muslim beys. Never mind that life in a harem might have been preferable to that of domestic slave with a disfigured face. I also heard of Aromanian women who, in a subsequent era when such abductions were no longer a threat, tattooed their own foreheads with crosses – out of loyalty to their mothers and grandmothers.

This is how, over time, love becomes indistinguishable from darkness.

★

The happiest photographs of Anastassia were taken here on the lake: swimming, boating. In one, she is by the jetty with her younger brother Slavejko, both peaky-faced and skinny-legged, children of hunger. She wears an elegant coat that looks threadbare, and he wears a Bulgarian cadet uniform (a fact that would soon become unmentionable in the new Yugoslavia), the too-short trousers flapping around his legs. But they smile with their sharp Levantine features as if to reassure us, the unborn, that everything will come to pass. She missed the bustle and anonymity of Sofia. Working as a council clerk, then a schoolteacher in nearby villages, while trying not to walk down the same street twice, was underwhelming after her dream of studying Law. She kept writing letters to the tall lanky guy in Sofia. Next to local men with whom life was a chronicle foretold – one of scrutinous mothers-in-law just like her own mother, Ohrid torta served with those doll's-house spoons, and fantasies of rowing to Albania and Italy – next to that, a distant romance had an edge.

Meanwhile, everybody hid under the table when explosions were heard in the hills, or warplanes thundered over the lake, sometimes dropping their cargo. It was said that Clement and Naum sent flashes of light to frighten the German pilots, and apparently it worked. By 1944, the family were back in their creaky old house by the hammam. When the war tide was turning and Yugoslav partisans came calling on Ohrid households, the family volunteered their elder son. He came through the war in one piece; they all did – physically.

Why did Anastassia go for a man she hadn't seen for years, and against all the odds? It wasn't only the man she chose. She chose a metropolis over a province, her own home over the perfection-or-death home of her mother Ljubitsa. She chose the closest to freedom she could choose, and I would have done the same. She strove for the boundless imagination, not for the mundane reality, and I inherited some of that creative capacity from her. It may come at a cost, but I am grateful.

My grandfather's last letter across the border dates from September 1947. I can't imagine how she felt when she opened it, maybe sitting here, with the lake before her. And how, after reading the typewritten text – he had handwritten all his previous letters, but he typed this one – she folded it, put it back in the envelope, in the pocket of her elegant but threadbare coat, and looked towards the distant mountains of Albania. The cormorants called. She walked up the charshia, past the beautiful mosque that would soon be blown up. The town knew of her liaison that had gone on for years, and she wasn't even engaged to him yet! Like father, like daughter. There was something vagabondish about the Gardeners, they couldn't settle down, their hawkish eyes were always scanning the horizon.

My mother would be born less than a year later.

And so we have had permission from the Ministry of Foreign Affairs and the Directorate of the Militia for your visa. In two days, we will also have the decision of the Balkan Commission [my future grandfather wrote, with characteristic pedantry]. I received your two letters and the photo, full of hope and love. You remain an idealist, unwilling to consider the ugly side of our decision.

Your arrival won't be greeted by anything pleasant. You will find me completely unprepared for marital life, morally and materially. There is love, but will love be enough to shelter us from the dark forces of dire need and privation? I think not.

It would be up to your feminine artfulness, perseverance and selfless love, strengthened by the legal bounds of matrimony, to make our marriage bearable, to shelter me inside it. It is a heavy chore, but once you have taken it upon yourself you must bear it without complaint and regret. I must take this final opportunity to present myself in my true colours. I do not wish to inflict more suffering on you. You have suffered enough already from your own family. I am writing this in all honesty, as I do not wish to be accused, one day, of being the coward who dragged you into the abyss of his own life. Think carefully before you take the fatal step.

The abyss. When Anastassia's departure was imminent, the former landlady Nadzie gave her a pair of silk quilts in Arabian blue. To remind her of the lake.

During the harsh Stalinist years, when everything in Sofia was bought with coupons, the spectre of hunger re-entered Anastassia's life. Proud like her mother, like her mother she had married a man who required sacrifices: crossing a border, exile, privation, isolation. For long months, her husband was recalled as an army reservist in some border drill, because Cold War tensions were high and the border between Yugoslavia and Bulgaria had unexpectedly hardened after a freeze-out between Tito and Stalin. Working but irregularly paid and alone with her daughter, facing the possibility of never seeing her *loved ones* and the lake again, Anastassia cut up one of the blue quilts. Out of it she made a dress for her daughter, who was in and out of hospital. Those were the last days of tubercular Europe. The girl was the apple of her mother's eye; in photographs she is wan, unsmiling, her face strangely old, a fragile blossom in the shadow of the mother-tree.

That blue dress was a flag of hope fluttering amid the grey Soviet days that stretched ahead, not at all the view Anastassia had imagined. Of course he had warned her, she could never blame him for being the coward who . . .

My mother remembers wearing the blue silk dress, past gaping bombed-out buildings. She remembers when old Sofia, wrecked by British and American bombers, was levelled by the Communists, and foundations were laid for the new ceremonial squares and avenues where people would parade, waving small frightened flags at balconies where men in dark coats stood motionless like Roman emperors.

She remembers wearing the blue dress and looking up at the faces of frowning men, faces flapping on banners, faces painted on the walls of buildings (Tito was a grimacing villain holding the bloodied hatchet of Capitalism in one hand and a bottle of Coke in the other), so that you always felt their eyes on you – looking up at them as she held her mother's hand. And through that hand, she felt her mother's hunger and her mother's fear. All they had now was each other.

My mother, a gifted seamstress, in our childhood stayed up late nights after work to sew clothes for us and herself. Just as her grandmother had done, and her mother. In my childhood, the shops were more than half-empty, and anyway with her exquisite taste and personal pride my mother didn't like factory-made clothes.

In times of poverty and tyranny, she and my grandmother had passed on extraordinary gifts to me: a love of language and literature, people and places, emotion and expression, independent thought and anti-conformity (neither of them joined the Communist Party or paid lip-service to its ubiquitous propaganda, although it would have brought benefits). They had sewn together, bit by precious bit, the wings on which I would fly. Even if they had tried to hobble me in the end by holding on with inhuman strength, heavy as anvils.

Here by the Lake, I finally understood why. The hunger and the fear had been too great. There wasn't enough to go round. With the partitioning of Macedonia, with the Cold War, with the cleaving of one people into mutually hostile national and ideological tribes, with each turn of the political merry-go-round and its *correct* diktat of reality, the psyche of the people had taken a hit. I was still reeling from it. The cumulative loss ran so deep that the prospect of any further loss, no matter how small, had become intolerable. And almost every change felt like loss – hence the frozen clock. Repeated emigration, like a magnifying glass, had made that loss look even bigger.

This is why for the women in our family, as in many others with similar histories, letting go feels worse than disfigurement. Letting go is like death.

The cormorants called. I sat on the low stone wall where the bouquiniste Elijah was setting up his stall for the afternoon. He was from the Village of Cherries and carried his books in a cart that he pushed along the street because he had no car. He always had a book or two to interest me.

For a man of books, he was very unchatty. When he finished, Elijah sat with me, and we watched the waves break over the promenade, the Arabian-blue lake and the distant mountains spread out before us like a silent poem.

We are the remnants of another age.
Like wolves tracked by the sights
of ancient guilt, we steal into
the land's forgiving solitude.

Nikola Madzirov, 2013

BESA

The crossroads of the lake led four ways. North to Kosovo, Serbia and Bulgaria. South to Epirus and Greece. West to Elbasan and the Adriatic. And east to Pelagonia and the Aegean.

If you head north and keep going upstream of the second major river after the Drim that empties into the lake, you glimpse a dark topography. A closed world of black-green forests casts a shadow over you for days after.

What looks like a gigantic unbroken chain of mountains unfolds – but it is several distinct ranges, just as the villages huddled within them are distinct cultures. The Christian villages are sparsely populated and unremarkable in appearance, with ruined houses in the hills. And every village harbours a secret. During the First World War when a road was built by the Bulgarian army, extraordinary necropolises full of golden masks and artefacts were found, dating from the seventh century BC (the Trebenishta gold), and locals are certain that there's more where that came from. In a village scattered over several hills as it crept down the mountain over time, the hilltop monastery holds Celtic stone crosses possibly a thousand years old, of unknown provenance. Here too is Belchista Wetland: a geological remnant from the great Dessaret basin of the Pliocene era five to three million years ago, whose other surviving descendants are Lakes Ohrid and Prespa. It has what is considered by conservationists Europe's cleanest water.

Then come the villages where a sombre flag flaps – black

double-headed eagle on red. The further north you go, the more
thin white minarets pierce the skyline. This is Muslim-Albanian-
majority country. But nothing here is quite what it seems. I visited villages that identify as Albanian but speak Macedonian.
In the outlying Struga villages, I saw families where the parents
speak Macedonian and the kids Albanian – after local politicians
had bribed the poor parents to send their kids to local Albanian-
language schools. Many of these people were and still are Slavic-
speaking Muslims, or Torbesh, who over time and under pressure
(poverty, the contempt of the Macedonian state) took an Albanian
identity. This process of cultural assimilation is not new. It is called
'Albanisation' by both Christian and Muslim Macedonians, and
is seen by them as an existential threat. With around a hundred
thousand Albanian Kosovar refugees housed in Macedonia during
and after the Kosovo War, Kosovo-Albanian ethno-nationalism is
feared for potentially driving a wedge into the Republic, which
could not withstand fragmentation.

At the edge of Mavrovo National Park, *sharplaninec*, sheep-
dogs, lay in the middle of the road basking in the sun, and you
drove around them – because this is their terrain, not yours. On
the western side of the Park is the Debar region with its lake and a
monastery that 'cures' addictions. The road continues north along
a tributary of the great Vardar River. If you cross into Kosovo,
you'll see the whole length of the rocky Shar Mountains, almost
nine thousand feet high and entering the border wedge where
Macedonia, Kosovo and Albania meet. This triangle is Gora, the
realm of the Slav Muslims known as Gorani, mountain people.
Even if you glimpse them from a distance, you see why the Shar
Mountains were known in the Middle Ages as Catena Mundi,
Chain of the World.

At Skopje, if you veer east towards Bulgaria, the alpine
Osogovo Mountains come as a new surprise; from the highroad
the rare villages look as if they've been tossed into the abyss. The
mountain ridges, like the backs of prehistoric beasts on their

glacial way somewhere, are a faded blue that seeps into you like weather, a Balkan blue.

This road I travelled by bus, one day. I wanted to see it because Anastassia travelled it countless times: by train, bus, and later in my grandfather's Skoda. The mountains are not welcoming. She liked nature, but in a romantic way, as a backdrop to personal drama. These mountains were also the wall between her Ohrid and her Sofia, between her sensual lake self and her intellectual metropolitan self.

It took seven hours from Ohrid to the Bulgarian border. The potholed Skopje–Sofia motorway was unmended since the 1970s, when Yugoslavia had her back turned to the poor cousin in the east, as if in an attempt to prove that there was no reason to fix the road, that all roads led to Belgrade, that Yugoslavia was forever. But the only thing that is forever are the mountains.

The mountains and relationships.

All her life, Anastassia would not let others be alone. When I'd lock myself in the bathroom, she'd press the door handle. Because to be alive was to be in constant relationship. To struggle, demand, reject, seek release and not find it. I always thought this was the way we are conditioned to be women – invasive or invaded, ever-pressured or self-pressured. But the longer I spent here, the more I saw that this was more broadly the Eastern way. To be oppressed and oppressive was the norm. The men were just as needy. I met men who confided details of their private lives within hours. Friendships and alliances were quick. Intimacies were like an assault. Conspiratorial and paranoid thinking was the norm. Exuberant warmth and vicious gossip alternated. Everyone was enmeshed in everyone's business, without being answerable for their own.

It must be the way of societies where industrialisation came late and feudal paternalism continues to be the default style of governance. You never learn to stand on your own feet, you're always leaning on *loved ones*, like a crutch. Poverty digs you deeper yet into dependency. In such a culture, there is nothing to challenge the supremacy of close relationship and clan loyalty – and the landscape only locked this further into place. Personal freedom had to be clawed back at great cost, almost against the grain of the land.

The East–West axis was, of course, the Via Egnatia. A section of this road – Ohrid–Elbasan – I travelled with my cousin Tino, Tatjana's son. I wanted to see it because three generations of our male ancestors had spent their lives on it.

My first meeting with Tino was by the jetty. A slim guy with dark circles around his eyes got up from a bench and walked towards me unhurriedly, the way the locals walked.

'I recognised you at once,' he smiled, and we hugged. 'You have something of the Gardeners about you.'

So did he. He had been seven at the time of his mother's death. I liked him instantly and within an hour had the feeling that we'd known each other since childhood. But without feeling put upon; Tino had a measured quality, something I'd come to recognise as a lacustrine quality. He was an urbane person of mild manners. His speech was gently self-deprecating and he was mentally agile, with a capacity for hard work and quick learning. But I also sensed a deep well of sorrow inside him, and he wore his insomnia on his face, like a distinction. Years ago, just as I was leaving New Zealand, he'd been ready to emigrate there for a new life. It would have been a strange unconscious swap between us, had he emigrated, but he didn't.

'That's how it was meant to be. And soon after, I met Nate.'

Since then he had pursued different jobs and businesses, moved to Malta, then returned to the lake and together with family ran Ohrid's iconic jazz club and an international jazz festival – until they had to close the festival for financial reasons. The town's former authorities had promised support but instead ended up filling their own pockets.

Tino was outwardly calm, but internally restless. Sometimes he stayed up all night working, or listening to jazz – anything so long as he wouldn't be left alone with the past, he said.

'I have spent my life running, forty years running from something,' he said. 'Yet here I am, by the lake.'

He and Nate, a social worker, lived in a flat with mountain views, in a tower block on the edge of town. I asked if they followed political events in the country.

'We've stopped,' she said. 'It was affecting our health.'

'I only watch sport and Nate reads books,' Tino said.

Internal emigration, a mass practice during Communism, had been revived here: you live in your country but only up to a point. In your mind, you are someplace else, more just, more emancipated, the way your country should be.

Tino shrugged, not wishing to dramatise. 'Isn't it like that everywhere? It's the times we live in.' During Macedonia's war up north, he had stayed here and followed events from a distance. He had no aggression, his anger had a tendency to turn inwards.

Tino had no memory of my family's visit in the oppressive summer of 1989. His childhood and youth had passed in a dark place. The more sensitive of the boys, he had been bullied at home after his mother's death, and had taken refuge with relatives. He'd moved out at fourteen to live in an abandoned house. His father had remarried immediately (he meant well, he wanted to have a woman to look after us, Tino said). The second wife destroyed the family albums before she tried to destroy what Tatjana had loved the most, her boys, so that Tatjana would not continue to eclipse her from beyond the grave. But she did. The town talked of Tatjana as if she died yesterday. The town loved its beautiful dead women.

'Yes,' Tino said. 'Everybody knew her except me. I've missed her all my life. Yet I carry so much of her. The restlessness is from her, and the creativity.'

Perhaps staying in Ohrid was for Tino an act of loyalty towards his mother who had loved the Lake, and him, as no one would love him again.

Loyalty carries especially heavy undertones in these parts. In northern Albania, the *Kanun* of Lekë Dukagjini was a feudal law laid down in the mid-1400s by the chieftain of the Dukagjini clan, though its practice dated to earlier times. In the Kanun, a *besa* is a pact, a bond, a word of honour, an oath that can't be broken (though in reality, it often is). The Kanun included rules about hospitality to strangers and, more importantly, a set of loyalty rules — to the family and the clan. If you break it, you pay with your life, or with the life of another of your blood. There may be a period of grace, during which the feud goes dormant, but once that period is over, there is no place in the land where the marked can hide. The Kanun was at the root of long-lasting blood feuds that stripped families of their sons. It was outlawed in the 1930s, but continues to this day in parts of Albania and Kosovo.

Although I was about to visit Albania for the first time, I already knew the besa and the Kanun. I think we all do. The Kanun is Cronos devouring his children.

'I think I've been running from things too,' I said to Tino in the car once we left Ohrid behind. 'But some things follow you. Like Furies.'

Tino smiled his accepting smile.

'Tell me about Furies!'

Tino got on with everyone. I would have found it difficult to see faces from my past all around me, and to stay loyal to my town, especially after that experience with the town authorities.

'Ohrid is beyond that,' he said. 'This lake is older than any authority.'

'And I'm not loyal to any place,' I said.

'You are loyal to intangible things,' Tino said. 'That's why you're here.'

We'd reached the last lakeside village before the border, past the Black Madonna monastery. The houses looked out towards the lake, like old people remembering. Behind them rose white cliffs, and a steep stairwell to the top.

'We built it ourselves,' said the owner of the fish restaurant on the water. 'And now people come to see the cave church from all over Europe.' He was tall and fair – another 'Celt'. Once a worker in the textile factory in Struga, he'd found himself jobless when the factory closed, and opened this restaurant. Business was good but, he nodded darkly at the establishment next door, his cousin was jealous.

'Typical,' Tino said during our breathless ascent to the cave church. The cousin had given us the heavy key. 'Envy, pride.'

If you had any breath left by the time you reached the top, the view took it away. The lake unfolded with careless magnificence, as if to say: there is enough for everyone, stop bickering. There is enough sky, enough water, enough air, enough earth, even enough trout. The rocky platform of the cave was plastered with guano, and someone had left a rolled-up kilim of the kind used in Muslim prayer, unexpected at the Church of the Archangel Michael. Inside were some of the last surviving frescoes of the days of artistic flowering on the lake, before the Ottomans. Those saints around the archangel whose faces hadn't been scratched out had their eyes closed, something I'd never seen before. The blinded and the wilfully blind.

'Maybe they didn't want to see what was coming,' Tino said.

But when we looked again, their eyes were open. It was disconcerting. We laughed it away, but the uncanny impression remained.

Above the village was the Via Egnatia, a small section of cobblestones still visible in the forest. We walked the white stones smoothed by two thousand years of feet and hooves.

'There were more,' said an old man who materialised from the forest, loaded with herbs. 'But folks used them for walls and barns. Blessings to you.' And he disappeared round the bend, a figure out of time.

This is how history looks on the ground – not a parade of great events but a quiet chain of recycling.

We drove on. Because the lake was already 2,500 feet above sea level, the road had to climb only another thousand, through a tunnel of leafy forest, to reach the mountain pass of Qafë Thanë (Chafassan) where a border checkpoint had opened twenty years ago. I was about to cross into Albania for the first time.

Today Chafassan was sleepy, but this pass had an eventful history. Since antiquity, it has been the boundary between Illyria and Macedonia. Chafassan is mentioned in most lake journeys over the centuries. It was involved in every siege, invasion and military movement in the vicinity of the lake. *Qafë* means neck in Albanian. There was a legend about a travelling monk from Mount Athos who claimed to have special powers. To verify his claims but also rob him of the precious icons he carried, brigands cut off his head here, at the *neck* of the mountain. It is not said whether the head miraculously reconnected with the neck.

A fine drizzle started. This was not Tino's first time in Albania. He'd even commuted to Tirana for work at one point, though you'd never associate the landscape ahead with commuting. Not unless you were a drover or a brigand.

The first thing I saw on Albanian soil was beehives. Bunkers and goats scattered over the crags. A shepherd propped on his stick, a woman gathering herbs. A statue of the Skoje-born Albanian Mother Teresa, stark against the scrubland, her hands in prayer. Here a spectacular crossroads opened up – one leg ran west to the Adriatic, over a switchback road and in the plains a patch-work of tilled land; another ran south, snaking downhill back to the lake.

We took the road west. Once we'd passed the clusters of fields and houses in the valley, and the fruit- and nut-selling roadside stalls, we started climbing again. We entered a landscape of brooding starkness. The road was overlooked by white cliffs and dark glades. Several times, the sight of vertiginously high aqueducts bridging gorges made me brake and pull over. We got out of the car and stood under the gigantic structures, these ghosts of feudal Communism built by political prisoners for the railway that would pass through this impassable landscape – and which had been out of use since the late 1990s.

The odd lone figure could be glimpsed walking along the disused railway bridge some two hundred metres above, crossing from one tunnel to another over the chasm, on some obscure errand, because if you were on foot the disused railway was a shortcut. But to where, it was not clear.

The landscape was like one of Escher's riddle drawings, asking: is this possible, or is it in your mind? You looked at it from all angles and still you had no answer.

Trees sprouted from the roofs of abandoned factories in the hillside – brick factories, cement factories, gaping quarries – scenes of neo-Gothic desolation. The soil was a clay-red, and everywhere there was water. As if the earth had opened its flanks after a tremor, and was churning out its subterranean humours. *Lavazhe*s, stations for washing your car, attempted to harness the water to profit, and skinny young men tinkering with mobile phones stood by hoses attached to taps as the mineral water flowed freely down the road, but traffic was sparse.

The only other activity along the road was the odd figure selling whole fresh walnuts out of sacks – an act so dwarfed by the mountains that at once I grasped why Albania is called Shqipëria, which is sometimes (incorrectly but memorably) translated as Land of Eagles. Because this was no place for humans. The humans had absorbed the qualities of the mountain – a stone-like endurance, a stealth, and a stubbornness that has ensured survival against impossible odds.

Bone-white Communist-era monuments, recently repainted

in an attempt to rescue them from post-Communist contempt, perched atop rocky outcrops. They commemorated the resistance fighters who had sporadically fought first the Italians, then the Germans, and most viciously each other. Once the Albanian Communist Party assumed power, and under the leadership of Enver Hoxha who'd already entrenched himself as secretary of the Central Committee of the Party before the Second World War, they began a merciless purge. Thousands of non-Communist partisans who had spent years fighting the occupiers were imprisoned, tortured and executed for having 'collaborated with the British' during the war. Which of course they had, as had the Communist partisans; without the help of British commandos flown in from Cairo, the resistance mightn't have succeeded.

The other kind of commemoration was the small gravestones along the road, where young men had died. We saw why, as drivers overtook in dangerous bends, heading blindly into the oncoming traffic. It was a Russian roulette that for some was exhilarating and for us a nerve-shredder.

'This is why I quit the Tirana commute,' Tino smiled.

Bunkers, car lavazhes and Communist-era ruins aside, this must be exactly what Edward Lear saw in 1848, when he rode with his dragoman Giorgio to Elbasan. His descriptions and sketches match what I saw one hundred and seventy years later:

'A most desolate and wild country does this part of Albania seem, with scarcely a single habitation visible in so great a space.' After the first crossing of the River Shkumbin, 'the landscape began to assume a character of grand melancholy not to be easily forgotten'.

He drew some of it. Lear did not follow the Via Egnatia, or not all the way, as it was almost completely destroyed by then. He used a combination of rough tracks and no tracks at all, really a mad scramble up and down muddy valleys, his horses laden with his drawings and frequently tumbling with their cargo. It was September. They forded rivers either by braving currents and getting sodden or using Ottoman and Roman bridges. At times he and Giorgio, like all travellers, used the 'government post-road', an unevenly paved causeway two or three feet above the ground, from which you could easily be dislodged by oncoming caravans and horsemen, down into the mud – or worse, into a ravine.

The terrain was so hard to pave or even shore up against floods that by 1900 the Ottoman authorities had given up. 'It was just as Nature and the Romans left it,' wrote another traveller. Foreign visitors were discouraged from journeying by land altogether.

The most gripping description of this roadless road is by the Scot John Foster Fraser in his *Pictures from the Balkans* (1906). He travelled with a dragoman and Turkish soldiers as escorts against brigands in the dangerous years after the Ilinden Uprising, when kidnappings and killings by komitas of all stripes were an everyday occurrence in Macedonia. The Ottoman administration gave escorts free of charge to Western visitors, to prevent expensive kidnap.

Once past Chafassan, Fraser's party started encountering 'tall, fearless-eyed Albanians', and became anxious. In Albania you were unlikely to be kidnapped or robbed, but more likely to be shot for no reason. In Byronic spirit, Fraser compares the Highlands of Albania with the Scottish Highlands: the view from Chafassan was 'like a Scotch moorland – humped, and for miles covered with bracken'.

They overnighted in Kukës, once a Roman station called Tres Tabernas and now a quiet scenic town with its back turned to the visitor. Its name had stuck in my mind after learning that a few of the twenty thousand girls and women of Kosovo who were raped during the Yugoslav Wars had come here, where nobody knew them, for abortions or to give birth to babies who were often abandoned. These survivors of horrific violence continue to live in silence, stigmatised by a culture of cognitive dissonance where cause and effect are conflated so that guilt and its enabler, shame, are collectively projected onto the victim, who must carry that burden alone so as not to 'dishonour' the collective. Together with her physical and psychic wounds.

It is easier that the shadow rest with the other, not with the self.

Here, where the landscape was starkly masculine, comfortless, almost turned against itself, it was hard not to feel that any great imbalance will remain in the land, as a reminder.

Fraser's party set off at night and rode for sixteen hours to reach the next destination. He captures the mood:

Now in the black of the morning we had to climb further. None of us spoke. We were too cold to speak. We had to ascend broken clefts of rock . . . Day came with the thinnest haze hanging over the world and clouds still resting in the great black ravines beneath us which looked like monster graves.

The torrents of innumerable centuries had worn out chasms . . . At the bends tumbling stone had obliterated the track. Rarely at such points was it more than twelve inches wide. At first one held breath, whilst the horse, picking its way as though on a tight-rope, walked round a precipice edge where was a sheer drop of a thousand feet . . . I turned my face to the slatey wall because to look into the gulf, which seemed to fall from my very knee, made me feel positively sick.

Fraser saw long stretches of the Roman road, then they'd suddenly plunge into a precipice, suggesting that the shape of the valleys had shifted over time.

Riding here around the same time, munching on oranges given to her by Elbasan's governor, Edith Durham notes that this section of the Egnatian Way was completely destroyed by the Turks in the wake of the Ilinden Uprising, 'in a blind rage, with the intent to destroy all communications as far as possible'.

Non-existent as it was then, this had been a major trans-Balkan itinerary, *the* highway between the Adriatic and the Aegean. Those who sought passage into the Balkans and Asia had to take it. Even now, on the tar-sealed road, we were never far from hairpin bends and tumbling boulders. Which gave me and Tino some idea of what it must have been like for our ancestors to move across this terrain at all times, in all weathers, and pretty much until they dropped dead from their horses.

My mother had given me an old family memoir. The author was a maternal uncle of Ljubitsa's, a civil servant in Bulgaria, where he emigrated in the late 1800s. Subsequent generations would acquire university degrees and sedentary jobs, leading to my life of books and Tino's nocturnal Internet vigils in stock markets and jazz clubs. We had long grown disconnected from the land. But our distant predecessors had merged with it. The early Gardeners had done it through gardening, the early Karadimchevs through road trade.

The Karadimchev clan of my great-grandmother's are traced back to 1700. There was an Ohrid man known as Dimche Karata, Dimche the Black. He was of darker complexion than usual – perhaps he had Arab blood. Dimche the Black amassed a fortune and left behind mansions by the kalé. He was a trader and so were his son and grandson, driving their caravans of horses and mules along the main trading route of the Egnatian Way: Salonica–Bitola–Ohrid–Elbasan–Durrës. They dealt in fish, mutton, olives, oil, wool, tobacco and other official and unofficial goods, and they also carried the mail between these remote stations, along the 'government post-road' – because there were no postmen in this corner of the Empire. Roads were too dangerous, conditions too gruelling.

The grandson was named Dimo, after Dimche the Black, and this Dimo had forty horses and a special *teskere* (pass) from the sultan, which served as passport and trading licence. Travelling traders like him were called *kiradjia*s, and this was the single most dangerous métier at the time. This is how we find our great-great-great-great-great uncle Dimo with his caravan. He was from Ohrid but spent most of the year on the road, where he was known as Dimo the Albanian. He wore the black-embroidered baggy trousers of white wool, a great hooded black woollen cape, and the white Albanian fez. He had a native's command of Albanian and Turkish, and must have spoken Greek and a Bulgarian dialect, or both.

In the 1700s, the British diarist Mary Wortley Montagu asked some peasants in western Macedonia, 'What are you, Muslims or Christians?' They replied: 'We are Muslims, but of the Virgin Mary.'

Later, in the turbulent months leading up to the Russian–Turkish War of 1877, the adventurous Briton Arthur J. Evans travelled on foot across the western Balkans, and observed that 'an Albanian will attend a mosque at noon and a church at night with the greatest sangfroid'. I had seen with my own eyes the Albanian Muslim women buying icons of the Black Madonna and phials of 'blessed' water. The essentially pagan belief in the magical properties of painted frescoes, curative springs, saints' relics, vilas and samovilas at full moon and the evil eye was shared by all.

Christians in the Ottoman Balkans had no right to carry arms. When Greek insurgencies became frequent, the sultan enforced a disarmament law. With difficulty and not without violence, Christian households in all of Rumelia were disarmed, to ensure they'd never revolt again (it didn't work). The only people allowed arms were the fierce Ghegs of northern Albania whom the Ottomans had always feared and never fully subjugated. Tino and I were on the road that nominally separated the Albanian north from the south, Ghegs from Tosks. Lake Ohrid fell along this very latitude. This road also cut through the heartland of the Albanoi, the Illyrian tribe first mentioned by the Alexandrian geographer Ptolemy in the second century, and who were to give Albania its name.

Dimo the Albanian carried arms at all times, and that was, I imagine, the most important part of his identity because it meant survival. At the time of the story told in the memoir, he was courting the daughter of the richest Christian family in Ohrid, friends and treasurers to the late ruler Djeladin Bey. Djeladin was a nephew of the formidable Ali Pasha of Ioannina, an Albanian ruler whose *pashalak*, or fiefdom, was a state within the Ottoman state. The Albanian pashalaks were a unique phenomenon across the Ottoman territories: autonomous from the sultan though nominally answerable to him, they gradually began to undermine the absolutism of the High Porte. The most powerful was Ali Pasha, who ruled Albania and southern Macedonia from Epirus to the lakes here. His nephew Djeladin (of Tashula fame) was in charge of Ohrid and Prespa. But after a long and bloody career, in 1822 Ali Pasha's defiance of the sultan had him beheaded and his fiefdom parcelled up among feudal lords still loyal to the sultan. A similar fate befell Djeladin, who fled Ohrid and died in exile in Egypt (possibly drowned in the Nile by secret agents of the High Porte). Both despots left behind young Christian widows. The lakes and their hinterland became more vulnerable than ever to casual brigandry.

One day, around this time, returning from Elbasan with a consignment of olives, Dimo the Albanian's caravan was stopped by a band of a hundred armed men at the pass of Chafassan. Fortunately, the band recognised Dimo – why, he was one of them, he's all right! – and shared with him their exciting plan. But the plan was to sack Ohrid, and specifically the gated town. They would share the spoils with Ohrid's own Albanian grandees, who would open the gates for them; Dimo the Albanian would be rewarded too. They asked him to take some missives to the Albanian grandees in Ohrid, under besa.

Dimo took the letters, gave his besa, and descended into Ohrid with the olives and the cold sweat that comes with impossible dilemmas. The sacking of the town would take place two days later. Ohrid hadn't been sacked since the barbarian invasions. Dimo went straight to the *kaimakamin* (the town's chief administrator) and showed him the missives. The kaimakamin was a local Albanian or Turk, and his loyalty was to his town. At once, he sent messages to the local beys, informing them that the town's cannons up at the kalé would shortly be turned in the direction of their mansions.

The town was saved, but as a result of the broken besa, Dimo had to go into hiding. Eventually, thanks to his wife's influential family, Dimo received another teskere from the sultan and returned to his old trading route and cowboy lifestyle.

When he had just turned seventy-five, Dimo's body was found by the Elbasan–Durrës road. His horses were there, with their cargo untouched. It had taken them over a generation, but the men from Chafassan or their sons had come for him. Dimo was buried on Albanian soil. He may well have had another family in Albania. Somewhere between Durrës and Ohrid, Tino and I may have distant cousins.

Dimo was killed four years after Lear passed through here, and I wonder whether the caravan laden with black wool that blocked Lear's narrow and precipitous path, somewhere before Elbasan, could have belonged to Dimo. And whether Lear tipped his awkward fez to the bulky, fully armed, black-cloaked seventy-one-year-old in the saddle – our great-great-great-great-great uncle.

'What's the moral of the story?' Tino smiled.

'That you can't have your cake and eat it,' I said.

'That sooner or later, you're forced to choose between loyalties,' he said.

'Still, Dimo did pretty well. Do you see yourself here on horseback?'

Tino spluttered with laughter and lit a cigarette. We could barely *drive* this road.

The postscript to this story picks up the theme of social, cultural and economic change. Dimo's wife's family were the treasurers of Djeladin. The townspeople found Djeladin Bey's trunks buried at the foundations of their mansion, full of gold and silk: a layer of gold coins, a layer of silk, and so on. Were they so scrupulous as to keep Djeladin's treasures buried, even after he was gone? It seems they were.

And another odd detail: they were one of four Ohrid families to be 'cursed for all times' by Ohridians for their role as collaborators of the Greek Patriarchy in the crushing of the Ohrid archbishopric in 1767, and so contributing to the rise of Greek influence in Macedonia. The curse was meant to deprive these families of progeny, but it didn't work, or not reproductively, for Dimo and his wife Arsa had six children.

'Maybe curses work in other ways,' Tino said.

'Have you sometimes felt like you're cursed?' I said.

We laughed, but the feeling of unease remained. Tumours, envy and pride, blindness and discord, sorrow and rage, stalk every clan. Once you let besa in, it's like a vampire – it's difficult to see it off.

Meanwhile, the Shkumbin led us into the fertile plains of Elbasan, where olive trees, orange groves and vines began to appear, the 'grand melancholy' lost its edge, and the air softened with Mediterranean light. A century ago, the finest silk in Europe was spun here.

Elbasan's low-lying centre was dominated by the ruins of the Venetian fortress and crowded with young people all dressed up, the European-style cafes full, and a vibe of idleness in the air. Albania is Europe's youngest nation. Youth is its great wealth. At the town's entrance, a large, overgrown Communist-era cemetery was being spruced up by gardeners – hundreds of simple gravestones of fallen partisans with a red star carved into their marble slabs. The dates showed how pitiably young these men

and women had been. From atop one of the towers of the Venetian fortress, we saw that Elbasan was at the bottom of a wide,
sea-bound amphitheatre. To the north were purplish alpine peaks
and in the south was the mythical Tomorr Mountain, its top worshipped every August by both Christians and Bektashis, to this
day. It was tempting to drive on to Durrës for a glimpse of the
Adriatic, but Tino had work in the morning and I'd be climbing a
mountain. This was my last week by the lake.

Dimo the Albanian's story marks the end of an epoch: his
was the last generation of traders to travel this ancient route. The
accelerated agony of the Ottoman Balkans brought the reign of
the brigand to this land. And as the era of the bandit waxed, trade
over the mountain passes waned. Traders swapped the Ohrid–
Elbasan–Durrës–Italy route for a land route to Budapest and
Leipzig. Leather and fur merchants from the lake frequented
central Europe's fairs where they bought Canadian and Siberian
furs and brought them to the lake, to manufacture luxury clothes
and sell them in Istanbul and Bursa.

We were back at the lake, back into the drizzle. Along the lakeside
road the odd boy stood with rain dripping into his collar, holding
trout for sale. Time had slowed down. It had passed fast on the
road to Elbasan. Mountains gobbled up time, while the lake gathered it. There was always more time by the lake.

The rain had drained the water of colour.

'No matter how many times I see this lake,' Tino said, 'it's
different.'

In the dusk, the outlines of Pogradec looked a blend of feudal and Communist. The streets' asphalt was broken and people
crossed without looking. Giant gilded statues dotted the tidy
lakeside park, and at first I thought they were remnants from a
past age that the townspeople had forgotten to take down, that
the gloomy bronze men with long coats and hard faces were all
Enver Hoxha and his commissars. But they were not: they were

made fifteen years ago and included the poet Lasgush Poradeci, in a fedora and a wind-blown raincoat, his face turned towards his beloved lake.

Men on old bikes pedalled slowly in the mist, and others sat in bingo clubs, their hands empty, staring into space. The concrete blocks were blotchy with water as if the town was crying.

'You have to find someone to show you round,' Tino said. 'On a sunny day.'

Along the lake front, a man with a deeply lined face where suffering had accumulated – an Albanian face – was packing up his battered van from which he sold home-spun rugs. His name was Eduard.

'Come back to Albania,' he bid us as we parted ways – him insisting on paying for our coffees at a waterside cafe where a familiar ballad played that sounded Italian to me and Yugoslav to Tino; and it was both – though the lyrics were Albanian. During Hoxha, you could get ten years' forced labour for listening to foreign music.

It was quiet at the St Naum checkpoint – as quiet as it had been at Chafassan – and both sets of passport officials waved us through with end-of-shift faces. The bells of Naum Monastery tolled for vespers. Like Chafassan, this checkpoint was opened in the early 1990s. For nearly fifty years, there had been no crossing point between the two countries of the lake. But you could not draw a real line between the Albanians and the Macedonians of the lake, only a fictional one – a line in the water.

The mountains were a divide but the lake was a gathering point of all that is shared by us, the people between the Adriatic and the Aegean, forever voyaging, forever recycling. Tino and I were of different nationalities but we looked so similar, we could be siblings. We *had* known each other since childhood, since before birth – through our mothers and grandmothers who had carried these mountains and each other until they could carry no more. Perhaps our restlessness, our tendency to dream of the road, began as far back as Dimo the Albanian.

We passed the last bunker and we were in Macedonia again.

The mountain road took us back to Ohrid. This was the road I'd walked in memory of Kosta: past the graffitied Italian bunker, past Trpejtsa where Nate's ancestors were buried. The limestone mountain loomed above us. The road was shiny with rain. No other cars. I read to Tino the messages I'd copied from the visitors' book in the Archangel Michael cave.

'Dear archangel, I would like another dog.'

'We are Ukrainian painters, grateful for the beauty of this place.'

'From England, with thanks to archangels everywhere – on the way to Mount Athos on foot, from the Lincolnshire Jews.'

'My biggest wish is for my daughter to be cured.'

'All I want is to be with the man I love.'

'I have a few wishes.' Tino put on some John Coltrane. 'But just one dream. A world without borders. Cynics will laugh.'

'But cynics don't dream,' I said.

'They're scared,' Tino said. 'Anyway, when are you coming back?'

Although I had gained new insight into family dynamics, and had got to know the Macedonian side of Lake Ohrid and my hospitable family here, it was clear that the wider journey had only just begun. I had to find out how the familiar patterns looked within the greater, yet lesser-known, landscape of the lakes. There was Albania, and there was Lake Prespa at a higher altitude, veiled in cloud and legend, barely explored, mysteriously under-written. I sensed that the rest of the journey would be less predictable. But for now, I felt so emotionally and sensorily saturated that it was vital to get away from here, to digest.

'You and I both like roads. Because a dream is like a road, isn't it,' Tino smiled, and for a moment he looked just like Tatjana in one of her radiant photos. Tatjana who, like my grandmother

Anastassia, had yearned for personal freedom but had not been able to claim it. The Kanun had been too strong.

The Kanun feeds on fear and guilt. Whereas a dream, like a road, takes you out of the tribal maw and sets you free, at least for a moment – and sometimes a moment is enough.

The lake is a crystal . . . It reflects the high vault of the October sky and the plunging mountain peaks where huge autumnal crocuses blossom, and wild cyclamens. When the sun sets, in the waves of the lake a ghostly palace of coral rises, and just as soon begins to disintegrate in the declining light . . .

A Scotsman from the Black Watch was brought into the field hospital. They called me in, to question him, but he is barely conscious. With a broken leg and a hole in his head, tall and gaunt, he lies upon the stretcher. Poor son of the Highlands, whose good-hearted father was a shepherd with melodious, green-lined bagpipes! . . . Perhaps a vision of the native mountains roams in his darkening mind, of handsome white herds scattered upon it . . . a cottage hearth, and the old Scottish song, Burns's song. 'My heart's in the Highlands. My heart is not here.'

Geo Milev, 1917

MOUNTAIN OF BONES

'You say you're leaving tomorrow, but you'll be back, you'll see,' Angelo said. 'It's the lake. It pulls you back.'

Angelo from the beach with the dead cow. We had met again.

In his twenties, Angelo had owned a trucking company that did business with Western Europe via Bosnia and Croatia, but then the Yugoslav Wars began, and after one close encounter too many with boozy paramilitaries at road blocks, he folded. Then he had a scrap-metal business and employed dozens of people.

'Lots of Gypsies. In Ohrid they speak Albanian, in other places they speak Romani. They work hard and they're ace people. Never trust stereotypes, trust experience.' But some years ago, he lost his business overnight to a shady company linked to the then-ruling party.

'Do you know what it's like to lose forty thousand euros in one night?'

The similarities between the outgoing government and the pashas of yesteryear were unmissable: Ali Pasha, Djeladin Bey, Tito and the creepily smiling ex-prime minister had treated this land as a private reserve, to be sliced up among their cronies like a cherry pie.

A mate of Angelo's suffered a similar fate with his business and shot himself with an army pistol. But Angelo was a survivor. Out of work, out of pocket and out of luck, he'd decided to lie low for a while and dedicate himself to his passions: mountaineering and paragliding. He was a mountain guide, and this is what we were doing today – preparing to trek to the top of Galicica Mountain where you could see both lakes, and where you didn't go alone unless you were Angelo. I had brought food that he packed into a rucksack.

Angelo spent the summers fishing and trekking, making a buck here and there from adventurous tourists. In the winter, he shut himself in the family house in the Village of Mean People, stocked up on logs, and carved objects out of cherry wood. This is where we were: at the family house at the foot of the moun-tain. Figs, black and white, mulberries, and even a pomegranate tree and a friendly sharplaninec called Hazel. It was paradise with a lake view. But the balcony was hanging off the house and the garden had gone wild.

'There used to be vines. My grandfather loved his vines.'

The indigenous grape is called *taljanka*, 'the Italian'. But the Serbs banned it and introduced another type of vine, the *correct* vine, he said.

'My grandfather kept growing his taljanka and ended up in jail.'

Angelo wanted to live here full-time, but how to make a living out of paradise?

The Village of Mean People had been prosperous for cen-turies. Above the village was Vojtino, today a wild hillside but once a Roman trading station and hub where travellers changed horses. The village had fat fields by the lake, and well into the mid-twentieth century had been the property of the monastery estate of St Naum. Twice a year, the fields were flooded by the moun-tain springs, which made them even more fertile. But in the 1990s when state-run factories in the region closed down and war raged next door in Serbia and Kosovo, people started emigrating en masse.

'Let me know if you have ideas how to make the garden pay for itself,' Angelo said, and started producing warm socks and jackets. It was a brilliant sunny day; I couldn't see why we needed them. You'll see, he said.

Angelo's distant ancestors had come to the lake on the ultimate one-way ticket: fleeing a Sicilian vendetta.

'There was a young man in Palermo, called Lazaro. One day,
they called him up with an order: to kill such and such a Muslim.
Some old vendetta. Sicilian vendettas are nothing to laugh about.
He gave his besa, but the Muslim he was supposed to kill turned
out to be his friend. What to do? He warned his friend and his
friend skipped town. Lazaro told them he'd done the deed. His
friend didn't come back for thirty years. 'Cause he knew they had
a long memory.'

'Who were *they*?' I said.

'Does it matter?'

True. But when did it take place?

'When, when. Do I look like some boring historian?'

He certainly didn't.

'Then let me finish my story.'

When the friend came back thirty years later, *they* remembered. And this time, both Lazaro and the friend had to skip
town. By now, Lazaro had grown-up sons and daughters. They
sailed to Albania, followed the Via Egnatia and arrived at St Naum
Monastery. This is where the two sons remained, to work on the
estate. The rest moved on east. It is not known what happened
to Lazaro and his wife, but it is believed that *they* followed the
daughters and murdered them. The only one who left progeny
was one of the sons. That was Angelo's ancestor. That's why his
surname is Lazaroski and his first name is Italian.

'I had Icarus syndrome,' he said when I asked him about the
paragliders in the house, folded up into coloured packs. He had
had a near-fatal fall which had broken his back, and didn't fly any
more.

We rode up the mountain road to the starting point of the
trek on his lightweight motorbike with a Bulgarian number plate;
Macedonians bought cars across the border because it was cheaper. No spare helmet for me. After many hairpin turns in the road,

we reached a lookout point. Coloured ribbons tied to the scrubby bushes flapped in the wind – reference points for paragliders. As the road climbed past 1,000 metres, the scenery changed – the walnut and wild fig trees gave way to moorland. It was all bone-bleached stones, mosses, and low-lying vegetation. The hill beneath was the Big Shadow that I'd glimpsed from the deepest part of the lake at Zaum Monastery. Despite the heat of the sun, the air was crisp and the wind pinched your face. From here, you could see the entire lake and it made you speechless. But not Angelo.

'Do you see now?' he said. 'The lake can't be taken in isolation. It works together with Galicica Mountain and Prespa. They are a system, ecological and spiritual. See the cross?'

Many Lake people were intent on seeing meaningful geometrical shapes and spiritual ley lines. Everybody's version was slightly different, but the most common belief was that a cross-shape was made by four manmade sites on the lake rim: St Naum Monastery to the south and St Erasmus cave church to the north; Ohrid town to the east and the cave church of Archangel Michael to the west.

Two bright paragliders passed overhead, noiselessly. One was doing pirouettes.

'Watch that, it's an air spiral!'

A friend of Angelo's had been sucked into an air spiral, lost consciousness and fallen to his death.

'There's a high mortality rate among paragliders,' he said; and looking at the pirouetting figure, I believed it.

'You never fly over the lake though, because it sucks you down. If you want to be over the lake, it's got to be over two kilometres high. The lowest you can go is eight hundred metres.'

If you fall into the lake from a great height, it can break your back. Like it had broken his. He had recovered, but had a permanent hump and breathing problems.

The starting point for the trek was halfway along the high road between the two lakes. We parked in a shadowy mountain dip called Mean Valley. I thought Angelo was making it up – mean village, mean valley – but then I looked at the map. The toponyms on Galicica were all like that. Beyond the peak we were scaling was another one named Coffin. Overlooking the Village of Mean People was a peak called the Abyss, and if we kept going east towards Prespa, we'd pass the ridge of Wolf's Lair.

'It's Mean Valley because the soldiers who fought here went through hell. Can you imagine scaling that mountain in deep snow, with heavy equipment?'

Mean Valley was a geological fracture in the massif, between two peaks of 2,270 and 2,254 metres. We were aiming for the second one.

'See those?' He pointed to aerials on a peak above St Naum Monastery. 'That's Albania. Those used to be their eyes and ears.'

We began the steep walk along a goat path. The craggy slope ahead looked almost vertical, but it was better than the shadowy side of Mean Valley towards Albania. There were no other paths. You had to know where you were going.

It was midday and I was hungry.

'Didn't you have breakfast?' Angelo said, without slowing down. 'Something you should know about Pogradec and Tushemisht,' he went on. Tushemisht was the first Albanian village after the St Naum checkpoint. 'They're all our people there.'

What do you mean, our people? I asked.

'We're all the same people on this lake, that's what I mean. Macedonians.'

Ironically, his Village of Mean People was first settled by Albanians, but Angelo was proudly Macedonian (even if he had a Bulgarian passport and number plate). Of course, he was right: the natural state of lake towns and border towns is to have 'our people' on both sides.

'Pogradec was wrecked by Hoxha. It used to be the richest place around. But in the 1950s, people were going hungry. That's because instead of fishing and harvesting, they were building bunkers. So there was this arrangement between families in my village and those on the other side. They'd send their children to us, to be fed. Over Mean Valley.'

They had a communication code from hill to hill – by means of horses and whistles. Naum Monastery had been the children's hiding-place on this side of the border, before they were sent to the Village of Mean People to eat for a few days. They were conveyed back the same way – via the monastery, over the mountains, out of sight of border patrol, with a local guide, as their families waited on the other side. But one day, it went badly wrong.

'Bastard of a priest in the monastery betrayed them and sent them right back over the border and the Albanian border patrol saw them and gunned them down.'

They gunned the children down, their own side's children.

The Village of Mean People was distressed. They felt responsible – those kids had been their responsibility.

'So a band of men, including my great-uncle, took their guns and came up here, to wait for the priest. They knew he was headed for Prespa.'

The priest had loaded donkeys with loot stolen from the monastery. They shot him on the spot and took the loot.

'The loot they donated to the village headquarters of the Yugoslav Communist Party. And the Party bosses built themselves houses with it. With blood money. I still have that gun. I hope I never have to use it.'

We passed various animal droppings: wild goat, wolf, and large dung that looked like—

'Bear.' He ran his fingers through it. It was dry and full of half-digested rosehips.

The trick was to keep to the main path (which I couldn't see) and not veer off it; bears keep to themselves except when surprised. From the height we'd already scaled I could appreciate the full sweep of Mean Valley, forested and deep in shadow, with pockets of snow. The peaks ahead were lit by the sun of early summer. Mean Valley and the cliff above it – called Bloodied Stone – had a current history in addition to their war history.

'One winter,' Angelo said, 'friend and I went climbing. It was hard going. Halfway up Mean Valley, we see this guy buried in snow up to the waist, as good as dead. He'd come over the mountain from Albania but his contact had stood him up. And he stood there waiting, the tears frozen on his face. With twenty kilos of marijuana strapped to his body.'

They gave him some rakia to warm him up and guided him to a safe crossing point, so he could make it back. He offered them two kilos as payment, but Angelo declined. And now – now they're best friends.

'There's been a lot of drugs with the Albanians. Drugs and arms. Mind you, Macedonian peasant houses always had a cake of top-quality afiyon. Sometimes a good hundred years old.'

What's afiyon?

'Opium, from poppies. Traditionally grown in the Vardar River valley.'

The expansive Vardar valley is the most fertile part of geographic Macedonia. *Afiyon* is an old Ottoman word, derived from the Hellenic *ofion*.

'People always had a stash, to calm the kids down, relieve the pain of the dying and the ill, sleep better. And of course, Alexander the Great's army used liquid afiyon to smear on their shields, and strategically positioning themselves in relation to the sun, they'd dazzle the enemy with their shiny shields. That's how they defeated larger armies. Now, see this?'

The face of the mountain began to show manmade scars. We'd come to a shallow cave in the rocky slope. The rock itself had been chiselled away painstakingly.

'Soldiers passing the time,' Angelo said, as if it had been yesterday.

During the First World War, the highly strategic Macedonian Front (1915–18) passed through here. It ran roughly along today's border with Greece, and over three major mountain ranges: in the east, Belasitsa above Lake Doiran; the Baba-Pelister Mountains on the eastern shore of Lake Prespa; and Galicica here, between the two lakes.

These three majestic mountain ranges are the southernmost glacial massifs of Europe, the southernmost alpine habitats, and a haven for rare species. And only a hundred years ago they were sites of catastrophic multinational battles. English, Welsh, Scots and Indian soldiers, alongside Serb, French, French Oriental and Greek troops, were deployed to the south of the Macedonian Front. They fought the formidable Austrian-backed Bulgarian army to the north (800,000 men fought on the Bulgarian side), who had entrenched themselves on one mountain peak after another. My great-grandfather Kosta was among those who answered the Bulgarian call for volunteers, though I have no idea where he fought.

There was one particularly terrible battle along this front, at Doiran (even though hunting dogs were passed between the Bulgarian and British enemy lines quite happily!). Appallingly, there were five battles of Doiran, and in each the Bulgarians were attacked by different armies. Over the winter and spring of 1917, despite being outnumbered, the Bulgarians repelled the British, inflicting devastating losses. Twelve thousand British soldiers died in just the First and Second Battles of Doiran. The Bulgarians lost two thousand men. That's fourteen thousand men in just two battles. At the end of hostilities, the Bulgarians buried as many of the British dead as they could, with their own, and the British cemetery at Doiran can be visited today. Some of these men rest in a military section of Sofia's Central Cemetery.

These numbers are hard to grasp. I can't even say *fourteen thousand men* without choking. And the Third Battle of Doiran was yet to come, the following autumn, again ending with Bulgarian victory and many more thousands of dead, this time Greek and French too.

One of Europe's finest Expressionist poets, Geo Milev, who fought in the Bulgarian ranks, wrote a poignant war diary, *By Lake Doiran*, where he describes how '[w]hen the night becomes a mirror in which we see the faces of distant sorrowful mothers and beloved women waiting for us, the night itself is sorrow'; and how '[s]ometimes, at night, the French sing. We listen to them. It gives me strange joy to write *the French sing*. I too would like to sing. I'd like to sing the Song of Solveig: "If you are in heaven now waiting for me . . .". How I'd like to sing it, in this moist, moonlit night. But we are all silent. Only the French are singing.'

At night, instead of the fishing boats with their dim fires, there was 'the broad radiance of a strange moon, the eye of the enemy projector, a foreign, roaming eye that sweeps lake and mountain, knowing not what it looks for'. That was the British and the French. Like the Highlander who was brought to the field hospital, Milev was wounded in the head and lost an eye. He survived the Macedonian Front – to be murdered by right-wing royalist police a few years later in Sofia, for his Socialist sympathies.

Here, on Galicica, to hold off the French Armée d'Orient from the south-east, the Bulgarians had hacked trenches in the rock, a Sisyphean achievement, and lived in temperatures of -25° Celsius along with cholera and malaria outbreaks. Malaria, typically rife in swampy marshes and the reedbeds of the lakes, was a major cause of death for all nationalities along the Macedonian Front. Amazingly, the remains of trenches were still here. You could see how the face of the mountain had been carved, and the trenches shored up with rocks. The sight left me speechless. I'd never before seen trench remains from the First World War.

'The French Oriental Army on the other side of Mean Valley shelled the Bulgarians but they didn't budge,' Angelo said. 'For four years. It was deadlock until the end of the war.'

I couldn't find any writing by combatants on Galicica, but the Scottish officer Edward P. Stebbing visited the equivalent of these

trenches on Kaimakchalan Peak to the east, only hours after a
particularly heavy battle which the attacking Serbs won at the cost
of over 4,600 men. Stebbing graphically described the 'ghastly'
scene of numberless dead Bulgarian and Macedonian men in the
trenches, many killed by gas, hoping that his account would warn
readers against future wars.

The Battle of Kaimakchalan changed the tide of the war on the
Macedonian Front, and therefore in the Balkans. Mass desertions
followed in the Bulgarian ranks. Men walked away, demented,
gunned down by their own command. After all the victories.
This war is known as the Second National Catastrophe in Bulgaria. The First National Catastrophe was the preceding Balkan War
of 1913.

'I'll tell you a war story,' Angelo said. 'My great-grandfather
hadn't been conscripted by either side in the Balkan Wars, don't
know how he got out of it. Maybe his mother broke his legs.
These things happened, you know.'

The anvil.

'One day in the latter stages of the war, a deserter turns up at
our village house. A Bulgarian soldier. Or maybe a Serb. I can't
remember. He says he can't kill his own kind, and begs the family
to hide him.'

Angelo's great-grandparents hid the soldier and gave him
clothes and food to start him on his long journey home. Who
knows how he made it back to Bulgaria or Serbia, but he did.
Because a few years later, when the First World War shook this
mountain again, Angelo's great-grandfather and a cousin were
conscripted by the Serbs, or perhaps the Bulgarians. They escaped
the front, but were captured and dispatched to a POW camp
near Salonica (which tells us the deserter must have been a Serb,
because the 'Salonica Army' was composed of the Allied nations).
And there, an officer recognised the man who'd saved his life.

'He gave them clothes and money and smuggled them out of
the camp.'

They walked over the mountains, through starving villages without men.

'When my great-grandmother saw an apparition in filthy rags approaching the house, she bolted the door.'

It had taken his great-grandfather eighteen months to walk home.

Angelo had seen 'Algerians' and 'Moroccans', presumably descendants of the African soldiers from the Armée d'Orient, looking for buried money here.

'They thought I didn't know what they were up to.'

Soldiers from the colonies, Senegalese and North Africans, had been stationed here for up to two years, so they buried gold napoleons that apparently still turn up among the rocks. Many were killed or died of exposure or malaria, and those who survived didn't have time to dig up the money, or couldn't find it in the snow.

'And then there's the people of the mountain villages, friends of mine, with Arab features. Guess why.'

In between shelling the enemy and getting sick in trenches like these, the soldiers on both sides raided the local villages without men. Some were friendly, others violent. Animals were 'requisitioned'. Children were born. An underground French field hospital was believed to be hidden somewhere on the Prespa side of this mountain, complete with a stash of gold rods, used at the time by military surgeons to replace shattered bones. Two shepherds in the 1960s found a Bulgarian underground warehouse, but nothing valuable in it, just cooking utensils. Afterwards, they had both developed a strange ailment, linked to the poison leaking from unexploded grenades in the warehouse.

Stebbing served as transport officer to the Scottish Women's Hospitals, stationed at the foot of the Baba-Pelister Mountains, and movingly describes their stoical work, and death, in his memoir. He was sympathetic to his own side exclusively, especially the Serbs who spoke to him eloquently of Macedonia as their 'ancestral land'. Stebbing couldn't know that many Macedonian men were forcibly conscripted by the Serb high command, to bulk out their ranks – or rather, he could have, had he bothered to talk to the soldiers. Those Macedonians who died on the Serbian side had already had their names changed and were buried as 'Serbs'. Although many Macedonians joined the Bulgarian army enthusiastically, like Kosta and other lake men, many were conscripted by force too. Two hundred thousand men from Macedonia fought in this apocalyptic war, sometimes not even certain which side they were fighting on, or why.

Another thing Stebbing didn't find out was that in the Macedonian territories gained by them – at the cost of utter human bankruptcy – the Serb army moved from village to village, making lists of ethnic Turks due for expulsion; their property was seized and divided among locals and settlers. As soon as the war was over, those 'Turks', some of whom were in fact Albanians, found themselves on the road to exile. Their families had lived in Macedonia for centuries. If you go to the towns and villages of European Turkey, you will meet their grandchildren and great-grandchildren; some still know Slavic words. Some are not even descended from Turks or Albanians, but from Slav Muslims swept up in the purge; they even look Slavic. Some had fled atrocities committed by the Bulgarian army too.

'Up here, it was the Bulgarians against the French Oriental Army,' Angelo said. 'But in Kaimakchalan, brother fought against brother, father against son. Literally, not figuratively. These border mountains are full of bones.'

We climbed in silence.

Many Macedonian émigrés had sailed back from America, hearing that Macedonia was going to be finally 'free', and elatedly joining in the effort.

In addition to soldier violence, civilians like Angelo's Village of Mean People suffered famine, cholera, malaria and dysentery. Women lost children to hunger and disease. Even the goats and the bees started to die off because every inch of land was seized by armies. The only civilians who travelled safely from village to village, because they had nothing worth stealing, were the *mechkari* − travelling Gypsies with bears on chains (*mechka* is bear). The bears 'danced', treading on the bodies of the ill, which was believed to bring relief. Ursine therapy was better than nothing.

In those Armageddon years, people said that with all the heavy fighting − the Balkan Wars, the First World War, seven years of assaulting the land − this land would eventually cave in, with its mountains and rivers, lakes and valleys; and floods would erupt from under the core of the earth, taking everybody down, soldier and civilian, human and animal.

'In the 1970s, a shepherd found a stash of French champagne in a cave,' Angelo said, to lighten the mood. 'He drank two bottles and got so drunk he smashed up the rest. Ever since then, treasure hunters have been rooting around caves for wine and cognac.'

As we climbed the rocky face of the mountain like goats − all traces of the path gone now − I saw that Angelo was looking for stuff. Collecting the scrap of history was second nature to him.

'I'm a scrap man, I look for scrap. You're a writer, you look for stories. In a mountain like this, everyone finds what they need, right?' He smiled with all the lines of his face, a vagabondish face. I was very happy to have him as a friend. But I was also very hungry.

'No,' Angelo said, and kept walking, 'you can't eat before we reach the top. And anyway, don't you want to test yourself? See how it was for those soldiers?'

No, I wanted lunch.

He turned to me, changing the subject. 'The lake reflects the mountain and vice versa.' He never got out of breath, despite the pack and his disfigured back. 'I've found as many treasures in the lake as up here. And I've barely scratched the surface.' He'd found iron camel shoes from l'Armée d'Orient (they used camels?), and he'd fished out a complete Ottoman brass narghile set, inscribed in Arabic. Whatever, I thought. Hunger was making me irritable.

'The lake has a memory,' he said. 'The mountain has a memory. They are a living organism.'

Large snail shells were scattered over the crags – mountain snails, some as big as a child's palm, the kind of thing you'd find on a beach. There were wild strawberries, alpine flowers, small orchids, fragrant herbs: marjoram, wild thyme, red gentian, and a prized green tea called *mursalski chaj*.

'Did I mention that if you see a metal object on the ground you don't recognise, for God's sake don't touch it. There are un-exploded mines. They were killing and maiming shepherds and kids and there was a big clean-up before I was born, but I've seen the odd one still, though not close to the main paths.'

He's exaggerating for effect, I thought. There can't be mines from the First World War here. Where did they discard the mines?

'In the lake. Where everything ends up. Mines, warplanes, family treasures, church loot stolen by mean priests and mean villagers, antique jewellery, Neolithic ceramics, inconvenient people, weapon stashes, saints' relics – you name it, it's in the lake. It's nature's safe box.'

Angelo picked up another dry animal turd. Rabbit, he said, you can tell from the herbs. When it's dry, you can put it in a joint and get off your head.

He picked up a piece of black rock. 'What do you think this is?'

'Basalt,' I said.

'Meteorite,' he said. 'I'll show you the craters later.'

I was so dizzy with hunger and sunshine, I didn't know what was true any more.

Then in a flood of light, we reached the top. A spacious plateau opened up. The blue of Lake Prespa glittered on the other side. We looked down towards Mean Valley, which was an impossibly long way down. There were craters in the hillside we'd just scaled.

'See the meteorite holes?' Angelo said. I nodded. But they were of course the scars of exploded mortar shells from a hundred years ago. Shell craters and trenches hacked in the rock – the mountain had not recovered completely.

A disused observation station stood in the middle of the plateau. It had been abandoned in the early 1990s. The whole mountain had been a militarised zone, and this observation point was one of the most strategic in Yugoslavia. The Yugoslavs and the Albanians across the border had faced each other off. Civilians had had no access here for forty years, but Angelo's uncle had been in the army, and occasionally he'd bring him up here to visit the soldiers. Angelo had loved hanging out with them, touching their weapons, and looking through binoculars at Greece.

You could see Greece without binoculars, on the other side of Lake Prespa. And you could see Albania, almost all the way to the Adriatic coast, mountain after mountain, an unfolding so beautiful, so immense and transcendent, it was hard to believe that was where the Italian-Albanian front had been only a generation later, in the 1940s.

'I told you it was worth it,' Angelo grinned.

At my feet was a white flower that looked like the rare alpine edelweiss. I bent down and picked it.

'What did you do that for?' Angelo lashed out. I stepped back and nearly fell off a ridge into a trench.

'Did you come all this way to pick this flower that has done nothing to you?'

I was aghast. I put the flower in my jacket pocket. He looked genuinely upset. The wind rose suddenly and filled our mouths. Angelo put up his hood.

'I shouldn't have done that,' I said.

The wind took my words and threw them away.

'That's right, you shouldn't have. Typical of you Bulgars, claiming everything here as yours. And you have to use force. Even with a little flower!'

I stared hard at him and he stared back. The wind tore at our jackets.

'And you?' I spat out. 'Poor Macedonians, always someone else's fault. Why don't you look at the pile of fabrications you call your national history!'

'Oh, and *your* history's the correct one!' he spat back.

'You've *no* idea, have you, you've been so brainwashed!' I said, not in my own voice any more. 'Macedonia's like a phantom limb to us!'

He snorted cynically. I could have hit him.

'Pass me the pack,' I said, and tried to turn my back to the wind, but it was coming from everywhere. There was no shelter. 'I need to eat.'

'You'll eat when we get down,' he said.

Now he truly looked like a native of the Village of Mean People.

'I bought that food,' I said with clenched jaws. 'Don't try to control me!'

'Oh really! And did you know, Miss Feminism, that we're two thousand metres above sea level and if you eat now, you'll be sick and I'll have to carry you down!'

'You're a bully!' I shouted.

Ignoring me, he headed for the disused observation station which looked fairly cursed, with its broken aerials and blown-off roof, debris strewn all around, as if after an explosion. The blood rushed from my head, making everything black for a moment. The emotions I was feeling were out of sync with the situation. It wasn't just hunger, it was something else, and the higher you went, the brighter the sun shone, the more bleached the rocks, the more sparkling the lakes – the more desperate it felt.

The ascent was also a descent. I stood on the plateau frozen, like that Albanian guy in the snow. I could go neither forwards nor back, and I couldn't believe I'd just said those things to Angelo.

How many frostbitten men had looked over these two lakes like eyes in an ancient face, and prayed for a truce? The mountains went on multiplying, majestic and empty like time itself.

After the war, Kosta stayed in Sofia where he met Ljubitsa, and her sister Tsareva met Taki, who didn't speak. He'd fought on the Macedonian Front.

One of the finest Balkan lyrical poets of the twentieth century, Dimcho Debelyanov (who was a pacifist), was killed at the age of twenty-nine near the Macedonian Front – in a battle with an Irish division. The opening line of his war poem 'One Dead' came to me:

'Now he's an enemy no more.'

Why do we humans have to experience death before we see the obvious?

Stebbing had watched the French make their way uphill, with their heavy artillery and thousands of mules laden with ammunition boxes; and the wounded in all their agony being taken downhill in haste on improvised stretchers – all this against the backdrop of Macedonia's majestic valleys and tranquil lakes. 'How absolutely out of place,' he wrote, 'how incongruous it seemed amongst these great hills, these eternal mountains, that man should have the effrontery to bring his petty strifes into their great silent spaces.' Yet here we were again, with our petty strifes. As if each lesson lasts a mere minute, then we forget.

Angelo walked back towards me. With his hoodie up and carrying a heavy iron bar he'd found in the ruins, he looked like history's tramp. He could kill me with a single blow of that bar. But he didn't look mean, just tired and sad, and I didn't hate him any more.

'Let me see that flower,' he said quietly. I took it out of my pocket. 'It's not edelweiss. It's a common flower.' I gave him the crumpled white flower and when he took it with his cold fingers, tears ran from my eyes and the wind blew them away.

'We are one people, aren't we?' I said, and a terrible howl rose inside me. 'Aren't we one people?'

Time collapsed and telescoped into a moment of irreversible loss.

It had always been there, that howl, it was older than me. It wasn't even mine. As if it came from the land itself. Angelo dropped the iron bar on the ground and hugged me.

''Course we are,' he said at last and wiped his nose. 'Isn't that the whole point?'

We went inside the ruined barracks. Gutted mattresses, broken windows, crates of empty beer bottles, insulation oozing from the walls. The frames of the iron bunk beds stood empty. Almost all of the recyclable scrap had been taken away. Angelo had seen men carting off metal doorframes, an iron stove, a fridge – on donkeys' backs, on their own backs – all the way from here across Mean Valley to Albania. It was hard to comprehend. I could not carry anything on my back over these mountains; I could barely carry myself. But perhaps I would if I really had to.

At our feet we found cartridge shells from the 1980s and 90s, and Yugoslav tin cans dated 1954.

'They weren't here before. There's always something new,' Angelo said.

The mountain kept churning up memories.

On the Prespa side of the plateau was a squat rusted toilet in the ground, the hole filled with stones. It had once been a cubicle but was now in the open.

'A shitter with the world's best view,' Angelo summed up.

From here you could see Baba-Pelister at 2,601 metres, and beyond it tragic Kaimakchalan, whose top was creamy with snow – in Turkish, kaimak is cream.

'I've spent so long climbing this mountain, flying over it, diving in the lake,' Angelo said, still rooting for objects of interest. The wind had abated and we didn't have to shout. 'It's like I'm looking for myself. Does that make sense?'

'Yes,' I said. 'It does.'

'And I'm afraid I'll be old and dead before I find myself,' he said.

★

The descent was subdued. My hunger had dulled. As we lost Prespa from view, the late afternoon sun moved towards the Adriatic. The mountain cast its stony shadow over Mean Valley. We walked downhill at a different angle, and passed scattered white bones that for a crazy moment I took to be human, but it was a wild goat. Two golden eagles circled above, looking for prey, or perhaps it was a mating dance.

Back at the house in the Village of Mean People, Angelo put the food on the wood-fired stove and brewed some mountain tea. Stars were lighting up the dark sky and crickets screeched in the undergrowth.

'You can sleep upstairs,' he said. 'In the room with the paragliders. With blankets from my great-grandmother, the one who didn't recognise her husband.'

He went to a chest and opened it. And there they were: shells from exploded mines and grenades from the First World War; the gorgeous ornate brass narghile inscribed in Arabic; the pair of camel shoes, manufactured in 1914. He added the newly salvaged iron bar.

'Everybody finds what they need, right?' He closed the chest.

Where was the rifle that had shot the bastard priest?

'Over here.' And so it was, its wooden handle shiny with use. 'Not loaded.'

Then he produced a Native American clay pipe and started filling it with grass.

'You're leaving,' he said, 'so we'd better smoke the pipe of peace.'

We went outside. To the north flickered the lights of Ohrid, to the south the lights of Pogradec. We sat on a fallen cherry tree with the invisible lake below us, and above us – the mountain of bones.

PART TWO

AUTUMN

In the village the creaking of a door.
On the lake the silence of an oar.
Over the Dry Mountain a distant eagle soars.

Lasgush Poradeci, 1930s

POETS OF POGRADEC

It was early September when I returned, and the smell of roasting aubergines sweetened the air. In the village houses, strings of red peppers hung from balconies: it was the season for making preserves. This time, I wanted to spend no time in Ohrid town – something about it now felt too small and claustrophobic – so I headed straight for the Albanian side of Lake Ohrid.

After the quiet St Naum checkpoint, the familiar faces of taxi drivers waiting for custom welcomed me on the Albanian side. The bunkers too, and the thick reeds in the shallows of the lake, so richly textured that they looked painted in oils. A spring called St Naum, inside a tiny whitewashed chapel built over it, bubbled from within the rocky shore and into the lake. Once inside the heavily militarised border zone, the spring was now a hub for Albanian youths on bikes who came to hang out in the evenings.

This was the way of the Lake: everything had its double and everything was connected. Pogradec (meaning 'on the rock' in Slavic) was the mirror image of Ohrid ('on the hill'); and there were two St Naum springs, now divided by a border but once a seamless system. A group of boys and girls in skinny jeans walked up the road towards the checkpoint, eating ice-creams.

The lake was serene, conscious, at one with the rocky mountain that rose above the red-tiled roofs of Tushemisht village and the apartment blocks of Pogradec. Lake and mountain were one. The world, when left alone, was one. I was filled with the exhilaration that accompanied arrival at the Lake every time – an exhilaration of wholeness.

Eduard was at his post with the kilims draped over his van, as if he hadn't moved since June. His ravaged demeanour and rustic rugs contrasted with the new hotels built, or partially built, in haste and with laundered money. His wife was here too, a woman with fine Mediterranean features, who kissed me like an old friend, though we'd never met before.

I had returned to the lake in a less personal frame of mind, to learn about the Albanian side and explore mysterious Prespa. In Pogradec, my home for the week was a room in a block of flats on the waterfront. My room had woollen blankets, a high ceiling and a glassed-in bathroom on the balcony, which looked out into the building's echoey courtyard. There was a summer stove on the balcony, exactly like the one from my childhood for roasting peppers in September that everybody had on their cramped balconies, which doubled as additional rooms. The neighbouring balcony belonged to my hosts: a retired professional couple whose American-educated sons were torn between emigrating and staying; one was abroad, the other was here. To supplement their income, they rented out this room to visitors. In the morning, the mother brought me hot doughnuts and surprised me by telling me, in broken Bulgarian, that her father had studied medicine in Sofia between the wars, but returned to Albania when the two countries severed relations in the late 1940s.

In the early morning when the lake was white and the first boats were going out for the day, I sat on the balcony with my coffee. The noises of the block's inhabitants echoed in the court-yard as if inside a well – coughing, doors opening and closing, even the clank of my spoon against the mug was magnified.

On the beach below, two homeless pals – a black dog and a white dog – came to run along the waterline, full of the new day. In the morning haze, up in the hills, the abandoned observation tower of the border checkpoint was the only manmade feature on the empty flanks of Mali i Thate, Dry Mountain. It was the same mountain I had climbed on the other side with Angelo – Galicica – but from this side it looked impossible to scale.

Men on Chinese bikes from the 1970s, some with transistor radios attached and playing Italian, Greek, Macedonian or Albanian music, pedalled up and down the alley on early errands. Rubbish bins were being rummaged by the destitute, while the first gleaming Mercedes of the day, driven by gormless-looking young men, began their ritual glide up and down the promenade.

The centre of the town, marked by the empty monolithic architecture of totalitarianism, had been spruced up in recent years, and when you walked down the pedestrian square to the lake, beneath your feet were memorial plaques to some of the great artists, scientists and progressive politicians of the Balkans and other European nations. But everywhere in the cafes, jobless men of all ages sat with empty hands, staring into space. Along the promenade passed joggers in trainers, dog walkers, but most arresting were the elderly couples, arm in arm, who were taking the air before the heat of the day – the men in full suits and ties, the women in dark stockings. After decades of murderous Communism, rapacious Capitalism, and the collapse of the money 'pyramids' in 1997 that pauperised the already impoverished and exploded into violent anarchy – after all that, here was a picture of gentility out of time.

One of these was Mr Bimbli, a retired ichthyologist. I met him later that day at the fish restaurant he ran next to my building. Mr Bimbli straightened his tie (with a tie pin) and told me at length about the fish of the lake.

He had an old-worldly distinction about him; in his brown suit and old but polished shoes, and his reserved politeness, I couldn't help feeling that he had walked out of a Bertolucci film. The fish of Lake Ohrid were the love of his life. He looked upset when I asked about endangered species, and instead of speaking produced

a booklet he had written about each species in the lake, under-
lining for me each endangered fish, with its Latin name, some
endemic to the lake: the Ohrid *nase*, from the half-extinct family
of Cyprinid; the Ohrid *koran* (trout), or *Salmothynus ohridanus*.
During Communism there had been strict laws, he said – and he
had been chief inspector of fisheries. But from the 1990s onwards,
in the 'transition', there had been overfishing in the lake.

'At one point,' he said, 'the fish became so depleted, the birds
went over to the Macedonian side. But they recovered, eventually.'

He quit his job fifteen years ago, unable to stomach the
corruption. Now he ran the restaurant, where I ate a fragrant
fish soup with orange rind, and where he sat at a white-napkined
table morning and evening, writing something in a big ledger.

At dusk, the promenade darkened with throngs of people –
friends, couples, families, sellers of corn on the cob and roasted
peanuts – the whole town came out in the evening to walk under
the chestnut and walnut trees, the olives and the willows, as it must
have done since its beginnings, as far back in time as Ohrid itself.

'How we longed to go to Ohrid!' Lazar said. 'We longed to see
the other side.'

Lazar and Liridon had volunteered to show me around,
though we'd never met before. They met me at the giant statue
of Lasgush Poradeci in the lakeside park, past the Hotel Enkelana
named after an Illyrian tribe and built in Communist-brutalist
style, past the plastic water slide that disrupted the pristine view
of infinity, past a plaque commemorating ten civilians of Pogradec
executed by the Germans for hiding partisans, past the men who
played chess under the chestnut trees.

Lazar and Liridon were a study in opposites. The younger
Liridon was polite and reserved. Lazar was effusive, excitable, and
stopped every few minutes to photograph swans in the lake, the
shimmer of the shallows, the drifting clouds. His face was open
and untainted, a young person's face, but his hair was white. He

was a high-school teacher and spoke English with native-speaker fluency, though he had never lived outside Albania or visited an English-speaking country – an East European phenomenon I recognised at once. We were the same age: the last generation to come of age behind the Iron Curtain.

Liridon, whose name meant Freedom, was born in the year Hoxha died – 1985 – and after graduating in history at Tirana University, he'd returned to his hometown.

'In those days, we were like that poem by Lasgush Poradeci, where the River Drim longs for the sea,' Lazar said. 'All we could do was watch the lights of Ohrid.'

'And I'd look at the lights of Pogradec, from Ohrid,' I said.

Lazar wanted me to love his town, but he also wanted me to see the truth.

'And the truth is, old Pogradec is being destroyed. It began under Hoxha and never stopped.'

It was hard to miss: along the water, ruins gaped open with their concrete viscera, broken glass and graffiti.

'New tourism,' Lazar said.

'New tourism' meant Communist-era buildings, and aesthetics to go with the 'new Albania' of Hoxha; 'old tourism' meant pre-Communist. And the wreckage of both new and old was everywhere, though I couldn't always tell which ruin was from which era. Up in the hills the remains of *fortesa*s, large bunker fortifications, and abandoned iron and nickel mines stood like sombre sentinels keeping watch over the town. Otherwise the hills were bare. Once forested, they were stripped of trees in the 1970s for maximum exposure and visibility, after one family's sensational escape by boat. The family had hidden in the forest first.

'And here was the old pontoon bridge,' Lazar said. I waded into the warm water in my sandals. In archival photographs, people stand on the pontoon in fine European clothes, their faces hopeful. Albanians had only three decades of relative freedom, between the Ottoman colonists' departure and the arrival of Communist totalitarianism. The submerged wooden stumps showed the contours of the old bridge.

'Submerged, like the past,' Lazar said. 'You have to know what was here to appreciate what's gone.'

But even if you came to Pogradec in ignorance, you immediately felt it: this was a traumatised topography. An assault had taken place here, a savage plundering.

'To understand a nation, you must look at its history,' Liridon said. It was the first time Liridon had spoken. I could see from his face that he too found the wounds difficult to live with. He wore glasses and spoke in a measured, sane way.

Liridon's people were from the mountains above the lake and had settled in the town only a generation ago; his parents were agronomists and non-practising Muslims. Lazar, on his father's side, was from an old lake family; they had come down from the obliterated fortress on the hill, inhabited by an Illyrian tribe from the sixth century BC onwards. The language spoken was Illyrian, which may well be the root of the Albanian language. The people of the fortress drew lake water through uphill pipes. It was only in the early Middle Ages that they started settling on the shores. Lazar's ancestors were Christians. Though Lazar had grown up in an atheist society (mind you, he said, my mother secretly dyed eggs at Easter, like everybody, and hid the family icons), in the early 1990s when the country opened its borders and Protestant missionaries arrived from Germany and the USA, Lazar became an Evangelical Christian.

'I was baptised here, in the lake,' he said. 'At the age of twenty.'

This was especially meaningful in the light of the total annihilation of Albania's clergy by the Hoxha regime – they were picked out for the most brutal tortures and executions.

We walked along the waterline.

'As kids we'd walk here and look for empty Coca Cola cans that had drifted from the Yugoslav side,' Lazar said. 'And display them at home, like trophies. We had nothing, but above all we had no information, and we were so hungry for the world!'

We had crossed into the old town, some of which had miraculously survived the bulldozers. Old Pogradec was a network of narrow lanes and two- or three-storeyed houses. You could still see the original low arched doorway, Ottoman style; the high windows, and the courtyards shadowed by immense vines, known throughout the Balkans by the Turkish word *asma* (with a stress on the last 'a'). Vines and roses everywhere. Some houses, dilapidated or derelict, were a beautiful blend of Europe and the Orient.

And here was the age-old Balkan method of warding off evil: a string of garlic hanging above the doorways; I saw it elsewhere in Albania too, including the distinguished old town of Korçë. It seemed that no amount of compulsory atheism could stamp out the belief in fate as a tangible force. If anything, the paranoid savagery of *Enverizm*, as the regime became known, had made people more superstitious. As if its fathomless cruelty only confirmed the existence of an irrational, wrathful force. And conversely – of the possibility of magical cures and narrow escapes.

'Paganism,' Lazar shrugged disparagingly.

Liridon smiled; he took the historian's long view.

Lazar knew everyone in the old town; women sitting outside their doorways kept inviting us in for coffee. The red-roofed house of Lasgush Poradeci was here too, and his poems were featured on plaques in the old town. Unlike some of his fellow writers, poets and journalists, he had not been imprisoned or put to work in the mines. But the regime tormented him in more subtle ways: Sigurimi agents shadowed him every time he left the house, his work fell out of print and he lived out his last decades in quiet desperation. Considered Albania's greatest twentieth-century poet, he just couldn't bring himself to abandon metaphysics and write in the *correct* form instead: Socialist Realism.

'He was ignored,' Lazar said. 'For a writer, that's a kind of death.'

Poradeci – a pseudonym he took to merge his identity with the town on the Lake – spent his last decades in his garden, tuned in to the Lake's seasons. His English translator, the late Robert Elsie, said that his verse was essentially pantheistic – which is true of Albanian culture in general. Lazar was a poet too, all his work inspired by the Lake. The family house where he lived with his parents was in the heart of the old town. Next door, the Orthodox Church of the Virgin Mary had been rebuilt from its ruined state – just walls and floor, no roof – after the fall of the regime.

'In my childhood, it was used as a storehouse, then a car mechanic's,' Lazar said. 'They poured concrete on the floor, and over the frescoes too.'

We could see the patch of concrete on the floor where cars had been dropped underground for repair. The priest, a tall, self-contained man in a long black cassock and with a boozer's nose, welcomed us in the rose-filled courtyard. He had been a horticulturalist until the 1990s, when he'd entered the seminary. Under the arched gallery, he showed us framed photographs of a medieval Bektashi tekke nearby called Shen (Saint) Constantin, destroyed during Hoxha. There was something very moving about seeing these memorialised images of Sufi life in a church, only a generation after both had been targeted for total annihilation by the regime.

A statement of tolerance by the Bishop of Tirana sat next to a citation from the Book of Matthew: 'You people who suffer under the oppression of unrighteousness and evil . . .', translated into English by Lazar.

'Albania would never make problems for Europe,' the priest said quietly, 'because we've always had mixed marriages. This is why fundamentalism can't take root here.' Both his children were married to Muslims, they'd had a church wedding, their children were baptised here – and they also celebrated Bayram and other Muslim festivals.

'This is normal here,' he said. 'Bektashis come to light a candle. As ever.'

Albania had been severely tyrannised from within and from without, but its most enduring quality remained tolerance, a live-and-let-live attitude that once characterised the entire Balkans. This seemed to me almost miraculous – and it has gone largely unacknowledged by outside observers.

Lazar's father had been the first person to ring the church bell in 1991, after the fall of the regime – a sound the town hadn't heard for decades – he was an atheist, but it was a question of freedom. There were two mosques in town, two Orthodox churches, three Protestant churches and one Catholic – remarkable for a place where any form of worship except Enverizm had been banned under pain of death. Though these days, Lazar was a private believer. He had grown sick and tired of dogma, he said, and in Christianity there are many doctrines, just like in Communism.

'I'm a poet,' he said. 'I need to be free. These days I'm simply a child of God.'

Lazar's grandparents had built this house, thanks to the fact that his grandfather had been a partisan. Though their old family property in town had been taken by the state, and not returned to this day.

'We're waiting for the building to fall down. You see, here there's no restitution like in other post-Communist countries. You can only repossess your property from the state when it falls into ruin. So, by the time it's yours again, it's only the land you get. Yes, it's crazy. Welcome.'

His parents were expecting us under the thick vine of the courtyard, where a long table and kilim-lined seats were set up next to the summer kitchen. In the garden grew roses and vegetables and I felt a lump in my throat – because this reminded me of the house of my great-uncle and auntie in the fertile pre-Danubian north of Bulgaria, a vanished world that had not vanished after all because it lived on here, in a land that until now had seemed 'other', a mirage of twinkling lights.

Lazar's mother had made crème-caramel, and we ate it with grapes and Turkish coffee. She was from the ancient city of Gjirokastër in the south; her father had been educated in a military academy in the Soviet Union, and posted to the northern border of Albania with his wife. Life in the north was harsh in the extreme. There were frequent clashes on the border with Montenegro: with *diversanti*, or saboteurs, the regime's term for those trying to cross the border into Yugoslavia. Killings of diversanti and soldiers were a daily event on the border in the late 1940s. But locals were protective of the family. Don't worry, local women said to them, while you're in our besa, we're answerable for you with our lives. Eventually, the family were allowed to settle here in balmy Pogradec, another border town but on a lake that was incomparably gentler. Grapes grew here, and the besa lost its edge.

We climbed onto the flat roof, which was like the floor of a yet unbuilt storey – and entered a forest of aromatic blue and white grapes. The same gnarled tree had been producing the small juicy sort known here as *bolgarka*, 'the Bulgarian', for fifty years.

'I pick them myself,' Lazar said. 'This year I expect about a hundred kilos.'

Each household made its own wine. Wine was such an integral part of domestic life that, in the old days, children were given bread soaked in wine and sugar.

'And opium drops,' Lazar said. 'To sleep better.'

Down in the garden, he kicked a concealed trapdoor under a vegetable bed. 'There's a bunker under that. Actually, there's a whole system of tunnels leading into the bunkers of the neighbours' house.' They had found the tunnels when planting the garden.

The clannish nature of traditional life in Albania had prompted the building of houses linked by small lanes and underground channels, and the Hoxha regime had capitalised on this culture of intrusion by harnessing it into a machinery for systemic surveillance that corroded communities from within, like gangrene. Every street had had its informant. Even among the children.

As a child, Lazar had successfully applied to the prestigious English Language College in Korçë, but his place had been snatched at the last moment by the son of a Party functionary. He resigned himself to learning English on his own. He was thirteen when he met two Greek girls at the drinking fountains of the old town. They were visiting relatives.

'I said: Hello. What is your name? The prettier girl said Maria, and gave me some chewing gum. I was so proud of myself!'

But chewing gum was banned as an imperialist product, and the conversation had been overheard by an older boy, the neighbourhood snitch, who reported to the local Party Committee. He'd gone to Lazar's house at once to let his parents know that their son was in trouble, without saying what the matter was, relishing the power he had – not only over children, but over parents too.

'When I went home, my parents were white as ghosts. What did the girls give you? Chewing gum, I said, but I spat it out, I didn't like it! It was imperialist chewing gum.'

In the end nothing happened, but Lazar's parents didn't sleep that night, fearing a knock on the door. Lazar's mother had been a Party member, but no one was safe. At school, there had been frequent alarms – for no specific reason, just to remind the kids that 'You should be vigilant at all times', as the slogan went.

'And whenever the alarm went off, a sinister voice accompanied it: "This is an alarm! Be alert! Be alert!"'

Lazar remembers the day in 1985 when the beginning of the end was felt by the whole nation. The day of Enver Hoxha's death was tinged with nightmarish hysteria. 'I went to school and all the teachers were crying. Classes were suspended, and a voice made an announcement on the loudspeakers: "Today, at 12:00, our dearest leader left this life." Then the wailing began. The whole school was wailing. It spread like an epidemic. My best friend was crying. So I started crying too. It felt like the world was ending.'

When he went home, his grandfather, the former border army colonel who'd been wounded during his partisan years and had a rod in his leg, consoled him: 'Don't worry my boy, our Leader is gone but our Party is strong.' But Lazar thought he caught a sardonic note in his voice. In a few years, Albania's borders would open and the long, painful 'transition', which hasn't yet ended, would begin.

'You know the funny thing?' Lazar said. 'We were asked to write a poem for our dear leader. And I did. It even rhymed!' He laughed. 'Of course it wasn't a poem, it was recycled propaganda, but you *could* say that the death of Hoxha made me into a poet.'

Later we drove over to Villa Arte, the former summer residence of the dictator at the Drilon Springs, and sipped Korçë beers by the water, Lazar busy photographing the swans, and Liridon and I gazing at the springs' mesmerising green pond. The water looked and felt cold, with a bubbling energy beneath. Amazingly, it came from Lake Prespa. It was filtered through the limestone of the Dry Mountain, that's why it was so limpid.

'The flow is seven cubic metres per second,' Liridon said. 'In Prespa, look for a place called Zaver. A karst cave where the water of Prespa is sucked into the mountain.'

Drilon Springs had a microclimate.

'Thirty degrees max. During Hoxha's visits here, giant fans were installed in the hills, to cool the air to the desired temperature. So he wouldn't be too hot.'

'The Macedonians complained that the fans were killing birds!' Lazar said. Of course, the locals had no right to complain about anything. They had no rights full stop.

The staff at the Villa had been vetted and there was a professional taster, to ensure Hoxha was not poisoned. Every year, during his month-long holidays here, the people of Pogradec would be treated to a month of Italian television's Channel One – a gesture of dictatorial munificence.

But the area around Drilon Springs was off limits to the people of Pogradec, though it was in their back yard. 'Except on 25 April each year – Border Day,' Lazar said. 'On that day, we could visit the Drilon Springs. It was full of barricades and soldiers. And cars of the Sigurimi. I didn't feel safe here.'

Ordinary Albanians were prohibited from owning private cars, so cars belonged to the Party elite and the Sigurimi. The Party elite drove a make called Aero, while a make called Gas 69 was used by the Sigurimi – and popularly known as *makina e tmerrshme*, the cars of terror. On the road between Drilon Springs and Pogradec was a complex of 'Villas' that had been used as holiday residences by Hoxha's entourage. The whole complex had been full of roses until 1991, when the gates to the Villas were opened for the first time to the public and the mob destroyed the rose gardens.

'It was sad,' Lazar said. 'Of course I understand that people were angry and fed up. But those rose gardens were beautiful.'

'Dictators like beautiful things,' Liridon smiled.

On the same day in 1991, the border with Yugoslavia was opened – for just twenty-four hours – and Lazar, aged twenty, walked with his parents to St Naum Monastery. It was an exodus, he said. Some walked all the way to Ohrid, others rode on their bikes. Their family had taken a picnic to the monastery grounds. Emotions ran so high that what was meant to be a day of happiness felt like a crisis.

'We had wanted this for so long,' Lazar said, 'that when it was actually happening, it didn't feel real. We almost couldn't cope with it.'

Then they had walked back to Pogradec, past the military barricades and armed soldiers, past the dictator's Villa, past the ravaged rose gardens.

When we stopped by the locked gates of the complex where the Villas had been, two unfriendly armed guards pointed at a sign by the gates saying that the site belonged – still – to the Ministry of Internal Affairs. An ominous silence hung over it.

The next day we set off for the monumental Illyrian tombs of Selcë, a remote part of the mountain west of the lake. Past the disused scenic railway which was supposed to be restored with a grant that never materialised, past the spooky abandoned factories up on the hills with their faded giant letters – GANIZIM, what was left of a typically meaningless slogan, *Dituri-Praktike-Organizim*, or Knowledge-Practice-Organisation – past the Chafassan border checkpoint and the Hotel Odessa fork in the road, winding up and down in low gear while the valley of the River Shkumbin opened up below.

'The lowest point of the Via Egnatia.' Liridon pointed at the faint ridge above the modern road. 'The Romans came from the west, the Turks from the east. Along the same road.'

We passed a village with a couple of mosques.

'Bektashi and Muslims,' Liridon said. 'It *was* wholly Bektashi, but at some point when Bektashism fell out of favour, people converted to Islam. Just to survive. There's still the *turbe* [tomb] of the founder here.'

His clear distinction between Sufi Bektashism and mainstream Islam surprised me.

'Bektashism was a liberalising influence in Sunni Islam,' he explained. 'A social movement. That's why it gained ground among people in the Balkans. And that's why it was persecuted by the establishment, eventually.'

This was in fact his mother's home village. Her family, before converting to mainstream Islam, had been Bektashis for generations. And before that, Christians. And before that?

'See the cliffs above the Rruga Egnatia?' Liridon said. 'There's a village there called Orakli. Named after the Cave of the Oracle nearby, an ancient pagan site. That's what there was before Christianity.' But the Cave of the Oracle had been destroyed during the rebuilding of this road, in the post-Communist years.

Later, Liridon showed me a photo of a girl with a large crucifix at her throat: his niece. Twenty-five years ago, his older brother had left home, aged fifteen, and walked to Greece in the first great exodus of Albanian men in search of work. He'd stayed in Greece, and now, under the influence of the Greek schooling system, his daughter had turned Greek Orthodox. It had far more social capital in Greece than being a Muslim Albanian.

'Nobody in the family minds,' Liridon said. Because they were the people of the vanished Cave of the Oracle and understood what it meant to go with the prevailing winds in order to survive.

As we turned our backs to the lake and continued up the mountain road, I felt we were entering a truly ancient realm.

'Yes,' Liridon said, 'this landscape is *i thyerne moshe*, broken by age. You say this of very old people but sometimes the land too. Because the land reflects the human experience.' Liridon was animated today, while Lazar was subdued – he was a lake soul, whereas Liridon was returning to his ancestral mountain.

In the hills above the road, the oak forest was an eerie rusty-red colour, no leaves, like premature winter. There had been forest fires in southern Europe all summer, and though the lake rim had been mostly spared, some forests had been quietly parched. Soon, the real climbing began, and with it – the vertigo.

Lazar and Liridon had mentioned that the old village road to the tombs was being renovated, but it wasn't until we reached what looked like a massive churned-up quarry with trucks, diggers and other heavy machinery that I grasped their meaning of 'renovation'. It was raining now, and the freshly sliced ridges of earth above were raining debris on us – rocks, stones, clumps of earth. The site was still open to private traffic – because it was the only access to the higher mountain villages – and seeing there was no turning back, I followed the trucks up the clay road, trying not to stall the engine.

Relaxed and snacking on walnuts we'd bought from a roadside stall at the lowest point in the Via Egnatia, Liridon and Lazar kept chatting as if we were on some dull motorway rather than clinging to a slippery ribbon of a track. Which in my mind made them truly Albanian. This was no country for the faint-hearted; the faint-hearted were the visitors.

We rejoined the old road which was one lane wide, passing one or two severe out-of-time villages where the stone houses were tower-like and windowless, with just slits, reminiscent of the *kullas* of the Accursed Mountains in the north where men marked by the Kanun would hide for months, years, as if buried alive, until the Furies caught up with them. Neatly stacked straw bales awaited winter, and sheep and goats grazed the hills. There was the odd church. The sprawling valley of the River Shkumbin opened up below. The coloured squares of the cultivated fields made it look like the earth was resting under a patchwork quilt.

'Praise the Lord, we made it,' Lazar said, but more out of politeness – for he hadn't looked worried at all. I was the only one with my stomach in a knot.

We abandoned the car by the roadside and took a path to a forested mound, snacking on wild sour cherries from the trees as we went. This was Selcë, or Settlement – yet another Slavic place name. Place names are barometers of changing political winds. In the 1970s, the Albanian regime had changed old Slavic place names in their campaign of 'Albanisation'. But since the fall of the regime, many had been returned to their original names. It was notable that the Albanians as a modern nation had been tolerant enough to keep at least some original Slavic names of the lake region, while next door in Greece they were systematically 'hellenised'.

A stunning series of monumental tombs made from gigantic

stone slabs lined the ridge, telling a story of the rise and fall of civilisations.

Excavations began only in 1948, but villagers had known about the tombs for hundreds of years, and by the time twentieth-century archaeologists got here they had been partially raided and locals had long used them for sheltering livestock. The most impressive tomb, Number One, was two-storey. The lower part had been found only in the 1970s by a local worker. Liridon showed us an image from that time – the giant slab that functioned as a door was still in place, closed. It had been untouched for two thousand years. Today, all the tombs were open to the elements, and unprotected from the depredations of treasure hunters.

'This is new.' Liridon kicked a broken slab lying on the floor, upset to see that the treasure hunters had been at work. 'I was here last week and it was intact.'

In the upper chamber was an indentation in the stone where the slave of the buried master had been chained, entombed and left to die of asphyxiation.

There were four tombs, each built in a different style and a different era, more than a generation apart, and their structural and decorative details told the story of the gradual decline of the Enkelana people – an Illyrian civilisation from the fourth century BC who were invaded by the army of Alexander the Great. The epic battle of 335 BC had lasted for months, and King Cleitus 'the Dardanian' of the Enkelana was holding out well until the Macedonians severed their water supply. Thus weakened, the besieged people had been overrun by the soldiers of Alexander, freshly enthroned after the murder of his father Philip the previous year, and bound for the conquest of the known world. It started with the Balkans.

One of the tombs had what Liridon described as a 'pagan cross' carved over the doorway, and the Albanian word KISHA, church. Liridon thought the tomb might have housed a makeshift church in Ottoman times. When we climbed up above the tombs to where the fortified antique town of Pelion might have been, we saw the remains of fortification walls and dwellings. It had barely been touched by archaeologists since 1950.

'After the Agrarian Reforms of the 1960s' – Liridon pushed up his glasses – 'this hill was treated not like cultural heritage, but like any other hill. It was turned into agricultural land. All the antiquities dug up by the peasants were discarded.'

He had a calm manner, but I saw him flinch as he said this.

'Liridon's pain is that he can't have this hill excavated, studied, and turned into a proper tourist sight, while in the meantime treasure hunters are destroying it,' Lazar summed up. 'And my pain is that I can't preserve old Pogradec.'

I felt their pain. In another country, Selcë would be a major site of excavation, and of cultural and rural tourism. The tombs were spectacular, the panorama of the river valley glorious, and the possibility that the remains might be from Pelion where one of the biggest battles in Alexander's Balkan campaigns was fought made this a highly significant site.

We stood at a lookout point to take in the Shkumbin valley – you could see why there had been a fort here. The visibility was 360 degrees: the Via Egnatia could have been seen, with its approaching enemy armies, caravans and pilgrims. When Cleitus had realised that all hope was lost, he burnt his own town, so as not to have it fall into the hands of the Macedonians.

Liridon handed me a small piece of brick-red ceramic he'd just picked up. It was at least two thousand years old, perhaps three, and though it felt wrong to take it, I have it still.

Lazar had a favourite hang-out in Pogradec, at the less visited end of the waterfront, where the town petered out and the rocky western coastline began. He called it The Club; it was a quiet cafe in the last house on the waterfront with tables by the beach. The customs building was visible from here, manned by two border policemen and operating boats between Albania and Macedonia

– but not for passengers, only for goods. There were no passenger boats because of the water border.

The Club sat on the last unspoilt bit of old Pogradec. We could see the thin stretch of sand that remained of Lazar's childhood beach, reclaimed by a widened road.

'We'd look up at the fortesas in the hills, the Italian ones and our ones, and when you wanted to explain distances, you said "between the second and third fortesa".' There were half a million concrete bunkers across Albania. They were difficult to destroy and remained in the landscape like eyeless witnesses to a false apocalypse.

'Anyway,' Liridon said, 'your tour with me ends here. There is an Albanian saying: Any more would be too much.'

I had one more day in Pogradec, and this was a formal release, the closure of his responsibility. It was the Albanian way: greetings and farewells felt ritualised – the idea of host and guest was still central. They had explained that while I was in Pogradec, I was their responsibility.

'That's a bit harsh,' I said. I didn't want to be anybody's responsibility.

'It's Albanian tradition,' Liridon said. 'There's an expression: my house belongs to God and to my guest.'

The Kanun was still a force, even in this lakeside town of grapes and roses.

'The Kanun had two main branches' – Liridon pushed up his glasses –'loyalty to the clan and hospitality.' If a stranger came to your house, you were obliged to take them in and look after them for as long as they wished. If something happened to your guest, you had to avenge them – starting a vendetta if necessary. Families who had the misfortune of something bad happening to their guest and failed to avenge him would be expelled by their community, their houses burnt.

'The cornerstones of the house were removed,' Liridon said, 'as a symbolic gesture of uprooting, so the family couldn't rebuild it. They were exiled because by letting misfortune strike their guest, they had brought disgrace on the community.'

If your guest was killed while on your watch, you were bound to avenge his blood by killing the murderer in turn. You still had a measure of choice whether to avenge the killing of a family member – but with a guest, there was no choice. A guest was more important to your honour than a blood relation. In these multigenerational honour murders, the gesture of murder soon becomes impersonal, detached from the man who commits it.

The Kanun represents a major archetypal aspect of the human condition: our collective death wish. It is our urge for self-destruction, masked as self-preservation. I'd much rather it had been exotic, confined to the Accursed Mountains, but instead it reminded me of our family, of many other Balkan families I knew, and more broadly – of human strife.

The Kanun was the anvil. It was the punishment for walking down the same street twice on the same day and the demand for absolute loyalty from clan members. It was the guilt, the shame, the pride, the love that maims, the projection of inner darkness by the old onto their young; the rage, the sorrow, the entombing of the spirit inside sunless towers, the adding of suffering to the family accounts already brimming with it. The Kanun made sure that repetition supplanted growth.

And all for reasons long forgotten but not forgiven. This is how we run out of goodness – when we act out of an inherited belief that we don't have the right to be at peace. As individuals, as families, as nations. That we must be constantly at war. The Kanun was the enshrinement of what Tibetan Buddhism calls *samsara*. Samsara, or the suffering-driven cycle of birth, death and rebirth, was defined by the legendary yogi Milarepa as 'a fortress of pain'. Milarepa himself had been an ancestral avenger–killer who renounced the tribal ways in favour of an individuated seeker's path.

My whole life felt like a bid to break away from the grip of my predecessors with their endless grievances, step after step, road after travelled road – as if awakening and seeing the light of the Lake for the first time.

On the bar stereo was playing the 1989 Italian pop song 'Felicità' by Al Bano and Romina Power, and all three of us hummed along to it. Italian music seemed to follow you everywhere on the Albanian side of the lake. It took me straight back to my teens full of anguish but also hope; and the splash of the lake on pebbles, the gentle, utterly un-besa-like faces of Liridon and Lazar, the very fact of being here, filled me with bitter-sweet hope: that not everything was doomed, after all. Not for as long as the Lake was here, and a few people who hadn't run out of goodness. The Lake was a constant reminder of that.

The fishermen were returning after ten hours on the water, with a haul in their nets. They would give it to their sons to sell, the boys on the road holding out whole trouts in the rain. Lazar rose to photograph them.

Albania no longer felt other to me. It felt like a lost homeland I was slowly remembering. While at first glance this side of the lake had appeared diminished, now everything was enriched with meaning.

'I'll walk you home,' Liridon said, and we walked along by the water, past the new and the old ruins, past the Hotel Enkelana, past Mr Bimbli who was writing in his ledger. We mingled with the people of Pogradec greeting each other under the chestnut trees, and the beautiful seller of corn on the cob, a woman my age, smiled at me for no special reason, revealing a dark mouth with the teeth gone, an old woman's mouth.

Because the suffering here had been fathomless, any grace that transcended the suffering had a particular beauty.

While we'd stood on the lookout point above the monumental tombs, Liridon had told us the following legend:

In the river valley below, once upon a time, there had been a village under a rocky mount called Hallmi. The mount was still there, Liridon pointed it out. Excavations had revealed the remains of a settlement, likely destroyed by an earthquake. The village was haunted by an evil bird which came out of the mount at regular intervals and cursed it. The villagers took turns to stand sentinel at the gates, and counter the bird with words of forgiveness for their village. The bird went away, until next time. But one day, a villager returned from abroad, and was chosen to stand guard. He was tired and irritable, and when the bird came out and cursed the village, he cursed it right back.

'And so magnified, the curse worked. Mount Hallmi collapsed and buried the village,' Liridon smiled, but a shadow passed over his face.

In the morning I sat on my balcony clinking the echoey spoon against the coffee mug.

Lazar and Liridon had returned from their years at university in cities with better job opportunities. They'd done it out of love for their town, for the lake and the mountain, a wish to be part of its healing. While others were busy laundering money in concrete hotels and driving Mercedes bought with money from drug and prostitution rings abroad, Lazar and Liridon were guardians of the Lake, full of forgiveness for their town.

There comes a point for us all when our inner reality, projected outwards, becomes the only reality we have.

The streaks on their faces and foreheads made them look as if they were wearing masks. Gjorg imagined how his own mourners would look when they had gouged their faces. He felt that from now on the lives of all the generations to come in the two families would be an endless funeral feast, each side playing host in turn. And each side, before leaving for the feast, would don that blood-stained mask.

Ismail Kadare, 1978

LIBERTÀ

'Up past the second fortress,' said Bashir Arapi in his Australian-accented English. 'Keep in mind that it was all forest back then. That's where I spent the last night and the last day, the 2nd and 3rd of July 1975. I had the boat with me, in a bag. Dismantled.'

He'd been sixteen years old. Looking at this bald man in an angora sweater and loafers, his heavy features, cosmopolitan manner, and countless businesses to his name, I would never have guessed that he was one of the sixteen individuals who made history as the only successful lake escapees during the Hoxha era. They were the ones mentioned by Tanas Spassé, and others: the family in a boat made in a basement, at night, without nails so as not to make hammering noises and alert the neighbours.

We had driven to the end of town, past The Club, to see the hill where the Arapi family had made their Houdini-like escape.

'Of course the moment the decision was made, we knew we were ninety-nine point nine per cent dead,' Bashir said.

A chill fog fell on the lake. A boat horn tooted as if from a past era: it sounded close to the customs house at the jetty, but I couldn't see it.

We drove back to the other end of the waterfront, to his quiet bar by the beach. We sat down with non-alcoholic drinks and he began to tell me his story.

The Arapi were an old Pogradec family, but they were marked as 'enemies of the people' the moment in 1949 when Bashir's grandfather had walked over the Dry Mountain, down Mean

Valley and into St Naum Monastery. After staying with relatives in Ohrid, he sailed to Australia. Back here, his wife and young sons were interned in a detention camp as 'enemies of the people', like Tanas Spassé's family. They eventually returned to Pogradec, but the stigma remained, ensuring that one of the sons, Fatos – seven years old when his father escaped – had an early taste of injustice, but also the secret joy of his father's escape.

In early photos, Fatos Arapi is a skinny, narrow-faced, blue-eyed boy; in later photos, he has a charmer's smile and a rakish fag in his mouth. He married at seventeen, still childlike on his bike and without his bride's family's approval, for he was the son of an 'enemy'. His bride came from another old Pogradec family, but they were quick to disown her completely, out of fear of being associated with 'enemies'. She moved, symbolically, to the other side of the river, and never saw her family again, or if she did, they wouldn't speak to her. Terror had assumed more power in people's minds even than clan loyalty – a true accomplishment of tyranny in a clan-based culture. Looking at photos of the couple, where she appears with the heavy features that Bashir would inherit, her fair hair braided into Heidi-like plaits, I am struck by the fact that not once is she photographed smiling, as if by the time Bashir was born, she was already regretting taking this extraordinarily diffi-cult road. For Fatos was no ordinary man.

In Hoxha's era, you became a political prisoner for any number of trumped-up reasons – from annoying your neighbour who could fabricate the right lie about you, to falling out with a friend who might be an informer, to listening to foreign radio stations; or, in the case of a relative of Lazar's who did ten years in a labour camp, for saying that Yugoslav-made socks were better. Although Fatos's first sentence (at the age of nineteen) was short – nine months, during which Bashir's sister was born – within a year he was re-arrested, this time on a serious charge: planning to escape by boat. His best friend had turned out to be an informer, and it was immaterial that the 'plan' was fictitious. Once a charge against you was uttered, it became true, and Fatos was sentenced to thirteen years' hard labour. He did ten of those, the last four at Spaç, the prison of the one-thousand-seven-hundred-year sentence.

Bashir and his sister grew up without a father. An indelible childhood memory is visiting Dad in Spaç – after a three-day journey by bus, foot and lorry into the bleak mountains, they would be granted an hour with Dad, though the guards reserved the right to refuse access to a prisoner, depending on their mood.

'Those mountain passes were like hell,' Bashir said.

There is a haunting oil portrait of Fatos unshaven, bruised around the eyes but with his mouth set in determination, against an Arabian-blue background, as if the Lake was peeking over his shoulder even in prison. It was painted in 1966 by a fellow inmate, clearly a professional artist, on a piece of fabric torn from a prison shirt.

After the ten years of forced labour, he returned home but new obstacles were put in his way. A qualified welder, he was employed in a nickel factory above the lake – one of today's ruins – but when he offered to build a crane to make life easier for the workers, the factory director fired him for being too clever. Enverizm was based on making life as difficult as possible, and keeping people as passive as sheep. Fatos was out of work. The only money father and son could make was by chopping trees in the hills and selling them as logs. Which was, of course, illegal.

'I was fifteen and I said to Dad, Why don't we escape? This is so unfair! And he slapped me. He said Don't ever say that in the street or we'll land another ten years in Spaç. Say only nice things about our country.'

One day, a telegram arrived from a cousin in Ohrid. It had taken months to reach them by the time the censors at both ends had checked it. There's a parcel to pick up, it said. Bashir and his grandmother went to the post office where a parcel was waiting for them, with wondrous items in it: silk stockings, seashell necklaces, gifts from the family in Ohrid. The customs fee, however, was equal to six months' pay and they couldn't afford to pick up the parcel, which was left for the customs officers' wives to enjoy. But they read the subtext behind the parcel: Fatos's father was in Ohrid, over from Australia, and this was a message from him that they must try to cross the border, sooner rather than later.

In fact the family had already made one attempt a couple of years earlier – they had started walking over the Dry Mountain one foggy night (with their three children), but the fog had unexpectedly lifted and they'd had to turn back. Now Fatos snapped into action. The decision was taken overnight with his wife and his two brothers (but not their wives).

'They said: It's time to go. There's no life here.'

The building of the boat began in a basement, with a stolen tent that would cover the precarious rudimentary wooden skeleton held together not by nails but by rope, wire, glue and nylon stockings.

'Mum stitched the canvas that went on top,' Bashir said. 'We built the boat in nine nights.'

When it was done, they dismantled it, put it into bags, and carried the bags at midnight up to the top of the hill, past the second bunker. Bashir was to guard the boat.

'That night and the following day, I had no food or water. But I was fine. I was excited.'

On the evening of 3 July, the fifteen other members of the family began to arrive, all from different directions, so as not to attract attention. A lie was involved too: Fatos's two brothers hadn't told their wives about what was to happen, for fear that someone would let something slip; they could not afford doubt and fear to sink the three families before they'd had their chance at rowing to freedom. Instead, the two wives were told they were off to a wedding that evening, and wore their best clothes. When they arrived at the top of the hill – God knows how they walked in their high heels – their shock must have been profound, and their terror too, but there was no turning back.

There were several children and a baby in the 'wedding' party. The task of making it to the lake shore, reassembling the boat and rowing across the lake under the sweep of searchlights and under the nose of customs patrol, border army patrol and Hoxha himself, who was staying at his summer residence at the time, was still ahead of them. It was an act so daring as to be almost insane.

'Either by boat or by the government, we knew we were ninety-nine point nine per cent dead.'

But one crucial thing was in their favour that night. Fatos had observed the movements of the border army units for years, and he'd noticed that during the dictator's holiday sojourns, all security was focused on the Villa. As a result, the army units in town were reduced. Furthermore, the giant projector lights that swept the lake's surface every two to three hours were reduced to only once a night – because their reflection from the surface of the lake onto the Villa disturbed Hoxha and his entourage.

'By midnight, the boat was ready. Me and my dad and uncles carried it down the hill, and took shelter in the reeds.'

After their escape, the enraged authorities eradicated all the reeds and cut down the trees on the hill. At the last moment, when the women and kids were making their way down the hill and across the coastal road, the baby cried: two men on bikes overheard them and stopped to ask where they were going at this late hour. A tense exchange took place, during which Bashir and his father and uncles, hidden in the reeds, had considered attacking the two men or even killing them and concealing their bodies there, but miraculously, disaster was averted when the women persuaded the cyclists that they were Gypsies out late gathering wood.

All sixteen of them were now in the fragile boat, tightly packed, no room to move, and Bashir and one of his uncles started rowing. The boat was untested. It could have disintegrated at any moment.

It took them eight hours.

'It looks close in a straight line,' Bashir said. 'But we had to row out as far away from the Albanian shore as possible, because we didn't know when the searchlight would sweep the lake.'

If caught by the border army, they would not only be imprisoned for life – the men probably executed – they'd be tortured first. The children would be sent to dire orphanages and 'correction homes'. Nobody would be spared. At one point, one of the kids, infected with the collective dread, started howling. She couldn't be consoled, it was a physical reaction. And of course sound carries with preternatural clarity over the lake. Her mother tried in vain to stifle her cries.

'Throw her overboard,' her father said to his wife. 'Or we all die.'

There was a moment of agony, then Fatos said:

'No. We die together or we live together. We don't get separated.'

Somehow, the girl stopped crying. The lake was kind to them that night.

'And that's how we did it,' Bashir leaned back in his chair and grinned.

I leaned back in my chair too. I felt exhausted.

'We arrived at St Naum Monastery drenched.'

A local saw them, and realising where they had come from, fetched an Albanian-speaker from the Village of Mean People. The two locals, awed by the family's courage, offered them a lift in their vans all the way to Slovenia – the northernmost republic of Yugoslavia. But the family wanted to see their relatives in Ohrid and report to the Yugoslav police – do it legitimately at this end, at least, not hide like criminals.

'We stayed in Ohrid for a few weeks. My dad and uncles were kept in custody for three weeks. The women and us kids were put up in some wagons in a lakeside camping ground. The women were crying every day. We didn't know what was happening. Maybe they were torturing the men?'

They were given meals at the nearest hotel. Holidaymakers and waiters stared at them in awe. Word of their escape spread.

'We made the Yugoslav news. The first and last family to escape Albania by boat.'

Not only that, but a newspaper published the date of their escape each year, as a commemoration – and a propaganda coup against Albania. Hoxha had isolated his country from the whole world. The boat is now on display in a national museum. Eventually, the Arapis left Yugoslav soil and flew to Australia, where Grandad was waiting for them. But since 1949 Grandad had only just made ends meet, and was not able to offer a base to his family, or even a loan.

A new chapter began for the Arapi family in Sydney, and this time the star was not Fatos, but Bashir. Sixteen years old and without a word of English, he started as a labourer in a foundry. Ten years later, he was the owner of a thriving textile factory, and a millionaire. He did it on nothing but wits and chutzpah, through what can only be described as entrepreneurial genius. And he had his father's desperate drive for freedom, self-fulfilment, and the courage to struggle against impossible odds. After all, what did he have to lose?

'In Pogradec while Dad was in jail, no one talked to us. Mum had no work. We were watched all the time. We were pariahs. But I figured how to make a few pennies.'

The family had had a vegetable patch and grew onions. Bashir had sold them in the morning, and in the evening went into the hills to gather wood. Having begged one of his uncles to give him a mule for the logs, he had sold the donkey to his father's friends during the night (because it was illegal) and continued carrying the logs on his back. He also sold apples from their garden to the Young Pioneers camp near the elite Villas. The same Pioneers camp where young Tanas and his brother had collected dry bread.

Albanian men in Australia, he said, married women from the Greek, Italian or Turkish diaspora. That must have been because

most of the Albanians *were* men – solo exiles like Bashir's grandfather, some of whom had left their families behind, to mop up
the mess for one thousand seven hundred years.

'I came back to the lake in the 1980s and stayed in Ohrid.
That's where I met my wife. She is from an Albanian family who
escaped to Yugoslavia in 1948.' During that visit, Bashir went to
St Naum Monastery and looked at his hometown of Pogradec
through binoculars. It was the closest he could get. The end of
the Hoxha regime was nowhere in sight.

There was something so extreme about the Albanian agony
that it made me think of ancient tragedies, of a black-clad female
chorus intoning 'Ninety-nine point nine per cent dead'.

I kept scrutinising photographs from the war, in which Enver
Hoxha appears as a chubby thirty-year-old partisan, and looking for signs of incipient monstrosity in his expression, but all I
could find were plump features and a small, greedy mouth. In one
photo, he reclines on the grass with fellow partisans and British
mission officers, smiling benignly. And yet, within months of this
photo, Hoxha would turn against his British allies in a Machia-
vellian volte-face. Already the Communists were bitter enemies
of the Albanian National Front, Balli Kombëtar. The British war
government, with Cairo as its regional base, turned a blind eye to
local politics and kept dropping ample arms supplies for the Albanian resistance, meant for both the Balli Kombëtar and the Communists – but it was the latter who benefited from the supplies.

Hoxha's partisans became the best-armed movement in
the country, and began murdering their way across villages and
towns, taking brutal reprisals on the civilian population where
'Ballists' might have been sheltered. The Ballists did the same, but
lost what had effectively become a civil war. At the end of the
war, under the orders of Hoxha, all non-Communist resistance
fighters and all fighters associated with the British mission were
rounded up, tortured or executed – including the translators and
other staff who had worked alongside the British mission for the

liberation of Albania. Many fled the country. The Communist Sigurimi would end up torturing poets, intellectuals, ordinary people, anyone who was an individual.

In the light of this history, it leaves a bitter taste to know that there are hundreds, perhaps thousands, of graves of young resistance fighters across the country, mixed with the bones of Italian soldiers abandoned by their own command, post-surrender, to starve to death by the roadside, be taken in by locals, or be executed by their own units. And it puts into context the fate of the Arapi family.

Everybody's fate was extreme in a time of extremes. But very few gambled their lives and the lives of their children for freedom.

Hoxha had borrowed from the Kanun even as he outlawed the Kanun. The contempt for the individual, the crushing power of a faceless authority (Hoxha recorded his statements, to be played in halls packed with terrified people), the futility of resistance, the ritual bloodletting, the premature burials, doomed births and poisoned families – all of that was played out during the long decades of Enverizm.

Fatos and his family stood up to the force that could issue sentences one thousand seven hundred years long, and simply said: No.

It was late in Bashir's bar. People kept coming up to greet him. It was a homely place, a hub for town parties, family gatherings, charity events. Fatos had died ten years ago of a heart attack, here in Pogradec, at the age of sixty. He never did get up to much, work-wise, either in Australia or back here once the family returned. As if once the mission of his life – freedom – was fulfilled, there was nothing left for him to do.

'He said, I worked myself to death in jail. I'm done working,' Bashir said. 'His last words were How quickly a man dies!' Bashir's eyes filled with tears. 'I miss him.'

But at least Fatos had lived to see his country open up, raise itself from the ashes. Fatos had returned from Australia in 1991, the moment he'd heard that the Albanian border was opening.

'He was first in the border queue at St Naum. But they didn't let him in. Because he was still blacklisted. He had to wait for a year to get in.'

Why did *you* return? I asked Bashir.

'Yeah,' he grinned. A familiar question. 'Everybody wanted to leave, and we were coming back!'

Seeing Pogradec again had shocked Bashir.

'Everything was devastated. No trees on the hills. Empty shops. Even Korçë beer tasted vile. I ordered a truckload of Coke and good beer to be brought to Pogradec. For people to enjoy, for free.'

Bashir struck me as a man obsessed with figures. He kept listing the global brands that his business represented, the areas in which 'we are number one'. Modest in his personal habits, he was addicted to profit. I also wondered whether at the root of his admiration for his father was Fatos's incorruptibility – his life had not been spent under the dollar sign but under the sign of freedom. A poor, harsh, admirable life.

But there was something exceptional about Bashir too. He was a man who had started with nothing and built an empire. And he was a man who had returned to his eviscerated homeland when it would have been much easier to stay on and enjoy the sweet life at Bondi Beach.

'You ask me why I came back,' he said. 'I was looking for a part of myself that I couldn't find in Australia. I grew up without a dad. And Dad grew up without a dad. There was a part missing.'

The night of their escape from Pogradec, Fatos had written on the wall of their living room: 'I'm not leaving my country because I don't love it, but because I can't tolerate the system.'

And Grandad, the one who'd done the first runner?

'In 1992, when I decided to return to Albania and said to him Come with me, he said "I'm only going back to that country in a coffin." He died two weeks later. That's how we brought him home – in a coffin.'

We said goodbye. I was due to travel to Prespa the next day and I slept fitfully, hearing the water splash as if under my boat-bed, though in the morning the lake was still as a mirror.

The black dog and the white dog were running along the waterline and the first fishing boats were already vanishing from view. Mr Bimbli, writing something in his logbook, nodded at me from his table.

On my way past the Drilon Springs, I spotted Eduard at his post along the main street. His van was festooned with the same bright rugs. Eduard and his wife wove them at home. After catching up over coffee, we got into an argument over the price of a large red one that I wanted to buy, pure wool. His special price for friends was so preposterously low that I refused to buy it, and eventually we settled on a price that was less of a give-away but still too cheap. Too much money, he said. This generosity explained, in part, why Eduard was selling carpets instead of running his own bar.

Eduard's story was revealing of the country Albania had become since the fall of the Hoxha regime. Like Fatos, he was forgiving of his homeland, though the reality was stamped on his face, and the reality was that if you insisted on doing honest business here, you were 99.9 per cent dead. Eduard had survived, but only just. He had in fact been the first person in the region to obtain a licence to start a private business, in 1990. He had been a grocer until then – by 1990, our shops were completely empty, he said. In 1991, as soon as the border opened, he crossed into Macedonia, paired up with a guy in Ohrid, and during harvest season they brought back a truckload of apples.

'People in Pogradec were stunned. They couldn't believe that something was actually coming into the country and being sold. That's how I started.'

Business was going well until 'the catastrophe' of 1997 – which is how people referred to the collapse of the financial pyramids in whose wake warehouses were robbed, including Eduard's own store – he lost crates of wine, hundreds of kilos of coffee. Law and order was replaced by teenagers with machine-guns. Shooting could be heard day and night. Parents locked their children in at home for months.

'Everything was destroyed. Hotels, restaurants and shops were gutted. Even the electricity wires were taken. Two boys in Pogradec electrocuted themselves while stealing wires. But we didn't care about the money we'd lost. We just wanted to keep the kids alive. Those were bread and salt days.'

An Albanian expression.

It had been difficult to resume business in the wake of the catastrophe. It was like starting from ground zero. Again. And in the last few years, Eduard had turned to carpets. Clearly, the carpets weren't selling. But apples were worse. There was a problem of overproduction, as imports from Macedonia, Greece and Italy displaced and devalued local produce. The fertile area between Korçë and here yields an overabundance of top-quality vegetables and fruit, everything from juicy onions to giant pumpkins, but because of greedy governmental policies on imports, tons of local produce are discarded every week. Simply thrown away. In this land of vines, grapes are imported from Italy.

'In Albania, we are used to hoping. Hope is what we have,' Eduard shrugged.

His words were interrupted by a bad smoker's cough.

'Come back next year! Do you have a jumper for Prespa? Prespa and Ohrid have different climates. When we have sunshine, in Prespa they have blizzards.'

Strange, how saying goodbye to Bashir who had an empire had been fine, but saying goodbye to Eduard who had only his carpets was a wrench. I was also slightly apprehensive of leaving the Lake of Light where I now had friends, and going to Prespa where I knew nobody.

He bent down to my driver's window. 'I don't know if I'll see you again. Life gets shorter every day. Be kind to people. Just be kind.'

Something about Eduard's smile broke your heart. It was a smile of the Lake, endlessly forgiving. Like Lazar and Liridon, Eduard was a decent person who bucked the trend by not selling out or giving up, in a land where 'the system' never quite ceased to work against you, one way or another. As each system stridently rejected its predecessor, it quietly borrowed its methods. Though you love your country, one day you may find that the system *is* your country.

Albania was a land kinder to the dead than to the living, though I'd fallen in love with it in less than a week. There was something uncynical about the people I met, an old-fashioned quality. It's easy to become a cynic, but what are we without kindness? Ninety-nine point nine per cent dead.

An empty lakeside restaurant was playing the 1987 Italian pop hit 'Libertà'. Like 'Felicità', it was forever linked in my mind to my teens when I'd sing along to it on the radio. Then the Berlin Wall fell.

'Freedom, tears are cried in your name. Without you, we are so alone.'

Forty years after the Arapis' escape, you still couldn't legally cross the short stretch of water between here and Naum Monastery.

I waved from my open window as I drove over the potholes up to the checkpoint, the carpet rolled up next to me, the Lake ablaze with light, and Eduard waved too – until both of us disappeared from view and only the Lake remained.

Lake Prespa and Little Prespa

Age: 1–3 million years

Depth: maximum 55m (Prespa), 8.4m (Little Prespa);
average 18m and 4.1m

Altitude: 850m

Highest peak in the area: Baba-Pelister Mountains, 2,601m

Catchment area: 2,029 km2 (Prespa); 189 km2 (Little Prespa)

Islands: Golem Grad (North Macedonia), Mali Grad (Albania),
St Achillius and Vidronissi (Greece)

First known name: Prespa (Vale of Snow)

VALE OF GHOSTS

Although the two lakes are only five kilometres apart as the pelican flies, it took an hour to drive over Galicica. As luminous Lake Ohrid waned, dark Prespa waxed.

Prespa wore a necklace of mountains only visible in their full diamantine majesty from the air. I could glimpse it only from the top of the road. Leaving limestone Galicica behind, I faced Baba-Pelister peak at 2,601 metres. To the north was Petrina (Stone) Mountain at 1,663, a sister mountain to Galicica, where Edward Lear passed on his way west. At the mountain pass, he came across a solitary guard-house with two armed Albanians and 'an irritable dog', ostensibly there to make sure travellers weren't attacked by bandits. Like me, he was travelling in September, and like everyone who passed through here and wrote about it he experienced a coup de foudre when he caught sight of Prespa, which appeared to him like a work of art — framed by forests in rich autumnal colours, a scene 'difficult to leave'. He returned from his base in Ohrid to spend a day painting it. He sat up there, flooded with memories of earlier travels; his seemed to be an endless journey towards an unknown destination.

Prespa, which means 'snowdrift' or 'vale of snow' in Slavic, felt to travellers far more remote than Ohrid, and still does.

'Soothing and beautiful is that vision of the Lake of Peupli,' Lear wrote, 'so dreamy and delicately azure, as it lies below ranges of finely-formed mountains, all distinct, though lessening and becoming more faint.'

There is a curious inaccuracy here: Peupli (today Lefkonas) is a village on Little Prespa through which he didn't pass. His map shows Prespa and Little Prespa ('Peupli') as tiny droplets next to a large Ohrid, though their actual sizes are not dissimilar. Lear relied on his dragoman for orientation. This tells me that not only were there no maps of the lake region available, but that the few maps that existed were wildly off the mark. The Ottoman Empire was as laissez-faire about cartography as it was about roads, and the cartographically gifted British Empire had no special awareness of the Balkans, yet. One of the first maps to show Prespa is the Mercator of 1589, which bizarrely showed a non-existent Prespa River flowing from a nameless lake. The same errors were copied in a map a century later.

Prespa had a way of remaining invisible, unknowable, almost unreal.

Lear's travelogue also tells a lot about Lear. He made little contact with locals except the occasional grandee – a basic exchange would have given him the name of the lake, for example. To him humans were merely an extension of the eternal landscape, and all his senses were occupied by the visual feast unfolding around him. Edith Durham, by contrast, had the advantage of speaking Albanian, and saw the landscape as layered with human narratives.

'Ploughing was in full swing,' Durham writes, between the two lakes, 'and in some fields the young green corn was already sprouting and promising food for the hungry land, and the big lake' – that's Prespa – 'was extraordinarily beautiful in the morning light. Ochrida [sic] is magnificent, but Presba [sic] is faery-like in its loveliness. My comrades held out hopes of a han' – a *han* was a roadside inn – 'and a possible fire, where we should rest and refresh at midday, but we arrived only to find it had been burnt down during the late insurrection, and a party of Albanian soldiers encamped in the ruins, as lonesome, melancholy, and comfortless as any Bulgarian refugees . . . No fire, no shelter, frozen ground, and a bitter wind.'

She was here in the wake of the 1903 Ilinden Uprising. By contrast, Evliya Çelebi, that great seventeenth-century voluptuary, came swanning along at a time of peace, when the Prespa basin was one of the prosperous corners of the Balkans. So seduced was he by the views, the spring water, the huge gardens and the flocks of sheep that his party stopped, set up camp in the woods, and for a week gorged on cherries, honey, wine and milk. They were true Oriental decadents, just as Lear, Durham and Fraser were true to the British pioneering spirit, revelling in privation. Durham gnawed charred lambs' heads and drank rough home brews, and Lear lived on rice and tea. Evliya would have been horrified.

But these vividly distinct writers on the lakes had one thing in common: the knowledge that they were from the ruling race ('race' was a fashionable word in the days of Durham, Fraser and Brailsford), that their people ran half the world, that the governments in their great capitals called the shots even here, among these 'savages' — as Durham refers to the peasants of Macedonia and Albania, even as she dedicates herself to helping them. In moments of crippling rheumatic pain from sleeping rough, thoughts of the British Empire 'cheered' her (and why wouldn't they?). And Evliya travelled across the Balkans as a favourite of a sultan who owned all the peoples of these lands, collectively called by Evliya *gyiaurs*, infidels. Each foreign traveller, furthermore, adopted a pet nation that they favoured disproportionately over the rest: Durham was a devoted Albanist and campaigned for their national cause. Rebecca West was passionate about the passionate Serbs. Fraser and Brailsford admired the Bulgarians as the most industrious, and on it went. A curiously irradiating effect that hasn't worn off with time, and leaves few who pass through here unaffected. The landscape has something to do with this, I think.

Until the Balkan Wars of 1912–13, Lake Prespa had never known borders. The members of the postwar Commission who

rode around the lake in a carriage to determine the new borders
would arrive in a village square and toss coins at the kids, then
listen to what language they spoke as they fought over the coins.
The overwhelming majority, including the Muslims, spoke a
dialect closest to Bulgarian. Even so, a three-way border sliced
up the lakes. In the 1920s, Greece ceded the western piece of its
Prespa pie to Albania, but held on to Little (Mikri) Prespa and
a corner of big Prespa with a lone fishing village called Nivitsi,
renamed Psarades.

To this day, straightforward circumnavigation of the lake is
impossible: a quick look at the map told me that. Or rather the
maps. I was wrestling with maps of bafflingly poor quality. No
national map included the lake territory next door. The lakes
appeared in blue slices, with only the national chunk offering
information, while the rest were blank, apparently gobbled up
by their neighbours and featuring no place names – sometimes
not even the rest of the lake! The hikers' map of the Galicica
and Pelister National Parks included nothing at all outside their
topographic remit, and their glossy Greek Prespa National Park
counterparts blanked out the rest of the lake, as if no people or
even landscape existed beyond the national boundary. In recent
years, vital trans-boundary projects for the preservation of the
lakes' biosphere have been started, and *all* of the Prespa basin
is effectively a protected wetland of international importance
because of bird migration routes and the very numerous endemic
species.

But whether as a traveller or a local, you still couldn't get a
map of the lake district as a complete realm. Maps tell stories, and
the fact that in the twenty-first century no such maps are sold,
while each local economy is desperate for visitors, told a story. A
story of petty ignorance, of wilful blindness to the bigger picture
so magnificently embodied by the lakes. Furthermore, although
Prespa flowed into Ohrid in the most vital way, their people didn't
mix. The mountain was no barrier to underground rivers, but it

was to humans. Even the two water-monitoring stations operated separately. Ohrid was a little afraid of Prespa because Prespa
was high and wild. Its most numerous inhabitants were birds, its
terrain was rough, its histories untold, its water opaque, its border
checkpoints sensitive.

I felt it before I reached the lake: there was something eerie
about this vale. It was a cold, silvery world. Unlike Ohrid, Prespa
was irregular-shaped, jagged with rocky peninsulas and islands, so
that distant peaks appeared and vanished and reappeared as something else.

A forest of juniper and oak lined the steep road, ringing with
orchestral birdsong. I passed only one other car, loaded with bags
of bruised apples – fodder for animals. The mountain road was
poorly maintained and rock debris had not been cleared by the
rangers of the Galicica National Park on the Ohrid side, who
collected a fee from drivers entering the Park while they themselves sat smoking all day in their kiosk. On the Prespa side of the
mountains, men with saddled horses were stacking logs along the
road. Logging was one of very few jobs left for Prespans. When
I came down to lake level, I drove over fallen apples and their
fragrance filled the air. The whole of upper Prespa was lined with
apple orchards.

Prespa had had three peaks of activity in its human history. At
the turn of the first millennium AD, the Romans arrived and built
towns, military stations and holiday villas on the fertile north-east
shore of the lake. In the late tenth century, Prespa became the
seat of the Bulgarian Empire of Tsar Samuil, terminated by a
Byzantine rival. And in the late twentieth century, Prespa became
a destination for Yugo-holidays.

Bird flocks crossed the sky in patterns that mirrored the swirls
on the lake's surface. The silence was so complete, I could hear
the flap of wings above. I was discovering Prespa in one of its
quiet centuries. There were no towns on Prespa, only villages.
The banks were green with poplars and elms, juniper, pine and

oak. Dotted in the rampant growth were ruins from the latest expired civilisation: the disused camping sites, workers' sanatoriums, Pioneers' hotels, and broken playgrounds of state-organised recreation.

Stenje was the first lake village you reached via this road and the last before the nearby Albanian border checkpoint, and this is where I found the only open hotel in the vicinity. Stenje was backed by the flanks of Galicica and bookended by a cliff. Typically, its name was meaningful in several languages: in Bulgarian and Macedonian *stena* is 'wall', in Greek *sten* is 'narrow', and in Serbo-Croatian-Bosnian *stena* or *stjena* means 'rock'.

The small hotel by the beach didn't have a name. The restaurant on the terrace played 1980s Yugo-pop incessantly. A wide beach led to the reedbeds. Parties of pelicans, cormorants, ducks and swallows bobbed on the surface, morning and evening. Seagulls and dogs rummaged in over-full rubbish bins.

'You know there's something wrong with a country when rubbish doesn't get collected,' said Tsape archly. He was the waiter in white shirt and black trousers, with a sleep-deprived face, and eyes that were watering with fatigue as if involuntarily weeping. Tsape wasn't his real name.

'In 1992 when the border opened and people started coming across looking for work, some guys called me Tsape. *Tsape* is goat in Albanian. The name stuck.'

Tsape drove a Zastava from the 1980s – the symbolic car of Yugoslavia. The hotel was a time trap. Framed on the walls were faded promotional tourist posters – a couple with 1980s hair and beige clothes smiling in a vale of snow; a 1970s man on water skis. The owner was surprised when I took a room for a week, and so was I.

His was the only hotel in Prespa that stayed open all year.

'So we have somewhere to meet and watch TV,' he said. 'The winters are long here. Just snowdrifts and howling wind.'

The owner was also the head waiter, and his wife did the cleaning when she wasn't working at the small textile factory nearby. Tsape too did night shifts at the factory, as night watchman. It was the only surviving enterprise.

'My job is to stay awake from midnight till dawn,' he said.

He made me feel like a regular customer, not a stranger. He'd joined me at an outside table in a rare quiet moment. Despite it being end of season, he was run off his feet. But why night watchman? Surely there wasn't much crime here – there were hardly any people left.

'After Hotel Europa burnt down, nobody feels safe,' he said.

Hotel Europa was the large burnt-out shell a few miles up the shore. Even from a distance it looked like a set from a horror film.

'Don't go there alone,' Tsape said emphatically.

He had been a construction worker in the early 1980s when it was built. Its first name had been Hotel Yugoslavia, and it had been used as a gated complex for privileged families, including staff of the Ministry of Internal Affairs. In winter, the complex would turn into a private hunting lodge for the Communist Party elite. Boar, deer, ducks.

'And in the 1990s, the new oligarchy moved in,' Tsape said.

Now nobody hunted, except poachers from the Albanian side who came over and used illegal snares. But Tsape and the rest were forgiving of their neighbours' petty crimes because the Albanian side of the lake was barren, just like Hoxha's regime.

'They've been through hell,' Tsape said.

'They're long-suffering people,' agreed the owner.

Besides, there were bigger crimes on this side, like the burning of Hotel Europa. Some believed the arson to be the work of the owners, but there were other, more outlandish theories involving curses. Prespa was an outlandish kind of place.

Of course, I ignored Tsape's advice and went to see Hotel Yugoslavia for myself.

It was accessed through a concrete arch of linked hands sculpted in Communist-brutalist style to hold the sphere of the Earth. A driveway overgrown with weeds led to once glamorous terraced grounds that now bristled with snakes. Only a hundred metres away from my car, I felt as if invisible shapes were approaching me from all sides. The impression was so vivid, I very nearly turned back and ran to the car.

The fire had started in the restaurant. The complex was similar to other derelict Communist-era sites I'd visited: though its demise had happened in time of peace – 2004 – it felt like a war ruin. The forest had moved in. Families of rats squeaked in corners. I climbed the carcass of the building with a metallic taste in my mouth, crunching over broken glass, steel and concrete. The lake was a shock of serenity through the building's gaping wounds. The rooms were gutted. Rubbish and graffiti everywhere: WHO ARE YOU-GOSLAVIA?

In one room, a dirty blanket in a corner looked momentarily like a covered body. When a crunching noise came from above, as if someone was walking over broken glass one floor up – but there were no other parked cars – my nerves gave out and I rushed down the broken stairs, got into the car and sped back out of the driveway and through the concrete hands holding the crumbling Earth.

A few hundred metres from the ruined complex, in a sparse pine forest, was a sanatorium for respiratory diseases whose buildings looked derelict with their broken windows and rust – until I was startled by people shuffling about in flannel gowns and rubber slippers among the pine trees and broken benches.

But what really spooked me was that they didn't appear to see me. As if I weren't fully here. As if I were a ghostly visitor from another time.

The sanatorium, Tsape told me later, hadn't stopped accepting patients since it opened. 'Because illness doesn't stop,' he said, and coughed through his cigarette smoke, laughing – a future patient of the sanatorium. In a stroke of metonymic felicity, the name of the sanatorium and of the whole area was Oteshevo, possibly meaning Consolation. It was in a quiet new hotel in Oteshevo, near the sanatorium, that the Greek and Macedonian prime ministers would come for lunch after signing the Prespa Agreement the following summer. To console themselves, knowing the road ahead would be bumpy.

Tsape leaned over the table and lowered his voice, though there was just me, him and the amiable hook-nosed old cook sitting in the flicker of the outside lights, while a gust of cold wind rose from the lake and blew sand our way.

'When we worked on the buildings for the Ministry and demolished the old ones . . .'

The old buildings had housed political prisoners, who were of 'bourgeois' origins, or Bulgarian-identifying, or other types of 'enemy of the Yugoslav people'. In 1948, they had been taken to Golem Grad island to hack rocks from the cliffs, with which they made the first buildings meant for recreation.

'And the road by which you came from Ohrid,' said the cook, 'they built that road too.'

'One day during the demolition' – Tsape cleared his throat – 'we found the remains of a man inside a wall. A skeleton in boots.'

The cook's face confirmed it.

'They had cemented him in,' Tsape said.

Alive?

He raised his eyebrows. His face did have something of the goat about it.

In Balkan lore, walling in someone's shadow – or living body – is meant to strengthen a building's foundations, but this episode had the flavour of a political execution. The story of that man remains untold, but what is certain is that Yugoslav apparatchiks had come to holiday with their families where political prisoners' mouths had been filled with quicklime. Apparatchiks like

Tanas Spassé's father: victims of one cruel regime, beneficiaries of another.

'Some say that when the construction work was done, the prisoners were taken to Golem Grad island, shot, and pushed into a big hole,' the old cook said.

But the bodies had never been found.

Throughout the day and later when lake and sky went pink, then charcoal, then disappeared from view, when the wind blew sand into our coffee cups and the phantom of Hotel Europa loomed white in the coastal darkness, locals came and went at the nameless hotel for gossip and a tipple.

There was a fat entrepreneur with shifty eyes who exported tobacco grown in the Pelagonian plains to the east and who was a living relic from centuries of fortunes and misfortunes made from tobacco, the Oriental sort known as 'aromatic gold' and once exported to all the corners of the earth. There were the odd German, French or Dutch campers or cyclists who would walk to where the cliffs brought an abrupt end to the beach and the road, open a map, and surrender by staying the night.

There was the cheerful taxi-driver Dervishevski whose surname went back to a story of two brothers murdering a dervish and escaping revenge by coming to the lake. He specialised in driving ill people from remote villages to the regional hospital, an oversized crucifix hanging from his dashboard. He told me of his healing powers, which he'd acquired through a lake stone that had special properties.

'Feel the energy' – he placed his hand on my forearm. He was convinced that the lake's healing energy permeated certain stones. He was rotund yet firm, so that when he ran, his flesh didn't shake, as if it were full of silicon.

'It's the stone', he said. 'It reverses your biological age.'

For years, he had been plagued by rage against a 'businessman' who had cheated him of his savings. His life's savings. 'But when

I found the stone,' he said, 'the rage began to melt away. Now I'm free. I realised how crazy I'd been. I'd been blessed by the lake all along.'

Next to the hotel stood three houses – the owner, an emigrant to Australia, had built them for his sons, identical so they wouldn't bicker.

'But the sons don't come,' said Tsape.

'Life is pretty quiet here. It's true that the few tourists who come are poor, but we see the lake every day, instead of seeing dollar-signs like Ohridians,' said a small friendly man who was the textile factory manager. 'Still, the shortage of women is a problem. Are you married?'

He invited me to his table for a coffee and said: 'I knew you were one of us before you spoke.'

Because 'our' people are easily recognised, he said, by three things: *torbeto, chorapeto, muabeto* – a sweet folk expression that puts three archaic Turkish words into the diminutive Macedonian form. It meant your wee bag, your wee socks and your wee chat; and by 'our people' – 'You know what I mean,' he said. 'We're all the same people in these parts. It's just that wicked politicians keep trying to divide us.'

'There are many mysteries in Prespa,' he went on. 'For instance, I saw giant human bones in a tomb on Golem Grad island when they dug them up. The shin bones and jaws were huge. A race of giants.'

I heard this from others too. But the most likely owners of the giant skeletons were island-dwelling monks, the last of whom was spotted on the island in the late 1930s. Unless it was the political prisoners.

One evening, I shared fried fish – *belvitsa*, a kind of bleak – with a squat, bespectacled customs officer from the nearby check-point who was skiving off his night shift. His name was Nezmi and he was from a village on the eastern shore called Nakolec, which in Slavic meant 'on stilts' – because remains of Neolithic water dwellings had been revealed over the centuries, whenever the lake receded.

'Nakolec is the oldest inhabited place on Prespa.' He pushed the plate of fish my way. 'The antique graves they excavated are of unknown origin. You see, the Skirtoni were old. We were the first people here. The Macedonians came later.'

Nezmi was an ethnic Albanian. He had waited for the others to leave before speaking to me openly, he said.

'They found stones with Illyrian script in Nakolec.' He watched my face for amazement.

But the existence of an Illyrian script is unproven.

'Many of the place names are Albanian,' he went on. 'But they don't want you to know that.'

It was hard work, sifting fantasy from reality. Nezmi was a native of the lake, his half-century's experience of it was genuine and his love for it deep. But he was vulnerable to political manipulation like everybody else here, where the poison of 'antiquisation' and other metastases of ethno-racial identity propaganda from both the Albanian and the Macedonian sides had invaded people's minds.

Nezmi had two university degrees. 'Yet I'm paid as a college leaver. Because I'm ethnic Albanian.' But everybody's salary was low in Macedonia, that's why so many were emigrating. On his salary alone he couldn't survive; he lived from his family's apple orchards. It was harvest season soon. Cheap workers would come from Albania to pick the apples, which he sold to Bulgaria.

The night had turned bitterly windy, and wrapped in all the clothes I had brought, I was drinking aromatic yellow Muscat rakia from a water glass to keep warm. Nezmi was delighted by my interest in the lake.

'It's a crazy lake,' he said. 'Unstable, with a mind of its own.' Two mountain winds collided over Prespa – a westerly from Galicica and eastern gales from Pelister.

'It's just as dangerous below as above water,' he said. 'There are at least four vortices where things and bodies disappear.' In the 1990s, fifteen children drowned by Golem Grad island. They'd been caught in cross-winds. Some of the bodies had never been recovered.

'My childhood friend drowned too. For three years, his dad walked up and down the beach here, looking for his body. Every morning.'

His friend's body had been sucked in by a vortex near the island where fishermen say giant carp lurk, two hundred and fifty kilos apiece, he said, and I tried not to look sceptical. But neither would I go swimming there. These holes sucked you in and spat you out in their own time, depending on water level, currents . . .

'And who knows what else,' Nezmi said. 'Prespa hasn't been properly studied. It's too dangerous for divers.'

He sighed.

'But the water has been retreating. We've lost seven metres.'

Prespa's levels had fluctuated through time, but the recent dramatic drop seemed permanent. The times when the lake was known to freeze completely were times of low water, like now. In the 1960s when Nezmi was born, the level had temporarily risen so that one of the churches in Nakolec had become an island. Nezmi was a Muslim, but in his village as elsewhere on the lake, churches and mosques stood side by side.

'We're peaceful,' he said. 'It's the lake. Water has that effect on you.'

But emigration haunted the lake. Nezmi's dad went to Australia in the 1960s, and Nezmi spent the 1990s in America.

'The only way to avoid the Yugoslav Wars. I didn't want to fight.'

When his country was tipped into violence ten years later, he had déjà-vu.

'It was horrific,' he whispered, though the only other person under the flickering lights was the owner-waiter clearing tables, who agreed. 'People became divided overnight. In Bitola, they

chalked crosses on Albanian houses and burnt them down. Thank
God it didn't reach the lake, but it came close.'

Nezmi went on to tell me a tale from the checkpoint – not
this one, but Chafassan where he'd worked before – involving
nine hundred kilos of marijuana he'd found in a Bulgarian truck,
and another one involving 1.6 million euros' worth of undeclared
branded sports shoes. He had done his job well, he said, but what
did he get in return? A demotion to the quieter checkpoint here.
For interfering in government-backed smuggling.

'This is our country,' he concluded, and packed his keys and
wallet back into his uniform pockets. 'They want us to live in a
poor, criminally corrupt, third-rate country. They won't let us
into the EU. They let Greece bully us. And we live with it.'

Who were *they*?

'The great powers. They've always decided our fate for us.
Like this business with our country's name.'

Europe, you Babylonian whore. But he had a point.

'Anyway, come to Nakolec sometime and I'll show you the
ancient stuff. Some of it's under water but it was there before us
and will be there after us.'

He trudged off to his car, then up the road to the checkpoint
without which the mountain would be as wild and pitch-black as
the first settlers had found it six thousand years ago.

Nezmi was right about the earliest-known inhabitants of Lake
Prespa, the Thracian-Illyrian tribe called the Skirtoni. Herodotus
wrote about them: 'On high stilts over the lake are wooden huts,
reached from the shore by a long narrow bridge. At the beginning, they all gathered wood for the huts together but gradually a
rule was introduced that whoever got married would bring three
new logs . . . and thus acquire a private hut with a trapdoor on the
floor which led down to the water.' When the Slavs arrived, they
adopted this way of life. And when the Slavist Konstantin Irechek
passed through here in the late nineteenth century, he noted that

the inhabitants were mostly 'Bulgarian Muslims', followed by Albanians. Identities have changed more frequently than the lake's fluctuating levels.

I swam in the warm dark water, and even drank from it, but only once – there was an unsettling feeling of something lurking beneath. One day, I drove round the lake to the Greek border. Maybe I could cross into Greece after all, even though people said the checkpoint had been closed for as long as they remembered. The road moved inland from the lake, making the lake feel out of reach. You could see it but you couldn't smell it or touch it. The colours of Prespa were deep and saturated, even on a warm day like today, and though the surface looked calm, something seemed to move underneath. Only the closest mountains had texture and reality. Those beyond were like a painted world.

I passed through miles of orchards whose apples looked so tempting that I pulled over and looked in the grass. It was the fallen, bruised ones that were being gathered now and sold as fodder. I passed through villages where only a cockerel or a barking dog was to be heard, and minarets and bell-towers alternated.

At a Muslim cemetery I discovered a mixture of old graves – anonymous mossy stone slabs – and fresh graves, each with a ceramic jug. A burial rite from antiquity! The jugs were to carry the soul to the next world. Treasure hunters had told me that jug fragments marked an ancient burial spot, but I had never seen them in a modern cemetery. The names and dedications were Albanian. This was the Village of the White Church, named after a large church that over time has vanished inside a glade. The population was now Albanian-speaking Bektashi, but it had once been Christian, and before that, Thracian-Illyrian, and before that – just the lake with its churning weathers, millennium after millennium.

Syncretism – the blending of religious and cultural motifs – was a speciality of the lake district, and of Balkan civilisation in general. It had two main features: survival and creativity, the

second in service to the first. It could even be said that the modern people of the lakes, the Albanians and the Macedonians, owed
their existential survival to syncretism.

'Oh I don't know any more,' said the man who ran an ethno-
graphic museum from his house in a nearby village. 'They used to
speak Turkish, now they speak Albanian. I can't keep up.'

He was a former folk dancer, and the costumes he had collected, both Christian and Muslim, were from every region of
Macedonia. They embodied a collective creative genius, a magnificent confluence of the Orient, the Occident, the mountainous
Balkans, and the mythical imagination. There was a woman's
costume three hundred years old – layer upon layer of wool and
linen, with thousands of Turkish and Bulgarian coins sewn onto
it. It weighed sixty kilos, his wife told me.

'So that the woman couldn't run away,' I said, but she didn't
laugh – to her they were like people. But I wasn't joking.

'If you can guess the purpose of this vestment, you can have it,'
the husband said, and held up a richly embroidered square throw
onto which tiny mirrors were sewn. It was a century old.

'I'll give you a clue. It's from the Mavrovo Mountains up
north, where the clothes women wore showed what stage of life
they were at.'

Of course. If you're a woman, everyone must know your sexual, marital and reproductive status at all times.

'Bridal?' I chanced, and he beamed. 'To cover the bride's
head.'

'Close! But I'm not giving you the cloth.'

It was for the horse, so that when a bride rode into her new
life, the little mirrors would deflect the evil eye – an essentially
shamanic practice. Another costume, from Mariovo, a canyon
region in Pelagonia made a ghost country by mass emigration,
featured headgear like a rolled turban, made from thick felt and
adorned with felt fruits, myriad mirrors and colourful beads. It
was a crown fit for a mountain queen. The town ones featured

furs. The Muslim ones were an explosion of colour, glitter and fine stripes, a celebration of silks and brocades.

And the Prespan ones?

'Over here.' He moved to a mannequin dressed in black. The little girl mannequin next to her was also in black. Black wool from head to toe, a funeral cortege of two.

To be female is to grieve. It had caught me out, once again, just when I thought I was safe, away from Ohrid. But something about these costumes touched a nerve.

'Prespan women were as good as widows,' he agreed. 'Because their husbands went abroad for twenty years on *gurbet*.'

Gurbet: Turkish for work abroad, or exile. In the Balkans, there is an entire culture of gurbet – gurbet songs, gurbet houses, gurbet fortunes, and gurbet widows. To this day. This is how, with the men absent or insufficient, mothers and daughters and grandmothers become betrothed to each other in a kind of black wedding.

'We don't get many visitors,' said the couple. 'Very few people visit Prespa.'

I bought some *white* linen cloth made by them in winter, when the lake is full of snowdrifts and howling wind.

I drove on and the malaise grew in the pit of my stomach, as if I was trying to swallow something indigestible. Black should not be worn for long periods of time. Was darkness this land's only reliable harvest? That was what this journey was about, after all – to get to the source of the darkness, and the love, and here in Prespa, to my surprise, I felt I was getting close.

Howling wind, snowdrifts, vortices and unstable lake levels were woven into the human history of Prespa. Like Macedonia's multi-layered costumes, the lake rose into a polyphony of plots and subplots.

In the collective imagination, Prespa was indelibly marked by the reign and fall of Tsar Samuil. People spoke of Samuil's time as if only a few generations had passed, not a millennium. The largest Roman town in the Prespa district, Pretor, had been the base for Samuil's royal guard. One Pretorian family, the Jonovski, traced their lineage to the medieval clan Sudjovtsi, ancestors of a nobleman, or *bolyar*, called Simeon. Simeon had been in Tsar Samuil's immediate entourage. En route to the border, I dropped into the family home in Pretor, unannounced.

A woman in black opened the door. She was widowed and lived alone by the lake, tending her apple trees. Her elderly brother-in-law, a literary translator, was on a visit from Skopje. He was an introverted man with a pained face, as if holding on to an illness or an old secret. His journalist father had written several books on Prespa. The family had always lived in Pretor, except for a spell in the eighteenth century when they left for Istanbul as Ali Pasha's men torched their way through villages here, just for fun. The family did well in Istanbul as orchardists and vintners, then returned home. Many became monks and nuns – an ingenious way, possibly the only way, to hold on to their extensive fields, by donating them to the nearest monastery and moving in. No one touched monastery grounds, or at least not in peacetime. There was still something monk-like about the brother-in-law.

Despite the mean-spirited denial and destruction wreaked by each new ruler on the previous ruler's legacy, Pretor kept churning up antique and medieval artefacts. The brother-in-law, pale at the garden table where the widow had placed a bowl of picture-perfect apples, squinted against the sun.

'The Macedonian Front passed through Pretor,' he said. 'Our people were on this side, and the Serbs, French and English to the south.'

He was writing his own book on Prespa, Tsar Samuil, and the family. There was a faraway look about him, as if he was more connected to the distant past than to the present of the lake. The widow gave me an apple for the road, and he told me to look for clues in the place names of Prespa. Place names were key narrators because so much material and written heritage had been destroyed. In the village of Wolf-Skinner people once hunted wolves and sold their skins. The Village of Bloodletting had seen massacres, and Preljubje, the Village of the Lustful, was named after an allegedly over-libidinous medieval Serbian prince who owned the province. Most intriguingly, the village of Asamati or 'the Bodiless Ones', a Greek derivation, referred to the spirits believed to watch over the lake.

The lake's name, like much of its history, is an enigma. Prespa appears in the historic sources of different languages as a lake, a vale, an island, a town, a royal palace, a river, and a religious centre of the ubiquitous lacustrine patron saints Clement and Naum. Even the quartet of novels by Dimitar Talev featuring the eternal Sultana is set in a fictional town called Prespa. But the only certain physical entity to have gone by the name of Prespa is the lake. In Ohrid, it was the water that seemed illusory at times. In Prespa, it was the very nature of reality.

One of the earliest recorded uses of the name is linked to the following story.

Some years after the deaths of the lakes' patron saints, a Byzantine chronicler wrote that a freakish winter had occurred, an immemorially cold winter. Animals and people perished from hunger. The lake froze over. In December 927, two messengers were travelling from southern Albania to the Pelagonian plains with an important missive. They were caught in a blizzard. They knew to follow the shore of a lake to the south-east. But there was no lake, just endless vales of snowdrift and ice. At the point of succumbing to a white death, they glimpsed a tower in the snow. It was Pretor. The Pretorians took them in and rubbed their bodies with snow and alcohol. When they came round, the messengers asked: Where is Pelagonia? It's east of here over that big mountain, the Pretorians answered, but it's all snowdrifts from here to there, *prespa* after *prespa*. Where's the lake? the messengers asked. You're on it, the answer came. This is Prespa. You've just crossed it diagonally. One of the messengers died of shock. The other continued on into the blizzard and a month later delivered the missive.

It is not said what the missive contained, but this tale is a reminder that the unsung endurance of messengers like these was vital in this difficult terrain. I imagine them as the long-distance lorry drivers of yesteryear – their lonely journeys across vales of snow, their nights of solace in villages where people speak forgotten tongues, their sealed cargoes more important than their lives.

Pretor touched the shore – and some of it was under water – but from here, the road went uphill again and so did the villages, only returning to the lake in the last few miles before the border. A cop waved me down. I got out of the car. Butterflies fluttered in the undergrowth that led down to a beach.

'The road ends here,' the border cop said listlessly.

You could in fact see exactly where it ended after the barricade, and on the other side was grass, as if there had never been a road. The cop was a large young man with a prematurely collapsed frame. He lit a cigarette and offered me one, glad of the company. I asked how long it had been closed.

He waved towards the lake to indicate infinity.

'The Greek colleagues are there on the other side,' he said. 'We get together for a dram.'

They spoke English, he grinned, though the Greeks understood Macedonian. 'And we've learned some Greek ourselves.'

This was the mutual way of checkpoints. Even disused ones.

The lake was veined with quivering threads of light, like mercury. The air was medicinally good. The first village on the other side was German (Agios Germanos), a couple of miles on. You could easily walk to it among the fruit trees and butterflies. But to get there legally, I'd have to drive over Pelister, east along the Via Egnatia into Greece, before descending again to Prespa.

'That's another hundred and seventy kilometres!' I said. 'And several mountain chains.'

'It sure is,' the cop shrugged, and returned to his kiosk, his body slumped like an old man's, his head in a halo of butterflies.

Like him, I sat slumped in the car, looking at the silver water.

The lake accumulated time but did nothing with it, not in human terms. It sucked it into its vortices, for some unspecified later use. The checkpoint had been closed unilaterally by Greece during their military junta, fifty years ago.

I had already decided to see Greek Prespa, driving the long way round. I'd arranged to meet at the weekend with an Australian friend from London, whose maternal grandparents were Macedonian exiles. I turned the car round and drove once more past the last village, called The Gouged Ones, in memory of the end days of Tsar Samuil's Prespa. There was a bakery there that made delicious stuffed pastry, but the severed road had stifled my appetite and I drove on to a higher mountain village instead, trying to make sense of Samuil's legacy. The Samuil narrative was a staple of national history in Bulgaria, and more recently in the Republic of (North) Macedonia. It came to life here, by the lake, through legends, place names, and physical remains of Samuil's days.

Samuil was one of four brothers of the Komitopouli dynasty founded by the Bulgarian Komita (Count) Nikola. All had Old Testament names, like their Armenian mother Ripsimi. The southern Balkans, including Byzantine territories, were roughly consolidated into an empire-like kingdom by Samuil and his brother Aaron. Their two other brothers had been killed. By the late 980s, Samuil had control over much of the Balkan peninsula, all the way south into Thessaly. His empire, which aimed to unite all Slavs, at least in theory, stretched from the Danube to the Aegean and from the Adriatic to the Black Sea. But with a neighbour like Basil II of Byzantium, such gains were always going to be contested.

Samuil's turbulent rule lasted thirty-nine years and the war between Samuil and Basil II thirty-one, a long time for a war but a short time for an empire. Samuil was able to repeatedly repel Basil thanks to the impregnable mountains of Bulgaria and Macedonia, much feared by enemy armies, and to his military talent. But Basil was hell-bent on retaking territory, battle by battle. He was a 'pathologically mean' man, in the words of one English historian. It was one of his life's missions to destroy Samuil politically. He couldn't forget the humiliation he had suffered when his army of forty thousand was annihilated at the Gates of Trajan near Sredets (Sofia).

But the destruction of Samuil's reign started from within – just like the vendetta story of Trena's mother in which 'the Turks' were only the catalyst. Byzantine intrigue, aimed at dividing the Komitopouli, had already infiltrated Samuil's family by the time he and Aaron reached forty. On learning about his beloved brother's supposed conspiracy with the Byzantines, Samuil had Aaron executed along with his family – an act after which, it is said, something in Samuil became permanently distorted. War with Basil II was now his main purpose in life.

A note of mercy is introduced at this point: one of Aaron's sons, Ivan-Vladislav, was saved from avuncular execution through the intervention of his cousin, Samuil's son Gavril-Radomir. The two cousins lived in Ohrid's royal court for a time. But mercy was not reciprocated: thirty years later, when Gavril-Radomir took over his dead father Samuil's throne, Ivan-Vladislav had him murdered during a hunt above Prespa, at the instigation of none other than Basil II – who had in return promised him exclusive powers. Gavril-Radoslav's Thessalian wife was also murdered, and their eldest son blinded. A pattern emerges.

As an act of punishment short of taking a life, blinding was first practised by the Persians on their captured enemies, and became de rigueur in the Byzantine world. A blind man can't be general or king. In centuries to come, the savage act of blinding would be unconsciously repeated in the digging-out of painted saints' and kings' eyes.

A prophet had warned Samuil of the rising levels of the lake, as the water approached his palace on St Achillius island. Take heed, the seer said, rising water bodes ill. But it was too late, the wheels of history were turning, and geography really was destiny: the simple fact of being next door to Byzantium determined the fate of Samuil's people. And so did the existence of the Via Egnatia: it was all about having control over that vital artery between Dyrrachium on the Adriatic, Thessaloniki on the Aegean, and the Bosphorus.

That same prophet had also warned, early on, that the Komitopouli would reign over a mighty empire – but tragically, for brother would kill brother. Perhaps, had Samuil spared his brother Aaron, things would have turned out differently.

The endgame came with the Battle of Kleidon, also known as the Battle of Klyuch, in 1014, won through sheer luck by the Byzantines in the gorges of the River Struma (Strymonas) where Macedonia and Thrace overlap. Both Kleidon and Klyuch mean 'key'. The two enemies – Samuil and Basil 'Bulgarochthonos', the Bulgar-Slayer, as he went down in history – never met. But legend has it that after the battle, Samuil's captured army of fourteen or fifteen thousand men was subjected by Basil II to medieval history's worst atrocity. All the soldiers were blinded, with a one-eyed man left for each hundred souls, to lead them westwards to their tsar.

It is a tableau of suffering on a scale not quite human. To blind fifteen thousand people requires an industry of blinders, but the Byzantines were fully capable of that. As if Basil II had wanted to maim not just the enemy, but all of humanity. There are sites along the returning soldiers' long east–west route across the mountain chains of Macedonia, where mineral springs gush from the skirts of the multiplying massifs in a sea of vapours like freshly laundered linens. There the blind army stopped to rest and wash their eye wounds, the legend tells. It was late summer. They took three months to walk the three hundred kilometres to Prespa.

I think of those eyeless men of many ethnicities and languages, returning to Prespa amidst nature's symphony of colours they couldn't see. Samuil's army contained many men from the lakes. The fastest foot soldiers were Albanians who came in their fusta-nellas, and Vlachs (Aromanians) who fought in their full furs, even in summer. The cavalry was led by ethnic Bulgars whose ancestors had come galloping across the Asian steppes. The most numerous were the Balkan Slavs, peasants largely of the Bogomil persuasion, the movement that resisted Byzantine-style feudal and ecumenical oppression and formed their own communes. They enjoyed unre-peated protection under Samuil, and some believe that his family were Bogomils too. Once Samuil's empire fell, the Lakes became part of the Byzantine *theme*, or province, of Bulgaria.

Some historians dispute the scale of the blinding, arguing that this tableau of mass mutilation was painted later as Byzantine propaganda to terrorise enemies, long after the miserable Basil II was dead. According to them, the memory of Samuil's blinded army may be partially fictionalised, to serve the wars of later eras, which were none the wiser. But this is an argument about scale rather than actuality. However many of the blinded had reached the shores of Prespa, thousands would have spent the remainder of their lives by the lakes. Soldier camps were set up here, in Asamati of the Bodiless Ones and the Village of the Gouged Ones. In the light of Samuil's annihilation of his own brother's family and the family vendetta, the soldiers' blinding by an external enemy takes on a more complex meaning akin to that of the evil bird that cursed Hallmi. An eye for an eye for an eye, until the one-eyed lead the blind. Some call this politics, others call it karma. Prespans don't call it anything. They just watch the rise and fall of their lake with a fatalism much older than them.

It is in fact the dramatic fall of the water levels – seven metres in sixty years – that is the real threat, ecologically and existen-tially. But in the collective imagination, as in my recurring dream, it is rising water that heralds trouble. In the twentieth century it rose to unprecedented levels three times: in 1903 (the Ilinden Uprising), 1917 (the First World War) and 1942 (Second World War).

At the end of a steep road that veered into the hills were two linked mountain villages I wanted to see. Above them were the Beautiful Oaks where a forest church high up occasionally rang its bell – in celebration or doom, I couldn't tell.

The cafe-bar in the square by the cemetery was full of red-faced men, and one mature woman in a pretty floral dress and with blonde plaits, who sat on the knee of one of them. The gathering had an unstable, fairy-tale feel. American English and broken Macedonian were being spoken. Alex from California told me that this was his first visit. His father, a lad from this village, had sailed to Detroit aged sixteen.

What do you make of the old country? I asked, and he seemed lost for words.

'It's not like America,' he said eventually.

'There are no luxuries,' piped his friend. 'There's power cuts, water cuts.' He was a construction worker from California, with the same story.

These were the children of the Village of Immigrants. The doctors, architects and economists who had studied abroad in the earlier twentieth century had stayed abroad too, and there had never been an economic incentive to return, only an emotional one. Every summer, on the day of the Ilinden Uprising, diaspora reunions took place here with folk singers, and hundreds came from all over the world to dance, drink, invoke the blinded soldiers of Samuil, be Macedonian – and go home.

'Some folks from the States, they don't even know where Europe is, let alone Macedonia,' Alex said. 'Then they come to Prespa and have all these emotions.'

'We don't even know where these emotions come from,' said his friend.

Out of nine hundred houses, eighty residents were left in the Village of Immigrants. 'Those of us who haven't died and the apple-pickers, that's it,' said a man from another table, and smiled amiably. He was a retired television producer who, after a lifetime in Skopje, had returned to try and breathe some life into his mother's village.

'Unsuccessfully,' he said. 'Nostalgia brings people back but no one invests.'

His name was Meto, from Methody. He asked me to come back the next day, because he had been drinking. 'I'm OK sitting down, but if I try to get up, you'll lose all respect for me,' he said. The next morning, I met him at the same place.

As Meto and I walked the lanes, he showed me the masons' marks on the stones of the old houses – a pentagon, a cross, or a crescent. These tower-like buildings with their generous balconies were typical of Aegean Macedonia.

'You'll see them in German too. I have cousins there. Before the Greeks closed the checkpoint in 1966, we used to cycle across and visit each other.' Agios Germanos was the first village on the other side of the border. German was its original name.

We walked up a forest track, a tunnel of foliage, to the remote St Petka Monastery. The only person we met was a beautiful old woman in black, gathering rosehips in a cloth sack, chewing something, time's eternal crone. She and Meto kissed on the cheeks.

'The woman I should've married,' he said, and she smiled girlishly. 'I'm like her son,' he added, but as he chatted she said nothing and seemed to suddenly vanish with her sack. This woman had known him since he was a toddler and she was the village beauty, but she never married.

Why was she wearing black, then?

'Because Prespan women are in eternal mourning,' he said simply.

Later at his house, he showed me a photograph of his grandmother with her three children. She is in her thirties, and although her husband is alive in America, she is dressed in black – black headscarf, black woollen dress, black leather shoes, black stockings. Meto's mother is a young girl with cropped hair and an old, old face. Sorrow permeates the scene like weather – a cold, waterlogged weather, like the lake in winter.

'Yes,' Meto said, 'my mother took on her mother's sadness. I don't know where it comes from. It's a Prespan thing or an Aegean thing, or both.' Prespa sat on the fringe of Aegean Macedonia where women traditionally wore black.

Some sixty thousand Bulgarian-speaking Aegeans were expelled into Bulgaria by the Greek state after the Treaty of Neuilly at the end of the First World War, and replaced with Greek refugees from Asia Minor and Bulgaria. Many Bulgarians have great-grandparents or grandparents from Aegean Macedonia. Others emigrated further afield. To have Aegean ancestors is to carry loss in your bones, one way or another.

No sooner had her husband returned from twenty years of gurbet than Meto's grandmother died of a heart attack, aged forty. There was something going on here, with the presence and absence of men. I thought of the distressed letters Grandmother Anastassia had written to her husband while he was away; yet she was no less distressed with him around. And I thought of the two first years of my life, which my father spent on compulsory military service; my mother's yearning for him seeped into me, along with her dissatisfaction later, when he returned. The yearning can never be matched by reality. It was not just the men's absence, alternating with their unsatisfactory presence, that made these women don black. What was it? I could not name it yet. It was something we carried within, long after its expiry date.

St Petka Monastery was built as a school for young monks in the fifteenth century. A chorus of birds greeted us in the court-yard, and we drank from the stone fountain where a tin cup was attached with a chain. It hadn't been a functioning monastery since the end of the Second World War, when the Yugoslav border army moved in. One morning when Meto was doing a spot of yoga, rising from his mat, he'd seen a bear on the path, looking at him. Then it had turned round and disappeared into the Beautiful Oaks. For half a century, only soldiers and bears roamed here.

St Petka looked strikingly like my grandmother in her forties. Which were the years I was in now, a powerful decade when you come to own your face along with your life. This is you, from now on.

The full oval, the heavy lines from straight nose to full mouth, the deep-set eyes and forcefully arched brows – it was the essential Levantine face. But the expression in the eyes made all the difference. Petka had the expression of one who had seen and transcended. Anastassia's obsidian eyes cut you up. She dreaded, then hated, losing her youth, as if there was nothing to take its place, as if she'd been robbed.

'It's a pity that this place isn't enjoyed by people,' Meto said in the dinge of the church. The smell of centuries was inside it, undisturbed. 'But maybe it's for the better. That way, it's preserved for those after us who may appreciate it more.'

What are a few generations to St Petka and the bears?

'See the top of the hill. That's the French Road, from World War One.'

It was also the route guerrillas and refugees took during the Greek Civil War. By the time we'd made it down the path to the village, a cold white fog had wrapped itself around the hills.

Back at his house, Meto prepared lunch with courgettes and tomatoes from his garden.

'This was the barn.' He pointed at the high beams. 'Here, my mother and grandmother sheltered the *detsa begalci* who made it over the French Road. They'd dress them, undress them, feed them, bath them and send them on. Eat up. I can't eat these courgettes by myself.'

The detsa begalci were the refugee children of the Greek Civil War. Some didn't make it. In 1949 when Meto was born, a group of refugee kids got lost in a fog and fell into the lake. Their bodies were retrieved and buried by people here. When I think of Meto in winter's snowdrifts and howling wind, in the house where children were dressed and undressed by the black-clad mother and daughter, I also think of his courgettes and tomatoes and how he wears his inheritance lightly, the way I'd like to wear mine.

The king had goat ears but hid them under his crown. Barbers were killed to keep the secret. One day, a boy's turn came. The king asked: do you have siblings? No, said the boy, I'm all my mother has. The king spared him but swore him to secrecy.

The boy didn't speak a word, but his mother saw he was unwell. She told him to go into the forest, dig a hole, speak his secret into it and cover it. A willow grew in the spot. Years later, shepherds cut whistles from the branches, and the whistles sang: The king has goat ears, the king has goat ears.

Realising that the truth can't be suppressed forever, the king was enlightened.

Balkan folk tale

OF MEN AND ISLANDS

'We can't go today,' said the old boatman to Danny.

'Yes we can,' said Danny, 'I've brought the group, I'm not turning back.'

'I know this lake and I'm telling you, the easterly's rising. It's the return I'm worried about.'

The boatman was gently spoken. The day was bright but the water turbulent.

'I've made this crossing forty times this year and I'm telling you it's fine,' said Danny. He was the guide.

The group was ten Dutch tourists and me. They had turned up at the nameless hotel and I'd joined them for the island crossing. The boatman agreed to take us but the concerned look stayed on his face. Water is always choppier than it looks from the shore, and already we were falling off our seats, laughing nervously, as the motorboat headed to Golem Grad island.

'Don't worry guys,' Danny shouted over the engine, 'you're safe with me.'

Pelicans bobbed on the waves.

'Pelicans are disappearing,' Danny shouted, 'because of climate change in the last twenty years. Prespa is one of the few places you can see them. Conditions here are perfect because they're perfect for the fish. Median water temperature is thirty-two degrees centigrade.'

Surprisingly, Lake Ohrid was colder by a few crucial degrees centigrade, and only sixty-five per cent of fish eggs survived, while in Prespa the survival rate was one hundred per cent. The pelicans came in May from Africa, about two thousand of them, the same individuals every year.

'In May, it's like *Planet Earth* here!' Danny said. 'And when they start hunting, it's like World War One!'

The pelicans attack schools of fish from the air, like bombers. Pelicans don't dive for fish – that's the cormorants' job, they dive up to twenty-five metres down, then the two share the catch. Which is lucky for the pelicans, especially in winter when fish sleep in the deep.

'In just one May day, fifteen tons of fish can be consumed on Prespa,' he said.

Old pelicans stay on Golem Grad island, up to forty years of age. Now, in September, their young were beginning their migration to Africa.

The island loomed closer – a high rocky outcrop with a petrified white forest on the top.

'Guano,' Danny said. 'It kills the trees.'

A wave hit the hull of the boat and drenched us. Handsome Danny took off his shirt so we could admire his lean, well-sculpted body. One of the girls blushed and looked away.

'Right now,' he said to me in Macedonian, 'I'm not in good shape but in winter I practise kick-boxing. So I'll be strong if there's a conflict.'

What do you mean, a conflict?

'Oh, how do I know? With the crappy politics we've got. Mind you, war is madness. All nuclear weapons should be destroyed.'

Another young Dutch woman was leaning overboard, retching, her friend holding her, with an accusatory look aimed at Danny.

'Hold on tight,' he shouted too cheerfully, ''cause the ride back will be worse!'

Another woman snorted cynically. We were all wet now, water dripping from our hair and faces.

Mali Grad came into view in the washed-out blue light, along with the arid Albanian coast. It was the smaller of the twin islands. The captain pointed out the burnt trees up on the hills of the mainland.

'Drought,' he said.

'Prespa is a dangerous lake.' Danny leaned over to me, switching to Macedonian, 'I don't want to freak them out but we're gonna have to do a super-fast tour of the island if we're to make it back. If we're unlucky enough to get winds from both Galicica and Pelister – well, let's not think about that.' Once, caught out by a storm, he was stranded on the island with a group and spent the night in a cave, building a fire and counting the stars, before they were rescued by a helicopter sent by the Dutch embassy.

'How are your survival skills?' He winked at me.

By the time we reached the island and the captain was looking for a safe mooring spot that didn't go against the wind, another young woman was doubled over with stomach cramps. The older women were tougher. We began the brisk climb through the petrified forest. It was a kingdom of snakes and turtles; juniper trees hundreds of years old, rosehips, and some other plant with barbed branches that slashed you like razors. It smelt of guano and birds, a stench halfway between life and death.

Bounding ahead, Danny looked for snakes and turtles to show us. This island used to be a herpetologist's heaven, home to some ten thousand water snakes, hence its nickname – the Island of Snakes. One time, an experiment was conducted: two mongooses were placed on the island with the aim of exterminating the snakes, which were freaking visitors out. It didn't work.

'But some years ago, the snakes disappeared by themselves,' Danny said. 'Where did they go? Nobody knows.'

'Maybe they moved to Mali Grad island,' I said.

The turtles too died en masse. Danny picked up the shell of a dead turtle.

'It's environmental,' he said. 'Climate change. The drought

burns the grass and the turtles are reduced to eating dead snakes or even the insides of birds. Believe me, it's heart-breaking to see a turtle eating viscera.'

He picked up a young snake and let it slither up his arm towards his naked chest. There were gasps, which was the required effect.

'It's all right, it's not venomous,' Danny reassured us. 'How to recognise a poisonous snake? It has split cat's eyes. The non-poisonous ones have round eyes, like us.'

He placed it on the path. Everything was white, scorched, thorny. White rocks covered in lichen were scattered like old gravestones. It was hard to imagine this island as a home. But it had been inhabited, on and off, since Neolithic times. Well into the mid-twentieth century it had been a monastic centre, and in the 1880s, during another of those freakish winters, Prespans had walked over the ice with their cattle, in the hope that they would survive in the warmer microclimate of the island. But a pack of hungry wolves had come down the mountains and across to the island too, and carnage followed, both of the cattle and of the wolves, which were shot by the Prespans. Or maybe by the monks – any hermit tough enough to live on this lake would have known how to deal with wolves.

The stone ruins where we now stood were from a basilica, but all Danny said was: 'We found skeletons in here.'

Skeletons of unknown origin, or unknown to him. They were the remains of monks.

As an aside to me: 'Some think Tsar Samuil buried his treasures here after his fall. That's why it's so dug up. But a proper gold detector costs ten thousand euros!'

A large fourteenth-century church from the reign of King Dushan held the remains of stunning frescoes, badly damaged by graffiti and gougings.

'Here's St Peter.' Danny turned to the group. 'In Macedonia, we have lots of churches. People believe in God. But God doesn't believe in people. That's the problem.'

And he bounded up the path because the lake now had white-crested waves and our captain was calling him to urge us on.

The return crossing was shockingly rough, with an emergency landing miles away from the usual spot, and even those with guts of steel were shaken as we climbed out. But the kind old boat-man kept reassuring us while the waves battered us that it was just one wind, not two, so we'd make it. Danny relished the whole thing.

Danny's grasp of the human history of his beloved Prespa may have been shaky, but he had perfected his routine of sexy-guide-in-safari-shirt, or without shirt.

'Look, I grew up by the lake like Tarzan,' he said to me the following day, when there was no group and he'd stopped acting. A different persona appeared, subdued and wearing glasses. 'So I trust nature. But history — nah. It changes all the time. Even though it's already happened. In just five years, with a change of government, history can be turned on its head. Imagine what can happen in two thousand years! That's why I stay away from history and stick to the snakes.'

I'd asked if I could see where he grew up. Danny now lived in Ohrid with his parents, but they'd spent twenty years in a prefab-ricated lakeside refugee camp. In 1991, before the Albanian border opened, several hundred people from the ethnic Macedonian villages in Albanian Prespa had walked over the mountain.

'When my parents crossed the mountain, they had just the clothes on their backs. Skinny, hungry. Things were so bad in Albania, there wasn't enough to eat.' His mother had been heavily pregnant. As soon as they arrived in Macedonia, his father was sent to prison for border trespass, and his mother to hospital where she gave birth to Danny.

We stood among the weeds in the Queenly Court grounds, which looked derelict but weren't. A few families still lived here and a dog came up, overjoyed to see Danny. The flimsy buildings were like a one-storey motel, all the rooms lined up and opening onto a communal corridor, with car ports below. Pinewoods led to the lake. Danny picked up a key from under a mat and unlocked the door. It was one room with a balcony view of the lake. This is where he had grown up with his parents. Queenly Court had been made up of several houses like this, fourteen families in each.

'There was a stigma about us, "the Albanians". Ironic when you think that my parents kneeled down when they crossed the border and kissed the ground,' Danny said. The ground from which they had been severed by the border for half a century.

'So I'd lie to my schoolmates about where I lived. A made-up identity. I grew up determined to make something of myself. To make enough for my parents too. So we are never ashamed again.'

One thing they did have as kids was freedom. In summer, they were out on the lake all day, and in winter they played in the communal corridor. The room was claustrophobically small and the sofas doubled up as beds. The kitchenette was on the balcony. On the wall was a photograph of a man, with black ribbon in the corner.

'My uncle. He went to Greece to work. But he lived rough for too long, caught pneumonia and because he was illegal couldn't get treatment. My auntie's still in black, fourteen years on. Prespan women grieve too much, you know?'

I know.

He locked the door of his childhood.

'And down the road is Hotel Yugoslavia where we'd go and hang out in the lobby and pretend to be kids of rich families staying there. Until the waiters shooed us away.'

There was one waiter who never shooed them away: Tsape.

'I can't bear to go there since it burnt down.'

Here, no one is too young to see the ruins of their youth.

Danny still went back to his parents' village in Albania, to see his grandmother. 'I haven't forgotten where I come from but I have a hunger for the world. I've seen misery close up. So I know how to appreciate life. Some people don't.'

Danny had found a job for his mother: she cooked for his groups and he paid her out of his own wages. He spoke of her with deep love. And soon, he said, he'd have a job for his dad too, because he was getting too old for packing apples in winter. Danny did have flings with tourists, it's true, he said, but that was just for experience. He wanted to marry by thirty, if he found 'the one'.

'Penguins are monogamous. The female remains in Africa while the male travels. Or is it the other way round? Anyway, I want to find my penguin. Wish me luck.'

I did.

'Remember to look out for Zaver!' he said when we parted. I waved him off and he drove up the mountain road to Lake Ohrid, built by political prisoners.

Zaver was the largest of the Prespa sinkholes, where water was sucked into the karst mountain and made its way sixteen kilometres through the limestone of Galicica, to rush out at three main spots on Lake Ohrid: Drilon, St Naum and Biljana's Springs. *Zaver* means vortex.

The hilly road into Albania was like the border checkpoint: deserted. I drove on. Nezmi wasn't working today, his colleagues told me, he was tending his apple groves. Vegetation decreased and an arid landscape emerged. There was something stripped, bone-poor, about the hills. I stopped to ask a man with a mule loaded with twigs where Zaver was, but he was mistrustful of strangers and shooed his mule away without a word.

Place names were signposted in Albanian and Macedonian, and posters of Macedonian politicians smiled insincerely from abandoned roadside shop-fronts. The Macedonian minority in Albania had two passports now. Many worked across the border and no wonder – jobs were non-existent here. There were no trees for logging or apples for picking, not even fish to sell by the roadside.

Pustec, or Dry Village, was where I was headed, because from there you could take a boat to Mali Grad island. I'd come before, in May, on a blustery day when lake crossings were impossible.

Women in rubber galoshes and carrying hoes and spades over their shoulders made their way up the village lanes. Hoes, mules, mud. There was nothing to indicate the decade. Their fair-skinned faces were sunburnt, some wore floral kerchiefs to protect their hair, their ages were impossible to tell because the harshness of life was etched into them like a birthmark. A man in an incongruous theatrical velvet coat was stacking logs against a wall, talking to himself in what sounded like verse, like some rural Hamlet.

Inside a concrete shop, an old woman sat at a table, counting coins. I sat with her. She had apple cheeks and laughing eyes that took me by surprise – here was the antidote to the black-crow widow.

'There are good things and bad things in every time,' she said in response to my question, whether now was better than during Hoxha's regime.

'The Hoxha didn't let us move. We were poor and the border separated us from loved ones. Now it's emigration that separates us from loved ones. And we're still poor.'

She seemed to find this amusing, and it was – 'the Hoxha' was her wordplay on the meaning of the word *hodja*, or religious cleric.

She had two daughters in Italy and Greece.

'And one here,' the old woman said with a wicked glint in her eye, 'to look after me.'

In the empty square, next to the outsized new Orthodox church built by the Macedonian government in place of the old House of Culture, and where the old church had been demolished by Hoxha's commissars, was a cafe. Here the remaining young men gathered from morning till night and scrolled down their mobile phones, with their jacket collars pulled up to make them look tough.

To my surprise, the boatman remembered me from May and even smiled, in his reserved way. Bojko was a man of few words. Weather's fine, he said, we can go. I sat in the cafe while he fetched his boat engine from home, and his timid friends looked at me out of the corners of their eyes. There was no work and no prospects in Dry Village. To get access to the Internet, you climbed to the top of the nearest hill.

To get to Bojko's boat, we drove past an open rubbish dump. People simply brought their rubbish and tipped it by the lakeside. A donkey mounted another donkey. Plastic bottles floated among giant reeds.

He installed the engine and pulled it into spluttering action, and the wind slapped into us without preamble. The island looked close, but it was three kilometres away, and the engine kept cutting out. Each time, Bojko restarted it with great effort, and I eyed up the oars and the waves, making contingency plans while trying to look relaxed. A dark cloud cast a shadow over the stony mountain of Dry Village. It was a forbidding fortress of stone and weather. A faint ribbon climbed up and into the hill and was lost from view: the road to the hinterland. There was one more village on the lake, then nothing. Dry Village was vulnerable, cut off, alone into eternity.

Though the boat shook as it hit the short choppy waves, Bojko stood steady at the helm, smoking in an off-hand way. His stance said: I can bear anything. When I'd first met him in May, I'd been put off by his wild face, but he was just unworldly. His expression mirrored the landscape: stoic and desolate. Though born the same year as Danny, he looked old, as if he'd never been young.

Bojko made a sort of living by fishing, he told me on the island. Him and a few friends.

'Mainly carp,' he said. 'In summer.'

And in winter? He looked away awkwardly.

The big waterhole where carp lurked in winter was in Greek territorial waters. If caught by Greek police patrols they'd go to jail, have their boats and licences confiscated, and get a five-year ban from visiting EU countries. In short, they'd lose the little they had.

'There's a cave church across there.' He pointed to the opposite shore, while giving me a handful of small figs from a tree in an unexpected gentlemanly gesture.

'There's a hundred and seventy steps hacked in the stone. Monks lived there once.'

I could see the dark hole in the karst across the water, it wasn't far at all.

'Where's the border?' I asked.

'Over there,' he pointed at the water. He could see something that I couldn't.

The way he spoke was clipped and matter-of-fact, like his father. I met his parents afterwards. We sat in their garden full of grapevines. His mother cut some bunches and put them on a plate: the small, sweet taljanka and the slightly larger bolgarka. Their house had a sweeping view of the lake.

'A whole lake at our feet.' She grabbed my wrist − 'But we have no water. Tell me, does that make sense?'

It was the communal pumps, they were too small, but the subsidies given for larger pumps had disappeared into someone's pockets.

'I have a bathroom, but no water,' she said. She was a small voluble woman. The father was quiet, his face packed with hard living. Before Hoxha's time, he said, all the men had been fishermen. But Hoxha decreed that only twenty men should fish, and their catch be handed over to the local Party functionaries.

Dry Village had fishermen who couldn't fish, lake women who had no water, men in the flower of their youth who were celibate and jobless.

'One cow was allowed per family. And a small garden,' his father said. 'Eight hundred grams of bread per person, but often there wasn't even that. We walked or took the collective bus to

Korçë to buy bread.' Korçë was an hour's drive from here. Some cycled, but there was a shortage of bicycles too. Now the family had twenty cows and some goats. Older people in these ethnic Macedonian villages on the fringe still didn't speak much Albanian – because we hardly need it, Bojko's mother said.

There were families in the village, his father said, whose men had emigrated to Argentina at the time of the Balkan Wars and never returned. During Hoxha, an electrified fence ran around Albania, which the father called the *klyon*. Its remains could be seen running up the hill, like a scar. They had cousins over the hill in Stenje, where my nameless hotel was, but they never met because of the border.

Bojko's uncle had been high up in the Albanian Communist Party because of his partisan past, and once in 1949, while travelling to the border area with a colleague, his colleague confided his plans to cross into Yugoslavia. The uncle handed him over to the authorities. Bojko's father told this without pride and without shame. And the man ended up doing twenty years' hard labour.

Why, I asked, why did your uncle betray his colleague?

'Because otherwise it would have been him doing twenty years,' Bojko said. He'd not spoken till now. 'It could have been a provocation, to test his loyalty.' Bojko understood the logic of that era because his whole life so far was its aftermath. He'd been born between two eras, two countries, two folds of the Prespa mountains.

'Tell me' – the mother gripped my arm – 'how's life in The Countries?'

I'd never heard this expression before. It designated places in the world where the rule of law operated and your son didn't have to risk his life on the lake, in temperatures of -20° centigrade.

Before I could say anything, I saw the tears streaking her face, even as she smiled.

'Take him,' she said fiercely, 'he's a good soul. Marry him. Or take him as your lover, take him to The Countries. For God's sake. There's nothing here.'

Bojko and his father sat looking at the ground. I opened my mouth but nothing came out.

I drove back to the nameless hotel. Over the mountain pass, past silent men and women returning with mules and hoes, and a well-spoken villager with the aura of a nobleman told me where to look for Zaver. But not before he'd offered me water from his house, seeing I was parched. There wasn't a single road fountain on the Albanian side of Prespa. He told me how, in his childhood, he'd jump in the water straight from the road and you could see the fish in the water as you walked along.

Where the lake had been, there were now allotments with toiling women and men.

The sinkholes of Zaver were dry too. The reclamation of water by the land was permanent. It was caused by orchard pesticides from the 1950s onwards, climate change, and some other, yet unknown, reason. Oddly, the amount of water coming out at the springs of Lake Ohrid had not gone down.

Even dry, Zaver remained the most symbolic sinkhole. The connection between the lakes had been formally verified in 1925 by a team who poured red paint in Zaver, and two days later, red water ran out at St Naum. The stories I'd heard of lambs and other gifts being pushed into a Prespa sinkhole, to appear at Ohrid, were inspired by Zaver.

The sunset made the lake look as if gold paint was being poured over the horizon. The lake was open, boundless. It was impossible to tell where each of the three countries began or ended, or why for pity's sake it had been necessary to partition one lake into three nationalities, to separate Golem (Big) Grad from its sibling Mali (Little) Grad. Pelicans, ducks and geese bobbed on the water. Only the humans were self-imprisoned behind invisible lines. Now the day was over, the pain of Bojko's parents caught up with me. I had swallowed it with the grapes. His mother's tear-streaked smile would stay with me, and Bojko too, sitting by the lake, waiting for the natal matrix to reabsorb him. His paralysis was not entirely personal – something of this land's fatalistic legacy had remained in the energy field of its people.

Although I was meeting more men than women, the Lake women felt more present. Dead or alive, they embodied the lacustrine element, the generative depths where desire and grief ceaselessly churned. I sat on the parched grass above Zaver. I imagined a procession: the women of the Lakes. Women washing linens, children on their backs, mending fishing nets, rowing against big waves in those coffin-like chuns, with loaded mules; and town women in high heels, with books and notebooks, and dreams of true love, great achievement – perfection, no less.

Water is indestructible. Among all the elements, water is the one that outlives the rest: it extinguishes fire, flows into earth, rots wood, corrodes metal, evaporates in the air, to return as itself. Water, not fire, may have the last word on Earth, engulfing islands big and small. The true women and men of the Lakes possessed the qualities of water: mutability, silence and endurance. The Lakes are their truest chronicle.

Water is also mercy. I imagined that the tears of all the women and men of the lake were sucked into these plugholes, drawn into the Earth's memory and filtered of impurities before they came out in the lower kingdom, three days later, to continue the cycle afresh.

I saw everything clearly now. It made sense to me that we had lost the war, that we had fed the fire, that our bodies had fertilized the cracks in the bedrock. It made sense that the enemy had triumphed. Better that way. Had we won, we'd be the enemy now.

I could see clearly. It made sense to me now that we survived, that we refused to be reformed, and set out to learn ourselves and the workings of the world, observing the greater laws that keep the world going, wondering what makes it seem still. It made sparkling sense that the vanquished, not the victors, should learn these secrets.

Stratis Haviaras, 1984

THE HOWL

The road to Pelagonia ran close to the ghostly Via Egnatia: from the apple town of Resen through the brooding massifs of Pelister. At the Gjavato Pass on the mountains' saddle, a small detour onto the abandoned old road where the Via Egnatia had passed took me to a symbolic water fountain. I'd read about it: a drinking fountain that naturally bifurcates. Some of the water flows east towards the Aegean and the rest flows west, towards the Adriatic, but it was hard to appreciate the natural part of the phenomenon, since the fountain had been cemented into two separate spouts. Like Janus twins, they faced opposite ways.

Gjavato Pass had linked the Via Egnatia with the Epirus road to the south, and was marked on maps of the Graeco-Roman world as *finis Macedoniae et Epiri*, the end boundary of Macedonia and Epirus. This is where the Illyrian and Macedonian lands began to overlap with the Thracian, to the east. The 'Jerusalem itinerary' brought the armies of the various crusades through this pass, and the multilingual army of Samuil during the decades of war with Byzantium. Nearby were the remains of the *castrum romanum*, or Roman camp, that guarded Gjavato. Even the Apostle Paul had allegedly walked this road on his proselytising journey, carrying the tools of his leather trade on muleback (and in his heart, a deep, irrational fear of women, one suspects).

I filled my bottle from the fountain and drove on, made uneasy by the spirit of dereliction that haunted the potholed road lined with plastic rubbish, and eventually bumped my way along a surviving cobblestoned road that retraced the original Via Egnatia. It linked a series of villages that looked as if they had been sacked by brigands. An oppressive pall hung over these once prosperous settlements with a millennial past and no present. Greenery engulfed the houses. Dogs with tumours hanging from their bellies lay in the street.

An old woman with herbs in a bag sat inside a broken bus stop where no buses passed, and cheerfully told me that she'd walked from Gjavato village five kilometres away to meet up with a friend but he hadn't come. Despite having no teeth, she wore lipstick and a nice dress. I was about to offer her a lift along the remaining cobbles of the ancient Via to her village, when three unshaven men in tracksuits got out of an old Zastava, lit cigarettes, then drove into the forest. Losing my nerve and with it my goodwill, I left the old woman and the cancerous dogs, turned round and rejoined the motorway.

The Gjavato Pass is gateway to the Pelagonian plains. The warm wind blew the car along, in the ghostly hoof steps of praetorian detachments, medieval armies, crusaders in chain mail, caravans with turbaned riders and veiled women; Aromanian shepherds wrapped in felt *yamurluks* (capes) and commanding the immense flocks that fed the peninsula, ascetic missionaries from Syria in hand-cut sandals that blistered their feet, mute peasants on mules gathering herbs and hiding rifles under blankets for the next uprising, messengers with sealed letters, tax-collectors; *komitadjas*, postmen, and men pursued by blood feuds as if by Furies. And of course Sufi dervishes with carved staffs in their hands and the ecstatic chant *la elaha ella'llah* – and if you walked here through the alpine meadows, one breathless view opening after another like a book of secrets, you'd be singing too.

The traffic of six empires had trodden over the Gjavato Pass. But if you forgot about this human density, you saw that Pelagonia looked the way it sounded: a landscape so ancient and empty, so prehuman that it could fit no political map.

From the sprawling city of Bitola and all the way to the Greek border, the shabby road had been patched up and the traffic consisted of trucks and beaten-up local cars. Fields of corn, fields of burnt grasses, and on the balconies of village houses – strings of bright-red peppers hanging like curtains, a festival of autumn. After the quiet Greek checkpoint, the expansive plain and distant mountains continued, only now the empty road and road signage were first-class and the cars more expensive, the result of decades of EU cash injections.

On the map, the road to Greek Prespa didn't look like much, but it was. Soon, it started climbing west into the Verno Mountains. The scenic mountain town of Florina, with its thirty-three-metre hilltop cross for the thirty-three years of Christ, was quiet. Many business premises were for rent. By the time you reached this last town in Pelagonia, you were cut off twice: by altitude and by the border. After Florina, the narrow switchback road plunged and climbed through beautiful dark valleys, where the only presence was the odd drinking fountain with its stone basin. I was glad that Nick was waiting for me at the end of the road, or I hoped he was – my mobile phone had no signal. He'd flown from London to Thessaloniki and driven to Prespa. In the two hours it took me to drive over the mountains, I counted just half a dozen cars and a log-truck. The road curves were so sharp, the tyres screeched in protest.

Road signs for Prespa began to appear, though there was only one fork: south to Lake Kastoria, and onwards to Prespa. You couldn't get lost on this road, only spooked. Disquiet stalked the sun-dappled mixed forests that rose on all sides. The only sound was the gentle bells of goats nowhere to be seen.

At the Vigla, or Sentinel, Pass, the highest point of the road where a Roman settlement had once been and a ski-resort operated in winter, the Vitsi Peak loomed close with its sharp Civil War monument. It was the site of the last battle of the Greek Civil War in the summer of 1949. A young couple had pulled over and were arguing viciously in what I took to be Macedonian, but it was Greek. The body language, the olive-skinned faces, the intonation, were the same. As I rejoined the road, an oncoming car found my presence irritating for some reason, and the bearded young driver gave me the fingers. Just driving here made you mean.

The road followed the steep valley of a river whose tributaries connected the Prespa basin with Lake Kastoria to the south, and with another mountain locally called Bellavoda, or White Water (2,177 metres), to the north, though it appeared on the map with a Greek name. In a village so small it was just a bend in the road, I stopped at a roadside cafe because there were people. Burly men sat talking, and a blind German shepherd dog came and sat by my feet like an old friend. I ordered a coffee. Inside, the house was full of musical instruments and photographs of armed men wearing white fustanellas and heroic moustaches, from the time of the Macedonian Struggle. A long-haired giant who looked like a brigand until I saw the gentle expression on his face, came to say hello, once the other men, rising heavily, drove off in their Jeeps. Clocking my registration plate, he switched to his local Slavic dialect. His name was Pavle.

It was an archaic dialect I hadn't heard before but understood perfectly. He and his brother and their wives ran this establishment which was also their home, but despite the dramatic topography and the adventure tours they offered, including hunts for wild boar, there were few visitors. It was the legacy of *Emfilios Polemos*, the Greek Civil War.

'You may not feel it,' he said. 'But it's here.'

Oh, I feel it, I said.

'In winter, it's just a few of us by the fire and the wolves howling in the hills,' he said. 'Last winter, two bears came to the front door.'

The village was called Antartiko, the Place of Guerrillas.

'The old name is Zhelevo,' said Pavle. After one Zhele, probably a komita.

The *andartes* (Greek) and the komitas (Bulgarian–Macedonian) were bitter enemies of similar practices. Both had roamed the mountains, where they'd vanish, leaving the villagers they supposedly protected to suffer the consequences in the hands of the enemy band. But villages like this *were* the mountains. During the First World War, the French Armée d'Orient had a base here. I can't imagine how the Senegalese and Cameroonians felt in these harsh mountains, but one French soldier left his impressions of the September harvest and, hanging in house windows, maize whose 'bright yellow explodes next to dark red peppers and scarlet aprons that give, under the sun, a wonderful colour tableau'.

'Always fighting,' Pavle said placidly. 'Why? Why are we always fighting? First the Turks. Then the Germans. Then brother against brother.'

Like many villages and some towns in Aegean Macedonia, Antartiko–Zhelevo had had a majority Bulgarian-speaking population. 'Before the fighting,' Pavle said, 'there were two thousand five hundred people, five thousand goats and sheep, and one thousand head of cattle. Now there are thirty old people and a few chickens. We're the youngest here.'

He was my age. By *the fighting*, he meant the Greek Civil War. There were two time planes here: before the war and after.

A man in a Jeep drove slowly up the road.

'Come meet a visitor,' my host shouted in Greek, 'from Ohrid.'

The man joined us. There wasn't much else to do here. He was another bulky type with a surprisingly gentle face, and though he understood *nashe*, he was reluctant to speak it and replied only in Greek.

Dopika ('local idiom' in Greek) or *nashe* ('our lingo' in Slavic) was how the local dialect was referred to here, in a careful avoidance of the taboo word 'Macedonian' or (more distantly but still undesirably) 'Bulgarian'. In the Greek nationalist project, dopika served to diminish the cultural weight a real language might have, spoken by real people who were not Greeks. Or not entirely. The project was helped by the fact that the various regional Slavic dialects of northern Greece had never been standardised into a national language and remained at a somewhat debased, domestic level.

'Before the fighting, there were twenty-five thousand people in Greek Prespa,' Pavle said. He had warmed up and seemed keen to get things off his chest. At the end of the war, there were just one thousand people left by the lake, all in a state of trauma. 'Now we are around three hundred. Even the lake is shrinking. When we were kids, we swam every day, the water clear as a teardrop. Now it's full of . . .'

He couldn't remember the Slavic word.

'Reeds,' a wheezy voice said. It was the old man in a wheel-chair under the awning, so desiccated he was mostly head. He'd been there all along, listening.

'Here's living history for you,' Pavle said. The old man looked at us but said nothing.

When the old man was a young lad with his flock on the hill, Pavle said, a German soldier came up to him and for no reason smashed his face with the butt of his gun and left him for dead. Once recovered, the lad was conscripted by the andartes of EAM (the National Liberation Front) to fight the German and Bulgarian occupiers near the city of Drama. No sooner was the war over than the Civil War broke out. Or rather, it had never stopped – for the different resistance factions in Greece had entered a bitter conflict, just like in Albania and Yugoslavia next door.

But Greece was already ticked off as belonging to the Western sphere of influence by Churchill and Stalin, in what Churchill called 'a naughty document'. On 9 October 1944, in Moscow, Churchill said to Stalin: 'Let us settle about our affairs in the Balkans. Your armies are in Rumania and Bulgaria.'

He scribbled percentages on a napkin, for each of the Balkan countries:

Rumania – Russia 90%, The others 10%
Greece – Great Britain 90% (in accord with U.S.A.),
   Russia 10%
Yugoslavia – 50–50%
Hungary – 50–50%
Bulgaria – Russia 75%, The others 25%

'I pushed this across to Stalin,' Churchill wrote in his war memoir, 'who had by then heard the translation. There was a slight pause. Then he took his blue pencil and made a large tick upon it, and passed it back to us. It was all settled in no more time than it takes to set down.'

So there was the fate of my family, of Pavle's, of Nick's, of tens of millions of others, scribbled on that napkin.

Starved and traumatised, postwar Greece swarmed with Nazi collaborators and proto-Fascist militias. Thanks to energetic British meddling, domestic Greek politics were manipulated into a state where it was possible to enforce the full disarmament of the leftist resistance fighters. Then deport them to prison islands en masse. The persecution and murder of resistance fighters by the Greek Nationalist Army and affiliated militias matched the Nazis' work in Greece. Rural populations like the Prespa villages lived in a permanent state of White Terror, though Red Terror arrived soon enough too.

This culminated in the 1944 *Dekemvriana* month in Athens, when militias opened fire on civilian demonstrators while British troops looked on. The resulting deaths and injuries sparked off an armed conflict in Athens which lasted a month and ended with the capitulation of the left. British troops under General Scobie took an active part. Their sudden new Greek allies were the thuggish Security Battalions and the Nazi collaborators of yesterday. Their sudden new enemies were their anti-Nazi allies of yesterday, the embattled Greek left. The situation went as far as General Scobie imposing martial law on Athens and ordering the aerial bombardment, during the Dekemvriana events, of a whole neighbourhood.

By 1946, when the Communist Party was made illegal, some hundred thousand leftists were rounded up and either executed, imprisoned or exiled. But the left regrouped in the mountains, and the full-blown guerrilla war that followed had its main theatre in the north-west of Greece: Pindus along the Albanian border and Verno here, for these remote regions provided two vital things for the newly formed Democratic Army of Greece (DSE): recruits and mountains. The Democratic Army was the military arm of the Greek Communist Party (KKE), and the inheritor of ELAS (the Greek People's Liberation Army) which had been the military arm of EAM.

The extraordinarily vicious Civil War lasted three and a half years and was won by the Greek National Army of King George, first with the help of Churchill's Britain, and after 1947, of Truman's America. The Greek king was a British puppet and in the wake of Greece's liberation from the Nazis, Churchill was hell-bent on reinstating him: he and the old ways were the best bulwark against Communism and the new ways. Greece was possibly the only country in postwar Europe where those who participated in the resistance against the Nazis were marked for elimination while Nazi collaborators were given political, military and judiciary power.

'Once again, our young lad was taken by the andartes,' Pavle continued. And when the Civil War ended, he was imprisoned on the island of Makronisos for having fought on the losing side. The official term for leftists was 'Communist bandits' or just 'bandits' – at the time and for decades after. The Greek Civil War – the first real war of the Cold War – ended with 158,000 dead and one million displaced, many permanently.

The old man pressed a button on his wheelchair and glided past us with a nod.

'He has perfect recall but won't talk,' Pavle said.

Why not?

'Fear.'

Fear? He survived the Nazis, the Civil War and Makronisos!

The two younger men sipped their coffees in silence. Fear, like grief, does not always need a current object.

'But I am not afraid,' Pavle said. 'Write this down. I am not afraid to speak our language. For twenty years we've been waiting for the old lake road to open. To bring some life back to Prespa.'

His Greek wife, who didn't understand dopika, had been sitting beside him all along, playing with his long hair like a bored child. She didn't let me pay for the coffee and invited me to come again.

They were a haunted bunch, living in the shadow of these blood hills. It was said that in the last months of the war, the earth turned red with the blood of the slain. The other brother's wife was a gaunt, pretty woman with a face so stricken that you couldn't look at it for more than a second. She was either ill or freshly bereaved. The brothers were known in the area as 'the priest's sons'.

I drove over the broken road out of Antartiko and several old men and women sitting on a bench waved at me with wordless smiles. Most of the village houses were abandoned, trees growing through the windows as if reaching out to grab you and tell you something.

The road to Little Prespa took the long, lonely time that roads to nowhere take. Just past the Prevali ridge, when I had almost given up hope of seeing the lake again, it appeared. What I was seeing was Little Prespa, and it didn't look small at all. It looked so majestic that my pulse quickened. The road descended. The flatlands at lake level were tame, agricultural. Monocultural, in fact: everywhere were bean fields, *fasoulakia*. But there were no people. I drove over the inlet between the two lakes, which had been a single lake before the water level dropped and mud was deposited in such large quantities by the nearest rivers that it had eventually been diverted into Little Prespa.

Little Prespa stretched towards Albania into a wetland wilderness, the water green with vegetation and brown with reedbeds. On the map, Little Prespa is a mini-me of Prespa, shaped by geomorphological and human forces into almost identical jagged teardrops.

The road began climbing the hilly peninsula that jutted into the lake like the head of a fish whose mouth was Psarades. I passed a small chapel called St George and a sign warning there were bears. Once over that pass, large Prespa appeared below, with its elusive gleam. Small, sharp, black hills rose from the water all the way to the north – dozens of them, a mirage. Prespa expressed something that cannot be put into words, or even feelings. High above the lake, I pulled over and sat in the car. I could not go on without adjusting to the majesty of the scene. Like the hills themselves, this place lifted you up and cast you down. In the still air, the juniper trees looked painted in silver. I wept without knowing why.

In the village square by the reeds, Nick was tucking into a green salad. Darkness was falling. I stumbled out of the car, hugged him, sat down at the table, and because Nick started laughing, I too laughed. My head was spinning.

'Can you believe this road?' I said.

'I know. It's a relief to see you, I have to say.' Nick poured me a glass of wine. 'I was starting to worry.'

Nick had an instantly winning quality, a warm and unaffected exuberance. With an unerring magpie's eye for the telling detail, an encyclopedic memory and boundless curiosity, he was especially interested in the former Soviet world and the Balkans, but really, his interests were omnivorous. Nick was a polyglot: he spoke five Slavic languages, Spanish, some Greek, some Romanian, some Mandarin, and some Hebrew (his partner was Israeli). His friends periodically asked: Are you sure you're not a spy?

'I recommend the catch of the day,' he said.

The fish was delicious, and of all the Prespan villages, Psarades alone still felt like a fishing village. Even its name meant The Fishermen. There were five restaurants open, mostly empty.

'European subsidies,' Nick said. 'As with the bean plantations.'

But after those mountains, I wasn't surprised that not many visitors made it here. It really was the end of the road.

Another Australian, a man from Perth, sat at the next table; he'd left here as a teenager fifty years ago. He always thought he'd bring his wife and kids, but they preferred Bali, so here he was like a cuckoo in the old family house. Of the two thousand people of this village once called Nivitsi, sixty were left. He spoke a mangled mix of lingos.

'Australian Lerinski,' Nick grinned, and the man nodded. Lerin was the old Bulgarian name of Florina and of the region.

'I grew up with Lerinski because of my grandmother,' Nick said. 'It's the first language I heard, before English.'

Nick grew up in Adelaide. His maternal grandmother had lived in a street full of exiles from Lerinsko, the region here. One day, on his way to school, one of them cornered him at the bus stop. 'And she told me how, after the Civil War, she'd gone in search of her children. They'd been taken by the Red Cross to Poland. It took her years, but she found them and brought them to Australia.' Another time, another old woman from the diaspora stopped him and without preamble told him how, when planes dropped American napalm on their village here in 1949, she and her mother were buried alive in a bomb crater. Next to their house. 'They dug themselves out with their bare hands. She carried her mother on her back to the next village. She'd never told anyone about it and needed to get it out.'

I pictured young Nick walking with his schoolbag and that woman's burden.

The final phase of the Civil War was called by survivors *the catastrophe*. Entire villages were obliterated by the army and paramilitary units. Children were burnt alive in houses, with mothers forced to watch, in revenge for the fathers joining the andartes. When women and children were forced away from their burnt houses in the direction of the nearest border, they often had nothing except the clothes they stood in; everything down to the last chicken had been taken by militants.

In the ethnic Macedonian villages of northern Greece and the Macedonian diaspora in Australia, there were code expressions like 'She's from Bapchor', to indicate a person who had been through unimaginable horror. Bapchor was one of the 'napalm villages'. Today it's neither on the map nor on the ground.

'I grew up with katastrofata,' Nick said.

He didn't know what it meant at first, he just soaked up the vibes.

'Growing up, there was anxiety about everything,' he said. 'Nothing was too small to worry ourselves sick about. Of course, the war was never discussed, it was too big. My mother picked it up from her mother. The anxiety. Even though she's Aussie-born and was an adult before she visited Macedonia for the first time!'

Nick's grandmother was from a nearby village, once entirely Slavic-speaking.

'We don't go there any more,' he said. 'It's been completely Hellenised. Not a scrap of its old identity remains. When my grandmother visited in the amnesty of 1987, she couldn't believe it. No one dared speak Macedonian. All the names were changed. People whispered about the war.'

Forty years after the war, people whispered about the war. They did even now, here – *seventy* years after the war.

'My grandmother said: this is not my village, not my home.' She never visited again. Her first husband had fought with ELAS against the Nazis, then joined the Democratic Army. Wounded in the last battle on Mount Vitsi, he died en route to the field hospital.

'He is buried in the family grave in the village, but his name appears in very small letters at the bottom of the tombstone,' Nick said. 'Like a pariah.'

One of Greece's many dishonoured heroes of the resistance. In the wake of the war, his family fell into the category of 'enemy'. Atrocities were especially rife against the Bulgarian-Macedonian villages here in the north, seen by the regime as a fifth column, as doubly 'bad Greeks': for speaking a non-Greek language and for being Socialist-Communist sympathisers.

The 1913 border that partitioned Macedonia had left hundreds of thousands of Slavic-speaking Macedonians and Bulgarians behind in Greece. This determined their harsh fate. Cut off from their compatriots in Yugoslavia and Bulgaria, they became an unwanted minority in a nation-state that was apparently allergic to ethno-linguistic and religious diversity. During the Metaxas regime in the 1930s, 'Slav-speakers and Turkish-speakers . . . were mercilessly persecuted, their languages forbidden in public, banned in the school-yard,' writes Fred A. Reed in *Salonica Terminus*. Things worsened immeasurably after the Greek Civil War.

Back in the village, the young widow who was to become Nick's grandmother was urged by her in-laws to disappear, before the paramilitary units arrived and torched the house. Australia was the obvious destination: her father, a gardener, had already settled there.

'My great-grandfather had arrived in Australia in 1929, just in time for the Depression!' Nick said. He'd left his wife and children behind. The young widow too left behind her two small children in the care of her mother, and sailed to Australia. A year into Adelaide, she met a young man at a Macedonian party and soon, Nick's mother was born.

The young man was a political refugee too – but from the Bulgarian Communist government. His family too hailed from Aegean Macedonia and had been expelled into Bulgaria in 1928 during the 'population exchange' between Greece and Bulgaria. By the late 1940s, he had fallen foul of the Bulgarian Communist authorities and, leaving behind a wife, a small daughter and a newborn son, he sailed from Naples to Australia on a ship called *The Nelly*.

'His escape was dramatic and clouded in secrecy. And as the years passed, increasingly sounding like something out of *Zorba the Greek*.'

In the wake of his defection, his family were internally exiled by the Communist state, treated as 'enemies of the people', and lived harsh lives.

'My uncle is an angry man. He says his life has been stolen.'

Meanwhile, Nick's mother didn't know she had half-siblings until they turned up. First her half-sister, then her half-brother, pale and serious in patched-up coats, just arrived from Greece with their grandmother, Nick's great-grandmother – yet another woman whose husband had gone away on a gurbet that had lasted a lifetime. But now that they were reunited, they fought constantly, Nick laughed.

By the age of six, Nick's mother was inseparable from her parents, accompanying them everywhere, on every trip to stores, governmental agencies, doctor's appointments. Because her parents never learned English.

'I know, it's amazing, but it wasn't so unusual,' Nick said.

'But why? Why did they burden their daughter like that?'

'Out of sheer bloody-mindedness, *inat*,' Nick said, using the pan-Balkan word for it. 'But also, I suspect, a delayed effect of trauma.'

A part of them remained frozen in time. And there had been the resentment of being strangers in a strange land, separated from their real identities while unable to go back, Nick said.

There was no way back. Not learning English was an act of protest. Oddly, they picked up Italian, from friends in the expat community. Even more oddly, they had initially spoken to each other in Greek – because their Macedonian dialects were so far apart that they had communication problems.

'As a kid I went between my grandparents who each insisted on their dialect version of simple words like potato! Because of *inat*. I'd translate between them.'

Although Nick had three siblings, it was him, the first-born, who carried the burden. Sensitised from an early age, probably from the womb, he formalised his commitment to his exiled grandparents by becoming a professional translator from all the Balkan Slavic languages.

'I remember my grandmother's tears of happiness when I started writing the Cyrillic alphabet at Masso school: К, Л, М, Н, О, П . . . Those letters meant so much to her.'

One of his early memories was watching the Olympics on television. His grandfather, who didn't contact his Bulgarian wife and children out of guilt and pain (he guessed their sad fate, and he knew there was no way back for him – he was, in the Communist state's terminology, a *non-returnee*, a dead man), rooted for the Bulgarian gymnasts and weight-lifters instead. He was proud of 'our boys and girls' when they won gold, and Nick was proud with him.

Nick's father, in turn, was one of the many young men who took the opportunity to emigrate from Tito's Yugoslav Macedonia. He had arrived in Australia with a friend in the early 1970s, seeking adventure. Though Australia failed to live up to his imagination and he returned home, by then he was utterly unable to toe the Communist Party line, and his own mother, afraid for him and the family's good name, urged him to leave again, back to Australia, whether he wanted to or not.

In Kanun terms, he had been banished by the tribe.

'He'd run away from Tito, but who was on the first page of all our Yugoslav books in Australia? Tito. *Tito, Tato, Mama*. Tito came first!' Another of Nick's early memories is of a city full of the portraits of a man who had just died. They were on a visit to Yugoslavia. 'Tito. I remember feeling bewildered by this mass sorrow.'

Nick's father, homesick after all those years away from his homeland, had wanted to bring his young family on a visit to Yugoslav Macedonia, to see whether there was any way back. But there was no way back.

Nick was born of the confluence of three Macedonias which together made up all of geographic Macedonia. Because of the borders, it was a confluence of exile, but it also meant that he had multiple identities.

To the north, the then Yugoslav Republic of Macedonia was his father's birthplace.

Aegean Macedonia to the south, now northern Greece, was his maternal grandmother's birthplace.

The province of Pirin Macedonia, in western Bulgaria, was his maternal grandfather's home.

Each came with its own internal contradictions and conflicts. Nick was like an Atlas carrying the weight of Macedonia on his shoulders, trying to stay cheerful – too cheerful sometimes – and not collapse, not get sucked in by the ancestral vortex.

'Maybe that's why you're always on the move,' I said, but the same was true of me. Nick and I mirrored each other in some respects. Because our family histories mirrored each other. 'Maybe restlessness is in our blood.'

He shrugged. His grandfather's restlessness, my grandmother's need to escape – these impulses had only been magnified in us by emigration. 'I just want to see as many places as possible before I get too old to travel,' he said. But he was only in his early forties.

In 1987, just two years before the fall of the Berlin Wall, his grandfather had arranged to meet with his grown-up son, the one he had left behind when he fled from Bulgaria. The dad had travelled from Australia to Yugoslavia, ostensibly for a family wedding but really to see his son, and the son had obtained permission to cross the border from Bulgaria into Yugoslavia, for one day. He had looked forward to meeting his dad his whole life. He was in his forties. But the Bulgarian border authorities kept preventing him, asking for more and more papers that he had to produce. Weeks passed. He could not cross the border.

'My grandfather extended his stay, but in the end, he couldn't wait any longer and made his way to Athens, for his return flight to Australia. You can imagine how he felt on that flight.'

Just hours after the dad had left Yugoslavia for Athens, and with the poisonous intent totalitarian regimes specialise in, the son was finally allowed into Yugoslavia.

'Everyone in the family strongly believes that this was too much of a coincidence,' Nick said. 'So there must have been a Bulgarian State Security agent tailing my grandfather in Yugoslavia all along, and once it was clear that my grandfather had left for Athens, then the border officials were tipped off to let my uncle cross the border.'

He did. Only to be told that his father had left a few hours before.

'And on hearing the news from his father's Yugoslav family, he just – howled,' Nick said. He had collapsed. He had crossed the border alone, and now he was alone in his sorrow.

'He howled like an animal, and the mountains picked up his howl and echoed it back. I think my uncle never got over that moment.'

A moment of irreversible loss. A parting like a death. The role State Security played makes this story not just tragic, but evil. This is how Communist regimes punished their non-returnees: by tormenting their children. The son did meet the father, years later – he travelled to Australia for it – but only in the last weeks of the father's life when dementia meant that the old man didn't know he was looking at his long-lost first-born. The son was never *seen* by the father.

The village and the mountain around it had gone black under the starry sky. The only sound was the treacly glug of water in the reeds. We went to our cold rooms in a stone house, and I slept like a stone at the bottom of the lake.

★

In the morning, when I walked across the sun-struck square, past the police station with its bored cops and their swanky 'Hellenic Police' motorboat, an impatient Nick and a smiling boatman in a captain's peaked cap were waiting for me at the pontoon. I was an hour late, not realising that Greece and the Republic of (North) Macedonia ran on separate times. A border wasn't enough. Closing the lakeside checkpoint wasn't enough. They also had to have different time zones. Even though, strictly speaking, they were Macedonia and Macedonia.

The smiling boatman was from the Macedonian-speaking villages across the Albanian border. He'd come over in the 1990s, like the woman who looked after our guesthouse for five euros a day, and who told me: 'We're all *nashi*, our people here, and the Greeks know it.'

'We all speak Macedonian here,' the boatman said, and we set off in his new boat. 'Just not near the police building.'

From our new vantage point on the lake, Psarades looked small, isolated, as if tossed into the water from the top of the cliffs.

'The real residents' – the captain pointed at the hilltop cemetery. 'We're all just visitors here.'

Because his mother was born in Greece and his father in Albania, he'd been called a Greek there and an Albanian here, though they were Macedonians. He didn't mind. He enjoyed himself like someone who had processed cruder forms of struggle in his life, and was now tuning in to the longer view. The lake view.

Two pelicans with enormous wingspans – three metres, the captain said – flew over us, landing not far from the boat, and bobbed about on the water. Prespa has one of only two European colonies of the globally endangered Dalmatian pelicans: the other one is on the Danube.

The captain told us an origin myth about the formation of Lake Prespa.

'A long time ago, there was a spring in the middle of a valley.

Two shepherds came to drink from it, but fell asleep and forgot to turn it off.' It is not said whether the shepherds survived the flooding, but towns were lost under the water which eventually became the lake. The spring remained forever open.

'Fishermen in Albania say that sometimes when the water is very still, they can see the outlines of lost houses in the water.'

When we asked about the water border, the captain pointed and said:

'Where there's sun, it's Greece. Where there's shadow, it's Albania.'

We could wave to Dry Village across the water and almost make out Bojko's parents' house. We docked at the cave Bojko had pointed out, and Nick and I climbed the hundred and seventy steps to the top of a vast chilly cavern forty metres above the lake. A humble church nestled at the echoey top, and the karst was nibbled by niches where fifteen monks had lived from fishing and hunting. Only juniper grew here, and in early summer, tiny orchids. On the shore across, there had been nuns. Perhaps they visited each other in those coffin-like chuns, and exchanged herbal recipes. The inside was painted in the early fifteenth century at the time of the Serbian lord Vukashin. The only reason Vukashin had retained his fiefdom during the early Ottoman decades was the remoteness of lower Prespa.

But the narrative of the church had been tampered with more recently: the Cyrillic lettering had been rubbed out, and either left blank or replaced with Greek script clearly newer than it should be. Christ held a blank book. This recurred in all the Prespan churches we visited. Diligent whitewashing had ensured that no Cyrillic script could be proven to have existed at all.

Charming scenes of miracles and natural phenomena abounded: the wind, human-faced and full-cheeked, a lake monster with teeth ingesting a white mass, maybe a swan.

'A cave is a mneme, a damaged cell of memory preserved when all that existed in the open air – peoples, crafts, cults – has rotted away,' writes Neal Ascherson in *Stone Voices*. His subject is the hermit caves of western Scotland and the Hebridean islands, once home to St Columba and early Christians of the north-west, who had 'turned their backs' to the warmer south as a gesture of penitence, to face the harsh Atlantic gales. Here, in the south-east, hermits had turned their backs to the violent land, to face the timeless light of the lake.

Looking at Mary's defaced countenance, it made sense that this place was called Virgin Eleusa, the Merciful One. Her face, even scraped out, managed to exude understanding. The space itself exuded quiet humanity. Mnemosyne, the Greek goddess of memory, is also the mother of all the Muses, and this cave held memories that were almost palpable, even after centuries open to the elements. After the cave, the light of the lake blinded us. Along the small jetty, a line of thin-necked cormorants perched like a welcoming party in black. Red ducks with black-tufted heads bobbed nearby. We were of no consequence to them.

A liberating thought: to be of no consequence.

'Great crested grebes,' the captain corrected me, then took us to a place in the lake where the three territorial waters converged.

'This is the deepest point of the lake,' he said. 'Fifty metres.'

We could wave to Nakolec and Pretor but go no further. The water boundaries pushed you away from the lake and back into its tormented hinterland. Even under a foreign occupier, the hermits of Prespa had been freer to move between islands and shores than the Prespans of today, who live in sovereign nation-states.

Back on the road, there was a place Nick and I wanted to see, on the fish-like peninsula that jutted into the lake with Psarades as its mouth. It was known as the Zachariadis Cave. It wasn't sign-posted from the main road but we could see the steps hacked into the hill. We took the steps, hard-going in the midday sun. And that was after breakfast and a good night's sleep, much more than the guerrillas had enjoyed.

Below us opened the silent fields of green beans, tied at their tops. But no people. Who ate all these beans? Later, I learned that the subsidised bean monoculture had killed off other cultures including animal husbandry, and that many absentee Prespans made profits from their bean plantations but lived elsewhere. The forest at the top had been a refuge for the Democratic Army at the end of the war, as they were pushed into the lake, and Yugoslavia. Then Tito slammed the door shut and it was endgame.

The villages of Psarades and German had been their arms and provisions bases. And up here, inside this cave, had been their HQ. Somewhere higher up, in another cave, was their field hospital. Nick climbed into the cave despite the feral smell.

'There's nothing here,' he reported, emerging cheerfully.

If Nick's grandmother's first husband had survived his wounds en route to the field hospital, Nick would not exist.

The forest held unspecified distress, and I was keen to leave. We took the stone steps down and just then, a park ranger rushed up towards us.

'Ah, good!' he said in Greek, and smiled. 'I saw your car. We have a bear with cubs in the cave. I came to check that everybody was OK.'

We thanked him, and I suspect I said to Nick, 'I told you it smelt feral!'

On the side of the deserted road was a small monument.

'Oh my God, this is new!' Nick said.

It was a humble granite piece bearing the mountain-like triangle, symbol of the Democratic Army (the DSE), and marking this spot as the centre of its activity between 1946 and 49. It had been erected by the Greek Communist Party (the KKE) this year.

Nick stood beside it, sombre-faced, elbow bent in the Communist fist salute. We didn't point out the sad irony of this moment because it went without saying. Neither of us was under any illusion about the ideology that had driven the Greek Communist Party's high command. Under Zachariadis, a Stalinist, they had highjacked the struggle of the left, hobbled their own cause through the brutality of their methods, and stamped the war with their particular brand of fanaticism and incompetence. They had planned a Stalinist-style dictatorship in the event of victory. Greece would have been gripped by the same tyranny its neighbours were already suffering under. But history had decided that it would be gripped by a different kind of tyranny.

Above a village called Orovo that didn't exist any more, Nick and I stumbled across another surprise monument, brand new.

'Oh my God, Vera Foteva!'

She was the figurehead on the granite slab. This meant nothing to me, but Nick had grown up with photographs of her and other partisans on the walls of diaspora culture halls. She was a hero in the DSE pantheon, and by all accounts a remarkable woman. Here was a monument to the Second Congress of the Pan-Hellenic Democratic Union of Women.

'The Communists had a way with words, didn't they!' Nick said.

Vera Foteva's story tells of the moral and political morass that was the Civil War. By September 1949, the Greek Communist Party under Zachariadis had capitulated. In a typically untruthful turn of phrase, Zachariadis proclaimed a 'temporary ceasefire'. Foteva and her comrades fled to Albania and later to the USSR. But the KKE, who regrouped in Tashkent, then in the USSR, undertook internal purges in the 1950s, ostensibly in search of those culpable for the failure of the Civil War. Foteva was accused of being an American spy. If the Communists wanted to frame you, you went down either as American spy or as Titoist, a punishable offence after the Stalin–Tito split.

'As an ethnic Macedonian and a woman, she was an easy scapegoat,' Nick said. He knew her biography by heart. She was tried in the USSR and did five years in the Gulag, after which she was internally exiled to Alma-Ata.

'But she never lost her spirit,' Nick said. 'Eventually, she was allowed into Yugoslav Macedonia where she married, formed a folk band with other refugee women from here called Kostur-chanki, Women of Kastoria, and remained a Communist to her dying day!'

In 2004, a few years before her death, the Greek government announced a general amnesty, and blacklisted refugees like her were allowed back into Greece.

'For nine days.'

Then they had to leave.

'Even the KKE betrayed us, once the war was over,' Nick said. 'They have never acknowledged the mass participation of ethnic Macedonians in the war. As if we never existed.'

Out of all the DSE combatants, up to forty per cent had been ethnic Macedonians and Bulgarians, including Muslims. With a lump in my throat, I photographed Nick with Vera Foteva, stony against the mute Aegean sky.

The following day, we drove south to Lake Kastoria of fur-trading fame and once on a trade route linked to Ohrid-Prespa in the north and Epirus in the south.

'The Communists banned love,' said a man in a village where many of the handsome houses had dissolved in the rain down to red stumps, with holes like gouged eyes. Others still hung on to their elaborate façades with dates, owners' names, and balconies.

'The punishment for love was death,' said his friend.

They were born during the Civil War. We had found them sitting in the shade of an old walnut tree. One of them had had a partisan mother and a father in the Nationalist Army – but this didn't mean much when so many conscriptions on both sides had been forced. Women between the ages of seventeen and forty were swept into the Democratic Army. In the last desperate year of the war, boys as young as ten were taken. The other man's siblings had been evacuated by the partisans to Romania. The father had survived Makronisos. Now a hundred and five years old, he'd never talked about it.

'What happened on that island can't be put into words,' he said.

I had read some documents and memoirs of Makronisos and had nightmares afterwards. Male rape and torture were commonplace.

'But the Communists were bad too,' said his friend.

'They shot their own.'

'Zachariadis brought katastrofata to this country,' said a massive old man with a young man's spark in his eye, who'd driven by in a tractor and stopped to chat.

'Greece has been devoured by her own,' said the man whose parents had fought on opposing sides.

'We all took a bite at Greece, and it has been eaten away,' said the massive old man.

'The dead outnumber the living,' said a younger man. 'See the cemetery by the church? There's a good twenty thousand souls buried there. And how many of us are alive? No more than thirty.'

Even his own daughter had left for America. He'd not finished primary school, back in the 1950s, because he had to look after the animals in the *orman*, he said, using the Turkish word for forest. The dialect here was full of Turkish words like *asker* for army, and of countless archaic Bulgarian words. They said *sinora* for border, a Greek word.

'It's true,' the men agreed. 'Our language has everything: Bulgarian, Turkish, Albanian, Greek.'

The many-coloured blossom of Macedonia, clinging to the bitter soil.

'You're looking for stories? My story is a short one,' said the massive old man.

He was one of the twenty-five thousand detsa begalci removed by the Democratic Army to Eastern Europe. He'd ended up in Poland, aged fourteen.

'We arrived in Gdansk in winter. We walked in the streets, but—'

His face suddenly twitched and tears came from his blue eyes, which he wiped with a cracked hand, then cleared his throat.

'But there was nothing left. No streets, no buildings, no people. Just big rags of snow falling from the sky. I thought to myself: My God, the Germans have really done it.'

He learned a trade in a factory and lived in a home with other refugees, Macedonian- and Greek-speakers. They helped rebuild Poland. He'd enjoyed his years there, he said, it gave him a chance to learn the ways of the world. 'Eight years later, they started allowing some of us back and I wanted to see my mother. I never went back to Poland. Here it's always been poor, but it's my home. This is the story. A short one, like I said.'

How do you sum up your life to a stranger two generations younger than you? He got back into his tractor and drove away with a cheery wave of his huge hand.

In a process known by the sinister word *paedomazoma*, 'the gathering of children', children had been taken from their families by the KKE, who feared, correctly, that the kids would be either killed in cross-fire or removed by the Government Army and placed in the government re-education camps known as *paedopolis*es, children's cities. Twenty-five thousand kids in fact ended up in these camps, under the tutelage of the monarchy, where they were provided for, educated, and indoctrinated in absolute loyalty to the Greek monarchy and Church. The only permissible language and identity was Greek. Like the refugee kids sent to the Eastern bloc, they were separated from their parents for years, sometimes forever.

Paedomazoma was historically associated with the dreaded Ottoman 'blood tax', and still strikes a note of dread, just like the expression *detsa begalci* sends cold shivers down the generational spine. And while the word *paedomazoma* contains the sorrow of forced departure from the homeland, *detsa begalci* contains the sorrow of impossible return.

'There is nothing here but orman and fighting,' said the

younger man. His grandfather had been an officer in the Bulgarian army. The other man's grandfather too. 'I am paying for my
parents' war. Can you tell me why?'

His daughter would never come back, he said. She didn't
speak nashe, only Greek, and her child didn't speak Greek, only
English. She wanted it all to *cease*.

'And I wish her well,' he said, with a bitter expression.

'But,' smiled the man whose father was a hundred and five,
'visitors make us happy. Thank you for visiting.'

Nick and I drove on to Kastoria in silence. He was used to
this level of psycho-geographic blight, from previous visits to
northern Greece. I wasn't.

Greek Prespa was a naturalist's paradise, but life here had been
harsh for generations. The men under the walnut tree told us how
superstitious the people here had been. Once, a villager was seen
walking the opposite way to where he was going before turning
back onto the right track. What are you doing? one of the men
had asked him. Trying to trick the evil eye, the villager said, so it
won't find me.

The war 'transformed the villages of northern Greece from
homes where children led difficult, but safe and secure lives
into battlefields of random violence and sudden death', write
the anthropologists Loring Danforth and Riki Van Boeschoten
in *Children of the Greek Civil War*. Many of the refugee children
in witness accounts said that 'the People's republics' had opened
their eyes to the world. Likewise, many of those housed in the
government camps cherished the education and worldliness it had
given them, in exchange for the stony besa of village life where
you are forever paying for someone's war.

By 1905, in the wake of the Ilinden Uprising, the lie of the political land was clear to perceptive outsiders. Henry Brailsford,
passing through Prespa, wrote that the traveller's impressions of
'the Bulgarians of Macedonia' were 'rarely favourable'. They

were a people 'with few external attractions; and [they] seldom trouble to sue for sympathy or assist the process of mutual understanding . . . [The Bulgarian of Macedonia] will not call on you unbidden at your hotel, or invite you to his schools, or insist that you shall visit his churches.'

This syndrome of obscurity was aggravated by the fact that 'all their best men are exiles in free Bulgaria. There is no educated class left to leaven the rest, or to represent the nation to the traveller.' Macedonian towns were like the people: silent, stubborn, inscrutable. Until, one evening in Pelagonia, he happened on a peasant family and heard them sing 'a song of revolt': 'From that evening onwards the air was always in my ears. Sometimes it was a schoolboy who whistled it in the streets; sometimes a group of young men who chanted it, with all its daring words, within earshot of a Turkish sentry.'

Doubly battered by the Greek clergy and the Ottoman regime who colluded when it suited them, too oppressed to even sing openly, the land sang for them. The mountains, the lakes, the forest glades vibrated with a spirit that couldn't articulate itself except in a 'song of doom, sung by the land itself'.

We could hear it still, in the empty valleys of Prespa.

Shockingly, Macedonian song lyrics seem to be banned from official events in Greece to this day. A great fear must lie behind this. But what lies behind the fear?

'The Greek term for Macedonian folk songs is *tragoudia dihos logia*,' Nick said. 'Literally, songs without words.'

At official events, people were still forced to play the songs instrumentally, moving their lips voicelessly. As if their tongues had been cut off. That was the aim, it seemed – to render them dumb, voiceless.

Xenophobia: fear and loathing of the other.

'Of course, private parties are another story,' Nick said.

The present-day 'Macedonian Question' of the name, as well as the politics of silencing, were a direct consequence of unresolved

bilateral, and national, trauma from the Greek Civil War. Danforth and Boeschoten call this 'memory wars' and the moving
case histories they present – of both Macedonian and Greek exiles
– shed light on the depth of the wounds that people sustained
before, during and after those tragic years. And on why the political ghosts of this little-known war are, in effect, Europe's ghosts.

I was intrigued to find that Aegean Macedonia and Thrace
to the east (an ancient region shared today by Bulgaria, Greece
and Turkey) were identified by the late pioneering historian Jean
Manco as the original homeland of what in linguistics is often
called the Balkan group of languages. This is the homeland of
the speakers of the unknown proto-parent of Armenian, Greek,
Illyrian and Thracian – our dimly remote ancestors who had
migrated here from Asia. The cultures of Macedonia and Thrace
– that is, the southern Balkans – were born out of a diversity
that survived many empires and thousands of years, only to be
assaulted in the last few generations by nation-states with a taste
for the biscuit-factory line of history, as Neal Ascherson has
called it.

The result? Human and environmental monoculture, and
rapid decline.

But we were in for a surprise. In a village above Lake Kastoria,
a man with sad blue eyes was delighted to have customers in his
cafe and told us, when asked, that his five siblings had all been
sent away during the war and two had never returned. Nearby
we discovered a cemetery with a locked church and a lake view.
Above the door, St Nicholas's name was scratched out and he was
left nameless as well as eyeless, but among the graves we stumbled
across a black marble slab that stopped us in our tracks.

'Oh my God!' Nick said.

The man's name was written twice: in Greek and in Cyrillic.
A common sight in Albanian Prespa which was openly bilingual,
it was unheard of here – not only for having been done in the first
place, in defiance of the seventy-year-long ban on Cyrillic, but

also for not having been defaced. The man had died a few years ago.

'Oh my God,' Nick kept saying, in shock. 'I never thought I'd see this in Greece. I wish my grandmother could see it!'

And tears welled up in his eyes. As they had in hers, when he'd written his first Cyrillic letters. They were the same tears, filtered by time as if by the karst. In the Cyrillic-Greek letters of this man's name was the hidden story of Aegean Macedonia, with its vanishing dialects, people, place names and songs. We stood by the grave of this man whose story we didn't know but whose face on the marble was stamped with endurance, and I was reminded of Edith Durham's sketch of an acquaintance in Ohrid: 'Being a Balkan Christian he has inherited a tendency always to expect the worst.'

'Yep!' Nick said and we laughed, though I too was crying now, for company. Though I'd never met Nick's grandmother or mother, I felt as if I knew them.

The Balkan Muslims had it worst in the second half of the twentieth century. Either way we, the distant offspring of this land, were not conditioned for good news. This quiet glimpse of tolerance in a landscape disfigured by denial choked us up. Good things brought us an unfamiliar sensation. Joy was a precursor to grief. Reunion brought fear of parting. And parting was like death.

We must have stayed by that tombstone for only a few minutes, but it felt like a long time. Small acts of kindness go a long way.

We drove for two days up and down the hills of Prespa, rarely meeting a soul. The only sound was the bells of goats we never saw, nor their shepherds.

For centuries, Prespa had been the domain of pastoralist shepherds known as Sarakatsani or Karakachani (from the Turkish *kara* and *kachan*, 'black smugglers', referring to their nomadic ways and black woollen dress, and their uncanny border-crossing skills). Here, they'd come up from Thessaly and the Pindus and spend the summer in reed huts above Prespa. Many others were based in the Rhodope Mountains to the east, and there is even a breed of Karakachan mountain dog in Bulgaria. They were an old subculture of the southern Balkans, deeply connected with nature's cycles. A handful of such families survived near Prespa, who'd gather in the centre of lakeside villages like German at the end of the season, with their cattle, then depart back to the south. They sold their milk to locals, for small-scale cheese production.

Dotted along the empty roads and packed with political symbolism were numerous monuments to senior Greek military figures from the Civil War. Some bore the Byzantine eagle that stands for ultra-Orthodoxy and the far right, and a couple were even inscribed in Katharevousa – literally, 'purified Greek'. 'Katharevousa on a military monument is a statement of ultra-nationalism in the Metaxist mould,' Nick said.

There were no monuments to those from the losing side, except a slab in a village listing the names of children killed by mines, and one memorial to a young partisan, just before the Albanian border.

'Rainbow tried to put a small memorial at Mount Vicho [Vitsi] next to the existing one, commemorating the Macedonian fighters,' Nick said.

Rainbow was a political party in Florina, representing the ethnic Macedonian minority. Their offices had been set on fire several times in the past twenty years. The monument was defaced instantly, then destroyed. Today, the far-right Golden Dawn gather at the summit every year.

'Every time we come here we swear it's the last,' Nick said, meaning northern Greece. 'It's like they're waiting for us all to die.'

'When you say *we*, who do you mean?' I asked.

Nick was quiet for a moment.

'Me and my mother,' he said. 'And my grandmother.'

Then he added: 'And my great-grandmother. 'Cause here's the thing: it doesn't even end with death!'

When his great-grandmother died in Adelaide and the family asked the local Orthodox priest to do the forty-day service, he refused.

'Because he was Greek and we were Macedonian.'

He'd called them *Skopianoi*, a Greek slur targeting their neighbours whose capital is Skopje. Even when they were in Australia. This contempt had a history, though not a very long one. But it is precisely these relatively modern Balkan *agonies* that get written off as 'ancient hatreds'.

In the Kastoria of the early twentieth century, Henry Brailsford met a Greek bishop who told him that the town hospital was for Greeks only, and Muslims and foreigners at a pinch, but that he would rather see Bulgarian-Macedonian women and children die than be admitted. 'Because they are our enemy,' the bishop explained, an answer 'so frank, so primitive' that the author despairingly concluded Kastoria to be 'the home of lost causes'. Meanwhile, since the majority of people in the Florina district didn't speak Greek, the Greek bishop was obliged to conduct the church service in Turkish as a compromise – which strikes with its comical absurdity.

We drove through Kastoria, where fortunes were once made from fur-trading. Shop signs in Russian were everywhere: 'Fur coats at warehouse prices!'

'Cyrillic is fine if it signals Russian buyers, of course,' Nick said. 'No end to the ironies!'

The irony was living testimony to the relativity of cultural meaning. Culture is all about created context. Meanwhile, no one was buying anything much in poor, pretty Kastoria, where old people with defeated faces sold plastic items at street stalls.

An English officer, consul at Ali Pasha's court in Ioannina, passed through here in the early 1800s and described Lake Kastoria – frozen, with buffalo-driven carts moving over it. Despite the warmth of the day and the beauty of the scenery, I could see it frozen, blackbirds overhead and wolves howling in the valleys.

Like Lake Prespa, Lake Kastoria and its outlying mountain villages where the few people we met had sad eyes, lost siblings, and things they couldn't put into words, left us feeling stricken.

'I'm glad we're leaving tomorrow,' I said. 'There's something very heavy here.'

'Welcome to my world,' Nick laughed.

We didn't want to talk about illness, so as not to fall into that ancestral habit – we had both noticed that across the Balkans, ill health was a favourite topic of conversation and there was in fact a disproportionate amount of disease and early death – but a decade ago, in his early thirties, Nick had been diagnosed with advanced cancer.

'And it's weird, but just hours after I got the diagnosis, my mother received a phone call saying her mother was about to die!'

His mother was trained in the catastrophic mindset, and here was catastrophe. When his grandmother died, the hearse arrived with a Greek flag on the bonnet. A war flag.

'The dynamics in the extended family have been a minefield of unresolved identity issues,' Nick said. 'Like an extension of the Greek Civil War. As if the war never ended.'

Family members were civil to each other, he said, but under the surface, tensions and the fear of association bubbled, which over time led to estrangement. It sounded familiar.

'My immediate family in Oz,' he said, 'by virtue of identifying as "Macedonian", were the black sheep of the extended family in Greece, with a constant underlying feeling that we were uncomfortable for the "Greek" family members. As if our very existence proved that they were not Greek after all. Rather than confront their self-made demons, they preferred just burying them.'

But how do you bury something that's alive? I asked about the health of his extended family.

'Outbursts of extreme neurotic behaviour, addiction, alcoholism, anorexia. And an extraordinary number of strokes at a young age.'

The struggle to own your name, your mother tongue and the letters of your alphabet, your past, your present, your children, the graves of your dead, to exist at all – this struggle, when passed down the generations undigested and further multiplied in a schizoid tug-of-war between cousins and siblings, is almost the definition of systemic illness. The entire system sickens.

This is a side-effect of 'Balkanisation', of the violent splitting into hostile entities of a complex matrix that cannot be divided any more than the child presented to King Solomon could be cut into two children. Nick, loyal Nick, had almost become the sacrificial victim of his family, by manifesting the collective disease in his body.

But his cancer had healed and he had been finally given the all-clear this year. To celebrate, he was travelling even more frenetically than usual. I kept wanting to tell him to sit still, be quiet for a moment, and stop looking up the latest news on social media. His restlessness infected me. It's as if he was constantly being engulfed by events and their consequences, and had no distance from anything.

But what about me? Even after years of retraining myself out of the feeling that good things only serve to invite catastrophe – despite my university degrees, fluency in various languages, travelling the world – even then, in my ancestral brain, I was not that different from the man who walked backwards 'to trick the evil eye'.

On the bone-dry St Achillius island of Little Prespa, reached by a long scenic walkway from the western side of the lakelet, all that was left of Samuil's great episcopalian basilica was the beautiful curved wall with three window holes, and columns propping up nothing, witnesses that are perhaps just as well silent. And bullet holes, as if from many executions. In the days of Samuil, there had been a natural isthmus and the island may have been a peninsula. Even now, when the lake freezes over, as it would in the coming winter, the few children of the island walk to school across the ice, as if across frozen time.

In the midst of the fighting in the winter of 1948, this island had seen the wedding of Nikos Zachariadis to his comrade in love and war, Roula Koukoula. Even if he had banned love for everybody else. He would hang himself many years later in exile in Siberia, after Roula betrayed him by voting for his excommunication from the Communist Party. They remained in an inner state of war to the ends of their lives.

Nick and I walked to the far end of the island, past the ruins of a monastery and a humble church with stirring frescoes. Hundreds of birds were scattered like crumbs over sky and water. But Little Prespa is changing fast – or fast in lacustrine time. The causes are human: the irrigation of the bean fields, which silts up the lake with unnatural speed. The bean fields are to Little Prespa what the apple orchards are to Big Prespa: deadly.

As the people of Prespa were driven away by war, the reedbeds – for centuries dwelling places for fishermen and their reed huts as well as sources of material for handmade goods – have been abandoned and are rapidly spreading, encouraged by the increased littoral mud. The shepherds whose livestock grazed the reeds and kept them under control are gone too. Until the 1960s, Little Prespa had water buffalo whose favourite food was reeds. Now, the spreading reedbeds nibble away at the wetlands, meaning less space for fish spawning, which in turn means fewer other species like waterfowl. After over a million years of self-regulation, it is twentieth-century war that may slowly kill Prespa, a process that has been under way for two generations now.

'The water plants are dying and decaying in the lake, which adds organic material, which in turn ages the lake and leads it to a speedier death: turning into dry land,' writes the Prespan naturalist Giorgos Catsadorakis. 'The extreme old age of a lake manifests itself in what we call marshes, swamps, and peat bogs. The corpse of a lake we call dry land.'

It was hard to imagine the death of Prespa, so far away in human time, but Little Prespa already showed the signs – the reedbeds were impenetrable forests inside the lake. Yet from our vantage point on the island, it looked like a place where nature, not man, would have the last word, where guano would always whitewash the ruins of our labours, where the illusions of empires and nations rightly come to the end of their road.

A Greek archaeologist who fell under the spell of Prespa began excavating the island in the 1950s. The inhabitants of the small fishing community of St Achillius are probably descendants of Samuil's Prespa – soldiers and workers, some of whom he brought with his army after his invasion of Thessaly to the south, whence he also brought the relics of Achillius, a fourth-century cleric. It was here, in Samuil's church, that the archaeologist found the sarcophagi of Samuil, his son Gavril-Radomir and his nephew Ivan-Vladislav: three men of different temperaments whose fate had been war, finally in a state of peace.

In another excavation on the island, a medieval necropolis revealed that the dead had Charon's *obols* (coins) placed over their eyes – the fee to the ferryman for the journey across the Styx. Those who didn't have the obol would remain in limbo, forever wandering the psychic landscape.

Back on the mainland, we recrossed the isthmus between the two lakes, back to the east side of Little Prespa. Villagers on the run from the Civil War had escaped towards Albania along here with their children, dodging shells. British bombers dropped shells in an attempt to blow up the bridge at its western end in Koula, 'Tower', its name suggesting that this had been an old observation point on the lake, possibly used in Samuil's time and even during the Romans'. Locals still find unexploded shells around Koula when the water level is low.

★

In the morning, in the mouth of the fish called Psarades, we said goodbye on the square by the reeds. Nick drove to Thessaloniki for his London flight, and I drove west into Albania.

A popular saying has it that *Makedonia* comes from *maka*, the Slavic for sorrow and strife. Of course, it isn't true – the 'barbarian' Makednoi are mentioned by Herodotus ten centuries before the Slavs arrived, and the root of the name is a word for 'high' or 'tall', as the apparently tall Macedons of antiquity were called Highlanders by the Greeks in the south (though the word was pre-Greek). Yet in the emotional lives of four Balkan nations, *Makedonia* has come to mean sorrow and strife – and at times *agonia*. But also survival against the odds. The emotional life of Greek Prespa was clearly out of sync with its official history – but on the other hand, history is also made going forwards because it is a living thing. From a certain point, it's up to the living, not to the dead, how history looks on the ground.

Only months later, in June 2018, this square by the reeds would witness a historic scene Nick and I wouldn't have thought possible, hereditary catastrophists that we are. The Greek and Macedonian governments would sign the Prespa Agreement, healing the rift of the last twenty-five years over the name 'Macedonia'. Or rather, of the last one hundred years.

Or rather, healing the surface of it; underneath, a chasm of discord and denial still gaped, maintained by both sides. Macedonia would agree to change its name to North Macedonia, and Greece would consent. The deal would be signed here by politicians with hopeful smiles, but the road ahead would be a turbulent one as nationalistic Greeks continued to rage at their neighbours and their government for using the word at all, and the Macedonians raged against *their* neighbours and their own government for reducing them to 'North'. When they were, *are*, here in the south too, still. But that is precisely what Greece had made taboo. Acknowledging the existence of a people who call themselves Macedonians and who are not Greeks, puts a dent in the 'biscuit-factory line of history' that goes neatly from Hellenic antiquity to Byzantium to the Macedonian Struggle and the modern Greek nation-state. All this might have been a lot easier, of course, had the manufacturers of Yugoslav and post-Yugoslav Macedonian national identity not gone to such extremes as to render the Bulgarian connection taboo and to claim direct lineage from warriors over two thousand years dead, respectively. This is how they produced their own biscuit-factory line, character-ised by that bathetic blend typical of all Balkan nationalism (and possibly of *all* nationalism) and which makes it so unsuited to actual life: pettiness and grandiosity.

Alexander would be pleased: his Macedon war goes on, though geographically much reduced.

Driving the roads of Greek Prespa, a line from a poem came to me, by the poet Yannis Ritsos who spent years on prison islands (first in the 1940s, then in the 1960s):

'The dead are increasingly in danger.'

This applies also to the unborn, surely. We must do things differently for their sake, if not ours. What was striking on that sunny June day in Psarades the following year, when an addendum to history was signed, was that the two young prime ministers with tired smiles looked like cousins. And that – as with the Ohrid Agreement seventeen years before – it took a lake to imagine peace.

The Albanian border was my aim. My final destination was St Naum Monastery. This journey was coming to an end. I needed to get back – not to Ohrid town, but to the Lake of Light. Prespa could be taken only in small doses, like medicine. To get to the Albanian border, I had to leave the lake again and for a long time follow a valley darkened by mountains, past comfortless Civil War ruins. Everything felt unstable, in time and space.

In Psarades the previous night, while eating dinner near the police station, Nick and I had started whispering, even though we were speaking English. After just two days, Greek Prespa had instilled paranoia in him, and resentment in me. I looked with mistrust at the cops with their ignorant swagger, and was all too ready to say to them, in a voice that wasn't mine: Do you have *any* idea how much these people have suffered! But what if the cops struck back with their own suffering? Prespa had taught me that their great-grandparents were probably exiles from Asia Minor, or poor pastoralists from Epirus, resettled here as part of the hellenising of the lake's hinterland. What choice had they had in the matter? They too were survivors of history.

It was no good, out-suffering each other, passing the parcel of pain as in some Beckettian play – I'll bury you. No, I'll bury you first. My people are more ancient than your people. No, we were here first, we're the autochthonous ones. We've suffered the most. You? You have no idea what suffering means!

We had to get out of this ontological loop.

'It made sparkling sense that the vanquished, not the victors, should learn these secrets,' wrote the child narrator of *The Heroic Age* when he grew up. This raw and beautiful novel by Stratis Haviaras is set in Civil War Greece. The child narrator is trapped behind the andarte line at Grammos with thousands of other kids. After time in a prison island for minors, he emerges with a new, life-affirming perspective, and that is the secret of his psychic survival.

It struck me now why Nick and his mother kept returning to Greece, even though it hurt them so. It was precisely because there was no acknowledgement that Nick felt compelled to become a monument to his ancestors' lives. He came to represent those who had been erased. He was the ghost haunting the denied hinterland.

A month later on social media I saw Nick on a potholed road deep in the mountains of south-west Bulgaria near the Greek border. He had gone to visit his maternal grandfather's village on the hundredth anniversary of his birth. Nick had retraced his grandfather's steps, returning for him, bringing back the errant spirit so that the howl would stop echoing in the ancestral landscape. He looked lonely on that godforsaken road, yet his expression said in no uncertain terms: Here I am. I made it.

But how many returns would it take? Will we know when to stop?

When I came across the term 'family homeostasis' to describe how families unconsciously strive to preserve the status quo, no matter how unhealthy, it made sense. Family homeostasis is the definition of moving on without moving on. In some families, it is embodied by a house. This is how inheritance issues grip generations in the name of invisible loyalty: the house becomes a mausoleum to the dead and the living alike. In our family, as in Nick's, after generations of emigrants there was no physical house for the spirits. We embodied them ourselves. In our maternal lines, the knowledge of loss and the fear of further loss had cast a deep shadow.

That was the dark force at our heels, the force that had manifested in mysterious pains, tumours, estrangements, and cellular anguish: the spectre of fear.

As with families, so with nations. The people of the lakes had been one people who, across time, borders and benighted policies, had become enemies. *Trauma* is Greek for 'wound'. A traumatic homeostasis had been preserved by ensuring that at any given time, someone or something in the family – in the nation, in the region – was wounded, that pleasure was spoiled by someone wearing black at the head of the table, that a shard from some past wreckage was lodged in the circulatory system, and the crisis maintained.

We were all good people, of course. We meant well, tried hard, felt deeply – and we were also unwitting servants of The Pain. This causes us cognitive dissonance that is so difficult to live with that we end up wilfully blind. Cognitive dissonance is when

individuals or groups (such as nations) fail to reconcile their sense
of being good people with the reality of having behaved destruc-
tively towards others, and themselves.

And here's the first infernal catch: we needed the relief of
external justice before we could be well. We needed an apology, a
commemoration, a gesture at least – from the State, from History,
from the Patriarchy. From Europe, that Babylonian whore
whose great powers had decided on the shape of our biographies
for generations, from our men who were absent or not perfect
enough, from our mothers like Furies, from our children who
ignored us, from the whole Earth that is witness to our suffering.

But here's the second infernal catch: what if relief didn't come,
not even after one thousand seven hundred years? For me and
Nick, time was running out, and illness had been a stark reminder.
We had to set ourselves free – and by doing so, release our ancestors too. Nobody was going to do it for us.

Actions, events, even intentions leave a blueprint on Earth,
because all is energy. In Prespa, the real source of my water dream,
I finally grasped this – not just with the mind, for the mind alone
can't accommodate all of reality, but at the energy level. Strife had
seeped into the matrix, creating an imprint we the distant children of this geography picked up, in a cycle of reinfection. Along
with the crystalline beauty which gave us a chance to rise above,
transcend, do things differently. If we don't, the task will fall to
those who live after us.

As with the private, so with the collective. It seems intolerably
cruel, as well as fathomlessly stupid, that yet more conflict may
visit the Balkans within my and Nick's lifetimes, but it is possible.
We both felt it. War thrives on denial. And here, the necessary
work of self-knowledge has not been completed. Self-knowledge
is needed for reconciliation – that is, for lasting peace. Not more
monuments to the 'winning' side, not more national martyrs, not
more borders and armies. Just more kindness and more understanding. We should try to make peace for those who can't

because they are trapped in the past. Even the young can be dead to the present, when sufficiently brainwashed by their elders. Cronos loves to devour his children.

Prespa, where I had no family history but where others' histories reflected my own, showed me this with absolute clarity. It is up to us to release ourselves from the cult of war. If we want a more peaceful world, we must learn peace ourselves. It's the hardest thing.

Seen from above, Ohrid and Prespa are a topographical image of the psyche – the light self and the shadow self, the conscious and the unconscious, linked through underground channels. Each contains the other without denying it, like a perfect yin and yang symbol. This is how they have survived as a self-renewing system for a million years.

Psyche is a Greek word meaning soul.

On a high road above Prespa, Nick and I had stopped to refill our bottles at a roadside water tap. We held a bottle to the spout but nothing came. It had dried up. I was reminded of the following story, told by a Greek man in *Children of the Greek Civil War*. He was eight years old, it was during the war, and he'd gone into the hills to fetch water from the spring. But by the spring, the body of a soldier had just been dug up by wolves. Three women appeared by the body and began to intone a lament. The wolves howled in the hills.

The narrator was eventually evacuated to a paedopolis, in a journey that began at a crossroads above his village. Such crossroads were commonly called *anathema*, or damnation, because it was at crossroads that men left for twenty years and children were torn from their mothers. Those who stayed behind donned black and cursed through their tears: *Anathema se xeniteia!* Curses on you, foreign lands! He was well educated in the camp, but for the next forty years he'd have the same nightmare: he goes to a mountain spring but as soon as he bends down to drink, the atmosphere darkens and he wakes up. He can never slake his thirst.

Until one year, he returned to the childhood spring, and the full memory came flooding back. He had repressed it – the spring, the body, the wolves, the three lamenting Furies. He held a small ritual there, for the victims on both sides. The nightmare ceased.

A man was tormented by darkness. In his waking hours, he'd think dark thoughts, and in his dreams he'd be attacked by beasts and torturers, he'd struggle trying to push huge rocks uphill and be overwhelmed by tidal waves. He was full of foreboding and sorrow, and sometimes, against his will, a dreadful voice would come through his mouth, not his own.

He was told to volunteer as a builder at Naum Monastery during the construction of the new quarters. Months passed, then one day while his fellow workmen were having lunch, he was seen running to the top of the cliffs and jumping in the lake. People rushed to help, thinking he was finally committing suicide, but he swam back to shore and came out, beaming. 'I feel good,' he said, 'I feel different.'

He was a changed man thereafter, and when people asked what had cured him, he said Naum. Naum had compelled him to run and jump from the cliffs, and as he fell in, all the darkness came through his mouth and dissolved in the water.

from *The Miracles of Naum of Ohrid*

HOW TO HEAL THE INSANE
AND THE MELANCHOLY

The arc of the sun and the cries of peacocks were the only things that marked time at St Naum Monastery. That, and the bells of evening and morning vespers. Every noise was muffled by the mountain above. Footsteps were gobbled up by the courtyard cobblestones as if by felt.

Each evening under the cypresses which turned black at sunset, when the last busload departed and souvenir-sellers went home, the grounds returned to their silence. Now you could hear the natural soundtrack: the rushing springs of Naum, which formed a large translucent pond and emptied their icy blue waters into the warm lake – and had done so for how many hundreds of millennia, I don't know – but our species arrived in Europe only forty-six thousand years ago. From this perspective, the monastery's earliest church huddled in the inner courtyard, and the few surviving original artefacts, seemed quite new at only a thousand years of age.

The hotel and restaurant buildings, by contrast, felt old, as old as my childhood. The two main wings of the hotel were called Konak I and Konak II – Turkish for quarters. They were called this in remembrance of the monastery's original medieval konaks, which had burnt down. The cavernous red-plushed Yugonostalgia, the residual Orientalism, the shy receptionist with an old-fashioned expression, the wool rugs that covered everything but didn't quite fit the corners – all this was redolent of the brown-beige holidays of the 1970s when the children sensed that all was not well and the adults smoked, their ash sprinkling the world. There were still heavy glass ashtrays in the rooms.

For a modest price, the monastery hotel provided a time lapse into eternal end-of-season holidays. Your summer clothes are suddenly too small, more time has passed than you thought, and you are now the person with white threads in your hair, just like the adults of your childhood. Many of them are dead or dying, and there is nothing you can do about it.

I was given a heavy wooden key to Konak I. Large and creaky, fit for a Party official or a corrupt cleric, my room was full of heavy dark furniture and overlooked both the lake ahead and the stone mountain behind. The extra blankets were needed in the chilly nights.

In the evenings, it was just me, the odd couple from Western Europe, the kiosk keeper Nomche whose beard reached his belt, the elusive resident monk Father Ambrosius, or perhaps Nectarius; a tiny gardener with a mullet, a mute Quasimodo-like man whose task was to scoop up the melted candle wax from the water of the candle boxes; and two slow-moving waiters in the terraced restaurant with folkloric table cloths, gloomy oil paintings and leather-bound menus. One waiter lived here, in a room below mine. He was a benign soul, a soul of the lake.

'I've got my Bulgarian passport and could work in Europe for five times the pay, but I just can't leave the lake,' he said.

Waiters earned two hundred euros a month.

The terraced restaurant had such a breath-stopping view of the whole lake that it didn't matter what you ate; bread, olives and water would be enough. To reach the restaurant, you walked past the pearl boutique which sold 'pearls' from the lake – not actual pearls but crafted ones, an Ohridian 'recipe' that was first introduced by an émigré from Lake Baikal. A heavily made-up girl sat chewing gum. She was new, the waiter told me. On his nights off, he made his way slowly to the small shop on the premises, bought a bag of crisps, and lay in his room munching. The previous pearl girl had been the love of his life, he said. But she had emigrated to America.

'I couldn't stop her. There's no opportunities here.'

He was grateful to have known true love, because some people don't get to experience it. To heal himself after her departure, he'd written a book of love poems and printed two copies, one for her in America.

'The other thing about this place is,' he said, 'three hours of sleep here are like thirteen. You have lucid dreams too.'

By the time he told me this, I had discovered it already. From the moment I arrived at the monastery and checked in for the week, I felt different, as if I'd drunk a potion. The mountains opposite looked fleshless and the air was lighter. There was space.

The monastery grounds and generally this southern bit of shore had a different atmosphere from the rest of the lake. Here you were stilled, as if by a hand. You were compelled to tune in to the beat of the waves on the sandy beach below the monastery cliffs, where nobody went because it was still a no-go border zone. Although there was no more border army, the wooded area between the monastery grounds and the checkpoint was still patrolled by a lone soldier. He swept the cobbles by his kiosk – fallen cypress cones and peacock feathers – there was nothing else to do. I looked into his eyes and saw that he had not seen the world yet. He was a child. If tomorrow there was another war, he would be the first to be cut down.

Each evening the sun cast its beam on the monastery, setting its windows on fire, then on the dilapidated checkpoint house in the hills, then onto Pogradec which, sunset-gilded, briefly looked like a mythical city.

In my room, the curtains to the many windows were of white satin, aquiver with draughts, so I could not only hear but see the unearthly light of the lake, even from my bed, even at night, magnified by the moon. The lake entered the room. On my first night, I had the distinct sense that some entity was moving towards me across the water as I slept. It knew me well. But I was not afraid, and the entity was eventually all around me, or I was part of it – not as myself, but as what remained of me once my dying self was out of the way. This was the exact antidote to my nightmare of rising water.

I experienced this subliminal presence without fail every night, until I began to feel that I was being dreamt by the lake. Always in motion even when still and still even when stormy, the lake was full of memories and symbols that were not wholly mine. We the creatures of the Earth are up to ninety per cent water. Anastassia loved this monastery and its then wild beach. Anastassia: a woman who, like so many others, had never felt properly held – except by the Lake. All women have an elemental desire for depth and connection; without it, we can become full of metal and war. That's why Persephone goes off with Pluto, or imagines she does: the Underworld provides depth. But in the Underworld, Persephone knows to sustain herself and all life with sunny pomegranate seeds, while her mother Demeter gives up on life and plunges the Earth into mourning. I thought of my mother behind closed shutters, curled around The Pain, and finally let her go. Some greater force not unlike this lake would take care of her, of all of us.

Here by the lake, it was clear: all that's left after our material existence is light. Even if we live behind closed shutters, the darkness that we carry will disappear, making us see, in one last breath, just how we have used this precious life. This life so precious that I didn't want to wait until my last breath to taste it.

Normally a late sleeper, I awoke early, feather-like in the mountain air. Squirrels darted up cypresses. The peacocks cried. The question had long changed. The question had long stopped being Who do you love most? or Whose are you? The question was: Whose life are you living? No, *really* living.

'I wake early here,' I said to Nomche one morning.

The courtyard was deserted except for the peacocks sweeping the cobbles with their tails, but Nomche was already in his kiosk, a giant inside a doll's house.

That's where he lived. He only came out for dinner and to sleep. Thirty years of this had given him a hunched, sepulchral air, compounded by his hermit's grey beard and waxy complexion, though his face was always relaxed. He looked like someone whose thoughts and emotions had been polished like pebbles on the shore. I could feel a similar effect. He sipped coffee and peered at me through the tiny kiosk window. Nomche was the diminutive of Naum. He was named after the saint, a common name here.

'It's the place,' he said. 'All you need is to be here, nothing more.'

Nomche was a man of modest vocabulary. He looked at people as they entered the courtyard through the stone arch, past the wooden gates studded with the flat heads of giant nails and said to be the original gates from the tenth century. Nomche said nothing as he sold the candles, small icons, books and crucifix chains to the annoying, shrill foreign visitors who spoke loudly to make themselves understood – but Nomche didn't speak languages and just gazed at them softly until they *ceased* and became quiet.

'I just look,' he said, and looked at me. 'I've seen so many faces, I know just by looking. I'm talking to you openly because I've looked at you and I know.'

'What do you know?' I asked.

'That you're gonna be OK. Many people who come here aren't gonna be OK.'

He said I looked familiar, had I passed through before? Yes, I said, in the 1980s.

'That's it,' he said. But I had been a child and he had seen a million faces.

'True,' he said, 'I remember the impressions, not the faces. Everyone leaves an impression behind them.'

A fortyish couple came through the stone arc – tall, gaunt,

quiet, the woman in a floral skirt. I had heard the engine of their car outside the walls. Nomche nodded and handed them a typed-out prayer in Serbian, as they explained in hushed tones. But he seemed to already know their affliction. They went inside and she kneeled by Naum's tomb, placing her arms on the velvet throw.

The church was a modest but harmonious amalgam of tiny buildings from different eras. Naum was said to have built the original chapel – long absorbed by subsequent constructions – with his own hands in 893. Remains of the oldest of those constructions, incorporated into later ones, dated to the early tenth century. The overall monastery complex too was a compendium of aesthetic influences: Byzantine, Islamic, Armenian, Moravian.

Both Christians and Muslims came for the tomb of St Naum, where his relics rested. His tomb was under a stone. It was believed that if you placed your head – or better yet, your whole body – on the tomb, you would be healed. The other belief was that you could hear the beating of Naum's heart through the stone, and although I remember hearing it as a child and being awed, now I couldn't. Either way, it was the rumbling of the underground springs you heard, the circulation system of the lake. Its acoustics were magnified by the layout of the monastery grounds with the chapel at its centre.

The large stone slab at the threshold of the church had been worn down by millions of feet. Heavy cobwebs hung like curtains high in the vaults. The church was a small but dense repository of memory – each chamber with its frescoes was from a different century, showing a changing perspective on power and pigment. Every square inch was painted with an expressive emotionality, and even the moon and the sun had faces – in the scene depicted in *The Two Brigands* only one of the brigands repents and embraces Jesus (the sun), Nomche explained to me. But there is another interpretation: the moon represented East; the sun, West. Yin and yang, female and male, the subconscious and the conscious mind, water and fire.

The church smelt of those long gone, of hope and long roads travelled, of something that would not die.

Here was the bitter-faced St Marina holding the devil by the hair like a trussed goat. Here was Tsar Boris I who converted the people of the southern Balkans to Christianity at a time when the tension between Eastern and Western Christianity was deepening, to culminate in the Great Schism two centuries later. And here at the entrance to the tomb was Tsar Samuil, with a white beard. His eyes had been dug out with some force. These people all wore haloes, as if to say: with time, The Pain diminishes. All wars end. All schisms heal. All that is left is light.

One portrait of Naum was slashed down the middle of his face, as if with a sabre. The icon above Naum's tomb bore what I took to be bullet holes. His hand was of cast silver, as if coming out of the painting and into this world.

Everything in the church was small, round, polished by time and by water, leading back to the centre. Up on the vaulted cupola, Mary held her narrow hands up in universal quietude. Her face was knowing and the ripples of her gold-edged red head shawl were a-flutter in the lake breeze – because inside and outside were alike. The lake was everywhere.

In one scene, Jesus was shown in a spaceship-like capsule of light, which is how pure energy was represented in the East. He holds in his arms a swaddled, dark-faced child with an old expression: *Jesus with His Mother's Soul.*

Over time, Naum had become a byword for purity that rose above the perishable. But who was Naum, other than missionary-theologian, Renaissance man and viticulturist? His most distinctive personal characteristic seems to have been peacefulness and love of nature; his alleged ability to heal mental ailments in particular was second to none. It didn't matter who you were, all you had to do was 'pray sincerely' and Naum would help you. Often, he appeared in people's dreams to give instructions and counsel. There were books for sale detailing his miracles, and the subsequent miracles fullfilled in the monastery grounds for those who came seeking cures.

The properties of the place clearly extended beyond the attributes of its founder, because the 'miracles' go on as I write. Just in the last twenty-five years, hundreds of sheep, lambs, rams and cattle have been donated to the monastery in gratitude for miracles rendered, and Naum continues to appear in people's dreams. A large proportion of the supplicants and donors, historically, were Muslim Albanians and Turks. Curiously, although the annals of Naum cover the entire period between his life and the present day, no chronology is offered, only themes: Naum helps the impoverished; Naum punishes sinners; Naum and the wild beasts; Naum heals the insane and melancholy.

To read this repository of oral memory and folk narrative is to rummage through the kitchen of history. Over the last ten centuries, 'miracles' have been legion. The place seemed to specialise in mental and emotional disturbances, but that was only one of the rubrics. Another was: the monastery provides protection, justice, nourishment, and the gaze of the silent witness in times of assault and injustice. A major theme was natural justice, or balance – some would call these karmic tales – featuring humans, wild animals and the lake itself. A wolf who had come down from the hills and eaten the guard dogs had returned the following night and lain down in place of the dogs. Some have the instructive morality of their times. Remember the woman who wanted to measure the depth of the lake and is punished for wanting too much knowledge? – here Naum the stern patriarch channels the lake's forbidding power.

'I'll show you something,' Nomche said, and taking a huge key from a nail above his head, squeezed himself out of the kiosk. The monastery had rooms for the mentally ill as late as 1945. Adjacent to the church was a locked, cell-like stone room with a high vault, now used for storage. Naum's tomb was just on the other side of the inner wall.

'This is where they used to put the most disturbed patients,' Nomche said. 'Next to Naum. Remember, there was no electricity.'

There were no windows, either. There was, however, a frescoed ceiling with a biblical scene. Perhaps the patient was expected to gaze up at it by candlelight.

It strikes me as significant that in some Slavic languages – that is, in the more Eastern understanding of human suffering – the equivalent to the reductively Newtonian 'mental illness' is 'ailing of the soul' (*dushevna bolest*). And that 'psychiatry' and 'psychology' come from the Greek for 'soul'. It is also intriguing that in some Slavic languages the words *duh* or *dusha* mean soul, and yet in others – ghost. The archaic meaning of the word was 'person'.

Nomche had nailed it: everyone leaves an impression, the ghost of themselves.

One of the 'Eight Miracles and Scenes from the Life of Naum' depicted in the church was entitled *Naum Treats the Nervously Afflicted*, where two blank-faced youths are lying down – or are they levitating? – with their feet shackled in a wooden vice. Naum stands by in the courtyard, praying with his arms wide open, against a rich midnight blue. It's a scene worthy of Chagall.

And here's the interesting part: in nearly all existing versions of *Naum Treats the Nervously Afflicted*, demons emerge from their mouths. This is also a recurrent motif in the recorded oral histories. Healing is achieved through utterance. Utter your truth, find your voice, name your pain, let your demons be released, shed the past, howl if you have to but let go – this seems to be the principle at work. It is ironic that Clement and Naum preached against the pagan ways – 'magic' and 'orgiastic dancing' were singled out for opprobrium – when they too used the principle of exorcism and energy healing. The purging of ill spirits, dark entities and shadow aspects of the psyche is part of the repertoire of early Christianity, Sufism, Tibetan Buddhism, Daoism and the shamanic traditions of Asia, Africa and the Americas.

Either way the mute, the grief-stricken, the obsessive-compulsive, the catatonic, the sleepless and the merely melancholy seem to have found solace here. Maybe it was simply time away from their homes that healed them. Here, there was no besa, no perfection or death. You could swim in the lake and be as weird as you liked. Though records tell that patients who were taken in by the monastery were also put to work – cleaning, making bread. Witness accounts tell of many a child, young person or 'bride' who regain their speech, their cheer or their usual self after being pushed into the lake, and specifically into the icy springs of the River Drim. The cure rate was high.

What was it about this place?

Nomche was having difficulty squeezing back into his little house.

'A miracle,' he said. He looked relieved as he settled in his chair.

Over time, Naum had become a byword for justice, health, peace, hope, plenty and destiny. Together, Naum and Clement were the lake people's conscience, their guardian spirits, and their gods. They were associated with phenomena involving blazing light, and legends told of how they communicated with each other across the lake with lights – another common image in Eastern Christianity and in mystical Islam.

The spooky well covered with an iron grid from my childhood was still here, and I peered in to see the glint of coins from past decades. At the time, you put your head on Naum's tomb and the Yugoslav state pocketed your fee, just as they pocketed everything the monastery had. From monastery estates and taxes to businesses, stealing was continuous practice here. Among the delightfully naive frescoes depicting 'Eight Miracles and Scenes from the Life of Naum', two are dedicated to theft: *A Monk Turns to Stone as He Attempts to Steal Naum's Relics* and *The Horse Thief*

Leaves the Monastery but the Horse Returns. This is why the people of the lake need Naum to provide mercy and justice, still. Because the state has failed to provide it for a thousand years.

Nomche was from the poorest family in the Village of Mean People, I'd been told. In the days before his monastery job, he didn't have two matching shoes – that's how poor he was. The monastery had taken him in, and now he and his wife were fixtures. He would be impossible to budge from his kiosk. I imagined him fossilised before being removed, hunched in his chair.

'A miracle,' Nomche summed up his life. 'Every day I thank Naum.'

Visitors began to trickle through the arch, and everybody bought a candle. The Quasimodo-like man stood by, looking fixedly at the melting wax that he'd scoop up with relish at the end of the day.

The many springs at the skirts of the mountain had been pagan sites before sandalled missionaries, desert hermits, self-proclaimed prophets and mystics started to arrive from Syria, Jordan and Persia. Thracian, Illyrian and Slavic nature rites were deeply connected with water. Communion with clean water is humanity's precious link with eternity – even when all else is lost. Behind the monastery grounds stretched a mixed forest. It was an enchanted, shaded world full of bubbling springs. You saw water, heard water, inhaled water, water was under your feet even when you couldn't see it.

At the main Naum Springs in the woods, I recognised the boatman – he was unchanged since ten years ago. He had one of those ageless faces. I'd remembered his name because he shared it with my father.

'Nikola,' I said, and he smiled as if he too remembered me. I climbed into his boat and we glided noiselessly over the lily-covered pond, bubbling, fairytale-like, with all the springs that converged here before the water reached the lake. Multiple streams from Prespa and thirty underwater springs met here, resulting in up to ten cubic metres of water per second discharging into the lake. The pond lived in its own time capsule under the weeping willows.

Nikola was the first boatman of the springs. He'd set himself up in the impoverished 1990s, when he and his mother survived by gathering herbs and mushrooms and selling them at the market. Since then, a dozen others had set up shop, but they were after easy bucks, I could see it. He was the only poet of the springs.

'Make a wish,' he said. The bottom of the pond glinted with coins, some oxydised green, thrown in over the decades by visitors – a coin for a wish. But I couldn't think of any – I already had everything I could wish for.

'It's the springs,' he said. 'I've had people weep in this boat.' Yet others became still and serene, and there were also those who became obsessed with the springs.

'A Japanese guy has been in my boat ninety times. You know the Japanese for spring? *Mizu no izumi.*'

Nikola knew the word for spring in dozens of languages. The reason why Nikola was light-hearted was that he lived above a giant spring that cleansed him daily. He had published books of photographs capturing the people of the Macedonian mountain heartlands, villages of old men and women, a land of wrenching beauty and neglect, but all his inspiration came from this spring, he said, even when he was far from here – like in Cambodia and Vietnam where he went last winter.

'It's like the Balkans,' he said.

Broken and fragmented in some ways, eternal and complete in others.

On my last day, a cold wind blew from Albania. Mean Valley filled with mist. In the morning, I was chatting to Nomche in his kiosk when a gaggle of young nuns arrived in the courtyard. Black-clad in capes like crows heralding autumn, they went into the church and began to sing with honeyed voices like a choir of archangels. Nomche and I listened. They sang in Romanian.

'A miracle,' Nomche said.

When they came out, the nuns were giggly and light, with a crystalline, limpid quality that contrasted sharply with what the bulk of visitors brought as they trod heavily under the arched doorway: depression, apathy, addiction. The ailments of the Earth.

Like Nomche, I had started to 'just look'. As the nuns fluttered down to the jetty, the head nun Nymphodora turned and called to me playfully:

'Pray for us.'

I waved back. I didn't know any prayers, and anyway it was not the nuns who needed praying for, it was everybody else.

On that last evening, I went down to the beach where the springs of the River Drim flowed into the lake. Each time we'd come to the lake in the past forty years, I would swim here with my dad – my dad who had given me the best of himself and asked for nothing in return. This was our place. It was thanks to him that I could swim out and swim back to the shore without fear. Thanks to him that I had broken free, knowing he was behind me, willing me towards the light. Like him, I'd always loved water and sunshine.

I took off my clothes and waded in, instantly losing my footing as the icy jet cut me at the knees and swept me in. You couldn't stay inside the root of the river for long, but you didn't need to because its nature imprinted itself on you instantly.

The jet pushed me into the placid warmth of the lake. I swam out. The water was so thin I could barely feel it on my skin. The mountains rose on all sides, bathed in a red sunset. I knew their peaks and their mean valleys. Past and future fell away. I saw a water snake's skin in the water – it floated transparent, the ghost of the snake. The further out I swam, the more it felt as if I was flying, and the lighter everything became. Then I turned round because I didn't want to be caught far out from the shore at night, and swam back to the beach.

All is one. Don't let me forget this, don't let the bastards divide me again. Our tragedy is fragmentation. It begins as a state of mind and ends up as destiny. It is the tragedy of our family of nations who hobble across this great peninsula, this exquisitely set Earth, like an army of blind soldiers a thousand years old looking for a place to rest. Let them rest. Forgive them, forgive me, forgive us. Our fear drove us insane and melancholy.

Yet the source was here all along. Every possibility is still at the source. All it asks of you is to stop struggling. Wade in, one September evening when the sky is African-red and the lake could be Tanganyika – it is the same lake – wade in and free yourself of the burden you've been carrying for centuries, become anything. Trout, eel, any of your ancestors still a child at one with the water and not yet ready to do the things that would lead to your birth, to the person you think is you, though what you are in the end is water, a spring that renews itself every second as it rushes in ecstasy to the lake.

ACKNOWLEDGEMENTS

I am grateful to my mother for sharing, over the years, stories and memories, and so enriching my understanding of the past and how deeply connected to it we are. Thanks to my relatives in Ohrid for their warmth and humour: Snezka and Krste, Biljana and Stefan, Tino and Nate, Maja and Jordan, Ognen and Hristina; also Bojan in Germany, Kiril in Portugal and Boyka in Sofia. Thanks to Vlado Zhura, Dejan Panovski, Nikola Puleski of Ohrid Town Council, specialist guide Katarina Vassileska, Chris Mounsey of Balkan Tracks, Christopher Buxton, Hristo Matanov for his counsel on Tsar Samuil's end days, and Alexander Shpatov for the Sultana conversation. Thanks to Andi Kosta and Ledi Zeqollari in Pogradec for their time.

Huge thanks to Nick Nasev who was not only an astute and enlightening travel companion, but also very generously gave of his time, energy and vast Balkan expertise – as well as his extraordinary family story. I know I haven't done it full justice here, but I hope it is a beginning, and that others may be encouraged to tell theirs.

My deepest appreciation to the vital Sarah Chalfant and Alba Ziegler-Bailey of the Wylie Agency who understood and supported this book from the very beginning and gave me the confidence to continue. Many thanks to Laura Barber at Granta for her sensitive and committed editing – and for being an all-round literary angel. And thanks to Sue Phillpott for her brilliant and devoted work on the copy-edit.

My love goes to TD who healed me, and Maggie McKechnie who enabled me to see the pattern behind the repetition. Another great teacher, Dónal Creedon, helped me to see where all war and peace begin – within us. I thank you for showing me that we have a choice.

GLOSSARY

bavcha, bahcha – a garden

belvitsa – a type of bleak, a fish endemic to Lake Prespa

besa – an oath, part of the Kanun

bey – a title for a local governor in Ottoman times

charshia – a market, usually along the main commercial street

chun – a traditional Ohrid Lake boat

detsa begalci (Bulgarian, Macedonian) – refugee children of
   the Greek Civil War, most of whom ended up in Eastern
   Europe; associated in Greece with *paedomazoma* (literally
   'the gathering of children')

ferman – an official document during the Ottoman Empire

gurbet – work abroad, often for long periods

High Porte – also Sublime Porte; the central government of the
   Ottoman Empire

kalé – fortress

Kanun – a medieval code of honour in northern Albania

keche – a soft skullcap, Albanian, normally white

kiradjia – drover, caravan-owner, travelling trader in pre-modern
   Albania and Macedonia

komita, komitadja – freedom-fighter, literally 'member of a
   secret committee', during the national liberation movements
   at the end of the Ottoman era; the medieval meaning
   was 'governor' – as in the Tsar Samuil dynasty of the
   Komitopouli

koran – see *pastrmka*

pashalak – fiefdom, semi-autonomous domain in the Ottoman
   Balkans; from *pasha*, high-ranking official

pastrmka (Macedonian), *koran* (Albanian) – a species of trout
   endemic to Lake Ohrid

samovila, vila – female shape-shifting entity in Balkan folklore

saray – mansion, stately quarters, for Ottoman rulers and their
   households

tekke – a Sufi lodge

varosh – inner town, old town

VMRO – the Internal Macedonian Revolutionary Organisation,
   originally a secret political organisation with many branches,
   aiming to liberate Macedonia from the Ottomans. Today, the
   name of political parties in North Macedonia and Bulgaria.

EPIGRAPH SOURCES

BIBLIOGRAPHY

Neal Ascherson, *Stone Voices: The Search for Scotland*, London, 2002

Marietta von Attekum and Holger de Bruin, *Via Egnatia on Foot: A Journey into History*, Via Egnatia Foundation, 2014

Edmond Bouchié de Belle, *La Macédoine et les Macédoniens*, Paris, 1922

Henry Noel Brailsford, *Macedonia*, London, 1906

Teresa Carpenter, *The Miss Stone Affair: America's First Modern Hostage Crisis*, 2003

Giorgos Catsadorakis, *Prespa: A Story for Man and Nature*, trans. Tim Salmon, Society for the Protection of Prespa, 1999

Naum Celakoski, Свети Наум Охридски Чудотворец (*Saint Naum, Miracle-Maker of Ohrid*), in Macedonian, Ohrid, 2009

Zhivko Chingo, Пасквелија (*Pasqualia*), in Macedonian, Skopje, 1968

Zhivko Chingo, Големата вода (*The Great Water*), in Macedonian, Skopje, 1971

Loring Danforth, *The Macedonian Dispute: nationalism in a transnational world*, University of Princeton, 1995

Loring Danforth and Riki Van Boeschoten, *Children of the Greek Civil War: Refugees and the Politics of Memory*, Chicago, 2012

Christopher Deliso, *Hidden Macedonia*, London, 2007

Bejtullah Destani and Robert Elsie (eds.), *Edward Lear in Albania: Journals of a Landscape Painter in the Balkans*, London, 2008

Edith Durham, *The Burden of the Balkans*, first published in
    London, 1905

Edith Durham, ed. Robert Elsie and Bejtullah Destani, *The Blaze
    in the Balkans: Selected Writings 1903–1941*, London, 2014

Robert Elsie (ed. and trans.), *An Anthology of Modern Albanian
    Poetry: An Elusive Eagle Soars*, London, 1993

Robert Elsie, *A Dictionary of Albanian Religion, Mythology, and
    Folk Culture*, London, 2001

Arthur John Evans, *Illyrian Letters*, London, 2005, first published
    1878

John Foster Fraser, *Pictures from the Balkans*, London, 1906

Liljana Gurović, Петкана (*Petkana*), Macedonian trans. from the
    Serbian, Skopje, 2003

Stratis Haviaras, *The Heroic Age*, New York, 1984

Herodotus and Aubry de Selincourt (trans.), *The Histories*,
    London, 2003

Julian Hoffman, *The Small Heart of Things*, University of Georgia
    Press, 2013

Nikola Janev, Маргиналии за мојот град (*Footnotes on My Town*),
    in Macedonian, Ohrid, 1998

Kiril Jonovski, trans. Metodi Jonovski, *Prespa*, Skopje, 2000

Kiril Jonovski, Преспа: историска енигма (*Prespa: Enigma of
    History*), Skopje, 2002

Ismail Kadare, *Broken April*, London, 1998, first published in
    Albania, 1978

Dimitar Karadimchev, 'Автобиография' ('Autobiography'), in
    Bulgarian, private archive

Anastasia N. Karakasidou, *Fields of Wheat, Hills of Blood: Passages
    to Nationhood in Greek Macedonia 1870–1990*, Chicago and
    London, 1997

Fatos Lubonja, trans. John Hodgson, *The False Apocalypse: From
    Stalinism to Capitalism*, London, 2014

Nikola Madzirov, *Remnants of Another Age*, trans. Peggy and
    Graham Reid, Bloodaxe, 2013

Jean Manco, *Ancestral Journeys: The Peopling of Europe from the First
Venturers to the Vikings*, London, 2013

Mark Mazower, *The Balkans*, London, 2000

Konstantin Mechev, Климент Охридски (*Clement of Ohrid*),
Sofia, 1966

Will Meyers, *People of the Storm God*, Oxford, 2005

Brothers Miladinov, Български народни песни (*Bulgarian Folk
Songs*), Sofia, 1981, first published in Zagreb 1861

Geo Milev, При Дойранското езеро (*On Lake Doiran*), in
Bulgarian, 1917

H.T. Norris, *Islam in the Balkans: Religion and Society between
Europe and the Arab World*, University of South Carolina Press,
1993

Branislav Nušić, Крај бреговите на охридското езеро (*By the
shores of Lake Ohrid*), Macedonian trans. from Serbian, Ohrid,
1999; first published 1892

Hugh Poulton, *Who Are the Macedonians?*, London, 1995,
updated 2000

Fred A. Reed, *Salonica Terminus: Travels into the Balkan Nightmare*,
Toronto, 1996

Stojan Risteski, Чудата на Наум (*The Miracles of Naum*), in
Macedonian, Ohrid, 2009

Anne Ancelin Schutzenberger, *The Ancestor Syndrome*, Sussex,
New York, 1998

Leon Sciaky, *Farewell to Salonica*, Philadelphia, 2016, written in
1946

David Smiley, *An Albanian Assignment*, London, 1984

Albert Sonnichsen, *Confessions of a Macedonian Bandit: A
Californian in the Balkan Wars*, Cosimo Classics, 2007; first
published 1909

Evtim Sprostranov, Дневник 1901–1907 (*Diary 1901–1907*), in
Bulgarian, Sofia, 1994

Edward Percy Stebbing, *At the Serbian Front in Macedonia*,
London, 1917

Nikola Pop Stefania, Охридски летописни бележки, in Bulgarian
    and Macedonian, Ohrid; first published in Sofia 1890

Ilche Stojanoski, Охридски вистини: Кажвиме за да не се
    заборајт 2 (*Ohrid Truths: We Tell It, We Remember It*, vol. 2),
    Ohrid, 2003, 2014

Dimitar Talev, Преспански камбани (*Bells of Prespa*), in
    Bulgarian, Sofia, 1952

Maria Todorova, *Imagining the Balkans*, Oxford, 1997

Yordan Velchev, Балканският човек, том 1 (*Homo Balcanicus*,
    vol.1), in Bulgarian, Plovdiv, 2014

Miranda Vickers, *The Albanians: A Modern History*, London,
    New York, 1995

Ed Vulliamy and Helena Smith, 'Athens 1944: Britain's Dirty
    Secret', *Observer*, 2014

Rebecca West, *Black Lamb and Grey Falcon*, Penguin, 1994; first
    published 1941

Blagoj and Vlado Zhura, Жура за Жура (*Zhura on Zhura*), in
    Macedonian, Ohrid, 1995

Gotse Angelicin Zhura, *The Cave Churches in the Ohrid-Prespa
    Region*, in Macedonian, English and French, Struga, 2004

Gotse Angelicin Zhura, Патописците пишуваат за Охрид (*Travel
    Writers on Ohrid*), in Macedonian, Ohrid, 2016

KAPKA KASSABOVA is a multigenre writer and the author of three books of narrative nonfiction: *Street Without a Name* (2008), *Twelve Minutes of Love* (2011), and *Border* (2017) which won the British Academy Al-Rodhan Prize for Global Cultural Understanding, the Scottish Saltire Book of the Year, Stanford-Dolman Travel Book of the Year, and the Highland Book Prize. It was also a finalist for the National Book Critics Circle Award. Kassabova grew up in Sofia, Bulgaria. As a young adult she lived and studied in New Zealand, and today lives in the Scottish Highlands. She writes for the *Guardian* and the *Economist*'s *1843* magazine.

Typeset in Bembo by Patty Rennie.
Manufactured by Sheridan Books on acid-free,
30 percent postconsumer wastepaper.